The
Brain's
Behind It

New Knowledge about
the Brain and Learning

Alistair Smith

Crown House Publishing Company LLC
www.CHPUS.com

The Brain's Behind It: New Knowledge about the Brain and Learning

Professional Development

© 2005 by Alistair Smith
Printed in the United States of America
ISBN: 1904424716
Published by:
Crown House Publishing Company LLC
4 Berkeley Street
Norwalk, CT 06850
www.CHPUS.com
Tel: 866-272-8497
Fax: 203-852-9619
E-mail: info@CHPUS.com

Every effort has been made to contact copyright holders of materials reproduced in this book. The publishers apologize for any omissions and will be pleased to rectify them at the earliest opportunity.

This edition is adapted from a book originally published in the U.K. by Network Educational Press Ltd., P.O. Box 635, Stafford, ST16 1BF.

Editing (of this edition): Kirsteen E. Anderson
Design and typesetting (of this edition): Sheryl A. Shetler
Illustrations: Trevor Bounford—www.bounford.com
Cover artwork: Geoff Tompkinson/Science Photo Library

Library of Congress Cataloging-in-Publication Data

Smith, Alistair, 1957-
  The brain's behind it : new knowledge about the brain and learning /
Alistair Smith.
      p. cm.
  Includes bibliographical references and index.
  ISBN 1-904424-71-6 (alk. paper)
  1. Learning--Popular works. 2. Brain--Popular works. 3. Cognitive
neuroscience--Popular works. I. Title.
  QP408.S62 2005
  612.8'2--dc22
                        2005003101

A wise man proportions his
belief to the evidence.

David Hume
An Essay Concerning Human Understanding (1748)

Making Sense of Making Sense!

'Participants will learn how to teach the right-brained learner.'
UK training program for teachers (September 2000)

OR

'You cannot give any one area of the brain any one function—it's just
one step up from phrenology!'
Susan Greenfield, *Brain Story* (2000);
from a talk given at Technology Colleges Trust (March 1999)

'Right now, brain science has little to offer educational practice or policy.'
John T. Bruer, *A Bridge Too Far* (1997)

OR

'Brain research in time will have a profound effect on how we teach
in schools.'
Rita Carter, *Mapping the Mind* (1999)

'Think of classroom management, not as a social coercion system, but in terms of its biology.'
Robert Sylwester, Brain Expo Conference, San Diego (January 2000)

OR

'I have a richer panoply of things which teach me than simply the connections between my neurons.'
Danah Zohar, *Spiritual Intelligence* (1999)

'We use only 4 percent of our brain's potential.'
Mike Hughes, *Closing the Learning Gap* (1999)

OR

'The myth that we use only 10 percent of our brain or less derives more from the self-improvement industry than it does from science.'
Stuart Zola, Brain Expo Conference, San Diego (January 2000)

Contents

Preface

The Brain's Behind It as a project began in one millennium and was completed in another. It is an attempt to make sense of what science says about learning from the point of view of someone with little or no scientific training. It endeavors to separate facts, fallacies, and fads and to identify scientific findings about learning of use to educators, parents, and policymakers.

Some of my excitement in writing this book came from my increasing realization of my own ignorance as I wrote it. I had been caught up in the excitement of the brain-based learning movement and had made some errors that I am now pleased to correct. This book is a snapshot of what I can find out about the science of the brain and how it relates to learning at this instance. It is now time to conclude the book. What I thought when I started is not what I think now. If I leave it much later, then my thinking will have slipped from me again.

The scientific activity I describe in this book considers what variables influence our capacity and willingness to learn. Some of the science felt familiar, some I have been persuaded of, and some has come as a revelation to me. In the early pages I try to address head-on some of the cherished but fallacious ideas that have fueled what has become known as the brain-based learning movement.

For purposes of simplicity, my use of the term *learning* in this book is deliberately broad. It is based on the idea of a permanent improvement of condition as a result of activation. Learning is often achieved through purposeful and distributed rehearsal. Although it does not occur without activation at some level, that activation need not be conscious. Thus, modeling and imitation are included within my range of learning strategies. So, too, are distributed rehearsal, processing time, focused and diffused thought, demonstration of understanding through varied means, and reflection.

When I use terms such as *neuroscience* in this book, I intend to include all disciplines whose focus is the study of the brain. This is a caravan of many members. It includes disciplines focused at the cellular level, those focused around imaging studies, and those that deal with clinical dysfunction. It does include neuroscientists, but I try to identify the work of cognitive psychologists separately. I do so for the purpose of distinction between the physical entity of the brain and what changes we can observe there, versus the cognitive functions that those physical changes may lead to. Brain and mind are often confused in the literature of brain-based learning. They are interconnected and must be recognized as such, but there is a difference between observable physical changes and conclusions about related behavioral changes.

I have set out to examine factors that influence the development of the human brain and to attempt to explain the possible damaging effects on learning capacity of physical insult to it. I describe the role of imitation and the importance of structured play in detail. The importance of multisensory engagement during sensitive periods seems to me as important in acquiring good learning attributes as appropriate leavenings of emotional security. Stress is good for learning in the short term but disastrous beyond that. What happens in the brain with practice? Distributed rehearsal is at the heart of any performance improvement, and maybe the place of rote learning ought to be defined. Is all learning of equal value in the brain? Are some experiences dependent and others expectant? If so, then all learning cannot be equal. What happens when we think mathematically? Are the same structures used for looking at pictures as looking at words? Is there a biological component to aggression? What about attention? Can a brain really have a deficit in attention? What happens to memory as we age? Would knowledge about the degeneration of memory in aging tell us anything about classroom learning? We are told that men are from Mars and women from Venus, and that boys and girls have such different brains we ought to teach them differently. Should we believe these views? Finally, the self-help industry will tell you that your left brain is logical while your right is creative. Is there any truth in this? If not, then why is this myth so pervasive?

I hope to clear up some of these issues and, if not, then at least to put forward a well-considered view. I cannot say with certainty if educators and brain researchers will ever be able to communicate meaningfully with each other. Perhaps this book will contribute to furthering the dialogue.

When I had only just started to write this book, a good friend discovered that a tumor the size of a mandarin orange had grown in her brain. She had just arrived in Vietnam on vacation. She was rushed by air taxi to Bangkok and within twenty-four hours she was operated on. The surgeons' phenomenal skill saved her life, but her prognosis remained gloomy. Some weeks later she was flown home to England and started her recovery.

Radiation therapy followed. It was unsuccessful. She had another lengthy and invasive operation. Chemotherapy followed. Again, unsuccessful. This operation scooped out what remained of the tumor and some of the secondaries. On recovery, she had some loss of mobility. She has begun to regain movement as she has recovered her health. The surgery would appear to have been successful. Fifteen months later, she is in the gym with a fixed smile that her friends recognize as uniquely hers.

It is impossible from a distance to get a sense of what fifteen months of hope given and removed, of pain and distress, of constantly having to be positive for yourself and others must be like. It is equally difficult to appreciate the skill of the neurosurgeons from around the world who operated again and then again with finer and finer margins and higher and higher levels of risk. The skill of the surgeons who helped my friend is built on the accumulation of hundreds of thousands of hours of dedicated research into the workings of the human brain, some but only some of which I can describe in the pages of this book. I hope that this book whets your appetite to find out more, to support those whose lives are devoted to furthering our knowledge of the brain and its workings, and to try some of the ideas I advance within it.

The final thing I want to say is that I am an educator first and foremost. I have acquired my scientific knowledge and training in much the same way as the Victorian amateur. If at any time I am guilty of "phrenological" thinking, then it has arisen as a consequence of enthusiasm rather than hubris. I have tried throughout to triangulate the evidence so it has more than one voice of authority behind it. Where there are omissions, I take consolation in knowing that brain science is indeed a developing science but some of the greatest brains are behind it.

Alistair Smith
February 2004

How to Use This Book

This book is organized to be easy to navigate through. I hope it facilitates different ways of reading it and is of interest to parents, educators, and policymakers. In it I provide an overview of existing scientific research into the workings of the human brain, starting with fallacies and fads. I follow this with a body of factual information from which a set of findings and specific recommendations emerge. Throughout the book, I keep the fallacies, fads, facts, and findings separate.

In the introduction I pose the question, Can brain research tell us anything about learning? I then attempt to identify a number of especially virulent fallacies and fads. Parts 1 and 2 are largely factual and lead into part 3, which contains the findings. Each chapter in parts 1 and 2 is broken down into clearly headed sections and opens with a summary of the sections and the questions that will be answered. Part 1, "Wired: The Development Cycle of the Learning Brain," is organized as a crude time line of brain development. Part 2, "Ready, Wire, Fire: A Model for the Learning Brain," is organized to demonstrate how brain science can be linked to formal learning. The chapters address topical issues.

Part 3, "The Brain's Finally behind It," contains a set of findings that arise from the book and separate sets of recommendations for parents, educators, and policymakers. Part 3 also includes an extensive list of questions and where in the book to find answers to them, recommended websites, and a detailed glossary. The final component is a bibliography organized by section, including recommendations for further reading.

Different Entry Points

The human brain is complex, multifaceted, and highly adaptable. So are you. In respect of this, I have provided a variety of routes through this book. You can choose

- to start at the beginning and read through to the end.
- to start by reading the fallacies and fads listed in the introduction.
- to go straight to the findings and recommendations found in part 3.
- to gain an overview via the illustrations. There are about sixty, and they are positioned carefully within each chapter to provide a distillation of the key learning points.
- to gain an overview via the chapter summaries. Each chapter is preceded by a set of summary points by section.
- to start with the questions found at the start of each chapter and duplicated in part 3.
- to start by looking up key words or topics using the index at the back.
- to put the book on a shelf to gather dust. Promise yourself that you will get around to reading it one day.

Acknowledgments

This book took a long time to research and write, and lots of people have provided support along the way. Janice Baiton has been very thorough and professional in her editing approach. Jim Houghton has not only given me complete freedom to choose my subject and write about it, but has risen above any pressures in a positive and pleasant way.

Nearer to home my wife, Ani, made me laugh and my niece, Connie, made me ham and tomato sandwiches. My brother, Ian, a very active man all his life, had his career as an airline pilot ended by a mild heart attack. The sections on the importance of physical stimulation and emotional stability are for his in-bed reading. Finally, my dad now resides in my memories, in my heart, and in a suitcase full of pictures under the bed, but he is still helping me. In his own way, he provided the motivation to write this book and will help with the others to come.

Introduction

Can Brain Research Tell Us Anything about Learning?

Within the space of two months I attended two events that addressed the question, Can brain research tell us anything about learning? One was in London, the other in San Diego. Both conveyed fascinating insights into what is fast becoming known as the brain-based learning movement.

The event in London was a one-day symposium held at the Royal Institution. It was a formal, carefully orchestrated day of neuroscientists presenting their position followed by educators presenting theirs. Presenters made careful arguments, summarized and discussed their positions, and invited the audience to comment. This all took place in the very lecture theater where Faraday and Davy had, in the eighteenth century, demonstrated their scientific discoveries. It was very British.

The Brain Expo took place at the Paradise Point Resort in San Diego, California. It was very different from the symposium in London. On the first morning three hundred delegates warmed up by doing the dance of neural networking. As a presenter demonstrated at the front, we were all encouraged—and found ourselves willingly participating in—simulating various neural structures. I was lifted off my seat as I suddenly became a myelin sheath. The woman next to me was being DNA when she should have been potentiating at the synapse. As the hysteria rose, I thought back to the wood paneling of the institution in London and wondered what the suited academics there would have made of all this. How readily—if at all—would they have collectively "gotten down" to the neurotransmitter boogie?

Suddenly brain research is sexy. Everyone wants a piece of the action (see figure I.1). Courses for teachers with titles like "Brain-Based Learning" beguile with promises: You can buy teacher packs of "brain-friendly worksheets"! You can become a licensed "brain-based trainer." Training

1.1 We are all neurologists—or are we?

companies with names like Brainsmart, Neurolab, and BrainLightning promise to enhance student performance, challenging teachers to "learn the seven secrets of your learning brain." These "seven secrets of your learning brain" look remarkably similar to the "five fundamentals of the Neurolab," which bear a striking resemblance to the "six steps to your lightning brain." Conference packs are filled with leaflets that implore you to "start your New Year with a sharp brain." Another proclaims the benefits of high-performance neuro-supplements" that not only "enhance IQ" and "prevent nerve gas toxicity" but also "accelerate the rate of learning by 40 percent." Yours for only $159.95 for three months' supply. What is going on?

What is going on is the coming together of breakthroughs in neuroscience with powerful, noninvasive imaging technologies, powerful computers, the information revolution that is the Internet, and, of course, the never-ending educators' quest for a definitive answer to the question, How do we learn? In the 1970s and 1980s, discoveries in brain science pointed to the possibility of an all-embracing model for learning. A few educators leaped onto this bandwagon with the adrenaline rush of a lion hunting quarry in the Kalahari. Books followed. Careers were realigned. Movements began. Now, for better or worse, the brain-based learning movement is a reality. Or is it simply a fad?

In this book I attempt to answer these questions. Is brain-based learning a fad? To what extent does it have a basis in real science? How much attention should those who are interested in facilitating the learning of others give it? Finally, is it possible, practical, and desirable that scientific findings about the brain should enhance learning in the classroom?

I can save you a lot of reading by telling you now the answers the book provides. They are, Yes, scientific findings about the brain can be used to enhance learning in the classroom, and No, scientific findings about the brain cannot yet be used to enhance learning in the classroom.

Are We Asking the Correct Questions?

The simple truth is that educators and scientists are asking different questions, which differ in their scope and purpose, their degree of complexity, and their level of detail. If you want a rationale for organizing the tables in your classroom, do not go to a neurologist for advice. If you want to know more about a specific piece of laboratory research that may give some clues to possible causes of a reading disorder, then some neuroscientists may be able to help.

Sir Christopher Ball chaired the previously mentioned gathering of teachers and scientists at the Royal Institution, London. This public seminar examined whether brain science could tell us anything about learning and, if so, what. He started the proceedings by posing his own questions:

- What is the balance between nature and nurture?
- How important are the early years?
- Does remedial education require special lessons, and why is remedial education so difficult?
- Are the links we make between natural development and artificial education appropriate? Are there differences?
- What is intelligence?
- What is emotional intelligence? Can it be developed?
- How does motivation happen?
- To what extent is learning age related?
- What can be said about different styles of learning?

His questions are the "Holy Grail" questions. They are considered and show balance, but they are also general and not susceptible to easy resolution. Finding definitive answers to these questions would transform learning worldwide. Scientists alone cannot provide them.

Educators use the terms "brain based" and "brain research" loosely. Perhaps we educators, more than any other group, are in search of the "Holy Grail" answers, the catch-all explanations of how we learn and why. These answers would provide solace for the teachers who do not know what to do with their low achievers on a wet Friday afternoon. They would stretch and test the academic who wants to test this theory against precedent. Are the answers forthcoming? Yes and no.

The members of the scientific community whom I have met while assembling this book have expressed not only a passion for learning, but also a passion for precision and specifics. Some of their research into the workings of the human brain reflects the interests of their funding sources. Much of the research provides very broad social benefits. All of the research operates at the limits of available technology. It is conducted within the known cases of, say, brain dysfunction. It cannot generate dysfunction for laboratory purposes. All the research operates within strictly observed codes of conduct and ethics. Each and every one of the scientists I talked to or read in preparing this book resisted generalizations around their work. This makes writing about it difficult!

In writing about learning, Sarah-Jayne Blakemore of University College London, the author of the Early Years Learning paper for the Parliamentary Office of Science and Technology (2000), says

 It is difficult to make direct links between neuroscience and early years education policy.

At the same time Robert Sylwester (2000, 72), another highly respected commentator on brain science and learning, writes

> Education must change from relying mostly on social and behavioral science to being based more on biology.

John T. Bruer (1997) reminds us that the scientific study of the brain and the scientific study of the mind evolved "separately and independently." He adds that it is only in the last fifteen years that neuroscience and psychology have seen "serious collaborative research to study how the biological brain might implement mental processes." He warns against expecting too much too early:

> Right now, brain science has little to offer educational practice or policy.

This is a bit like suggesting that physics has little to offer computer science. In the same year another author writing about the human brain offered a more positive spin:

> Brain research in time will have a profound effect on how we teach in schools. (Carter 1999)

There is a strong desire within the education community to have science affirm our professional instincts about the complexities of learning. This is an age of rapid breakthroughs in brain research. It is also an age where the divisions between disciplines are being questioned and in many cases broken down. Publications emerging from esteemed educators, such as Howard Gardner, draw from multiple disciplines, including neuroscience. Those books that popularize ideas such as emotional intelligence obtain some of their legitimacy by reference to neuroscience. So we have communities looking over the fence at each other. It is an exciting time in the fields of education and in brain research, but it is also a dangerous one.

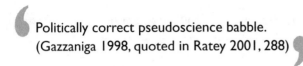

> Politically correct pseudoscience babble.
> (Gazzaniga 1998, quoted in Ratey 2001, 288)

In this quotation, Michael Gazzaniga, a highly respected world figure in neuroscience, is writing about the idea that you can "hothouse" your child's language development, and thus intelligence, by an early exposure to the rules of grammar and structured dialogues (Ratey 2001). It is not unheard of for solid scientific findings to be published, translated by an intermediary, popularized, picked up by the media, and used to shape educators' thinking. In the blink of an eye, every pupil in every school is drinking water, listening to Mozart, and rolling their ears between their fingertips. Taking scientific ideas out of context can lead to the creation of damaging pseudoscientific generalizations, which in turn, can begin to shape policy. This can happen very quickly. I estimate that I have given more than five hundred separate, detailed presentations to diverse audiences in the last five years. I get calls from time to time from the press. The parts of my presentations that get the attention of the media are the sexy stuff: "Can you tell us about using classical music in the classroom?"

It is never the research that is ringed with caveats and with tight controls. It is never the considered learning model. It is the slightly eccentric but entirely peripheral suggestions sometimes given as an afterthought that catch media interest: visualization of patterns of success as a taught activity, tai chi for autistic children, sponsorship for the afternoon sessions from the local grocery.

I have vivid dreams. They are generally pleasant. I rarely find myself falling through space, being chased by shadowy figures, or drowning in gravy. I have in recent dreams lined up to compete in the Olympic hundred meter hurdles alongside a hippopotamus complete with athletic vest and running shorts. I have also done a lot of surfing, though in reality I've never been on a board. My dreams usually have a narrative, albeit a loose one. They often arrive and leave in snatches with any moral left hanging. Last night it was rats.

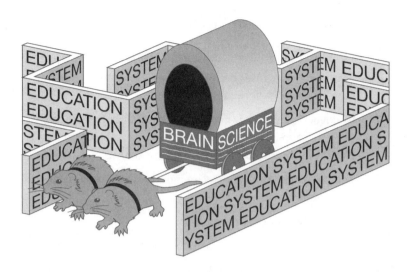

I.2   What influence, if any, will brain science have on our education system?

The rats were not Orwellian. They were not the product of any phobia, at least none I am aware of. They were laboratory rats, and they were pulling covered wagons (see figure I.2). The wagons were of the Wild West type and the lab rats were pulling them West, pioneer style. What they were doing felt important. There was a lot of Wild West dialogue with words of three letters: "git," "yip," "paw," "maw." At one point the rats circled the wagons. The prairie chickens, known for their depravity, were on their way. What happened to the pioneer rats? I never discovered. I awoke early. When I woke, I puzzled as to their fate. Where had that dream come from?

At some point in the last year I had read an article where the author used a metaphor about laboratory rats pulling the heavy wagon that is brain science through the maze that is our Western education system, or something along those lines. It obviously stuck. It is a good metaphor.

Our limited knowledge of human brain function must not be too readily applied to the cognitive potential of children developing in a society with very different demands and expectations than that of their forebears. Brain science alone will not provide the answers but, as ever, educators need to operate in an environment where there is no primer.

Brain science faces problems in answering the questions that educators pose. First, there are the broad difficulties:

- Brain science focuses on highly specific questions, whereas educators ask general questions.

- Discovering how a chemical is secreted at a synapse does not easily lead to a hypothesis about a learning behavior, nor is it the scientist's job to make such a hypothesis.

- The neuroscience research community is vast, and no one individual has an overview.

- Funding influences the research.

- Technology and access to technology influences the research.

- Dysfunction, particularly dysfunction that has a profound community impact, is of more interest than typical learning.

- Research findings often derive from case studies, morbidity, invasive surgery, trauma, or dysfunction. This is the "crumbs at the rich man's table scenario." You get what is left over.

- In the everyday world, only laboratory rats live in impoverished environments. You cannot, for the benefit of science, deprive children of stimulation in order to research enriched environments.

- Like any research community, neuroscience has its own language and its own means of communicating findings.

Then there are the more specific issues that make it difficult for neuroscientists to answer educators' questions:

- Human brains are different from those of monkeys and rats.

- The brain develops differently in different species.

- Different parts of the brain develop differently.

- Each brain reflects the environment in which it developed— and no two environments are the same (ontogeny reflects phylogeny).

- Different modes of learning depend upon different brain systems.

In an age of rapid breakthroughs in brain research, the focus needs to remain on the individual child, not on any category of function or dysfunction into which we can fit that child. I am, however, confident that neuroscience offers the promise of a science of individuality rather than generality, and of function rather than dysfunction. Neuroscience offers the possibility of identifying and helping children with conditions that can be clinically defined and recognized. Such conditions may be directly related to learning—such as dyslexia and dyscalculia—or have a more general effect on a child's willingness or readiness to learn—as do schizophrenia, depression, or autism. As scientists better understand human brain function, the list of conditions that research can identify and help remediate will expand.

Our understanding of conditions like attention-deficit/hyperactivity disorder (ADHD), trauma, anxiety, and aggression benefit from improved scientific research techniques. This understanding in turn may contribute to a shift in perspective away from a ready categorization. The child who is inattentive and may be labeled with ADHD is the same child who may benefit from more structure, more tightly focused and negotiated learning challenges, more use of time out, and more attention to diet.

The human brain is marvelously plastic and resilient. It develops through its complexity and responsiveness. Perhaps we can start to respect it by asking more exacting questions, particularly around fallacies and fads.

Fallacies, Fads, Facts, and Findings

It is incumbent on educators to show responsibility in this area, particularly with regard to asking more precise questions of neuroscientists. Follow the instincts of parents in the presence of a doctor. They describe their own child and his or her quirks of behavior in elaborate and loving detail. They ask specific questions and give supportive detail. Educators could benefit from a more disciplined and scientific approach to the questions they ask of themselves and of others about their classrooms.

Scientists could benefit from knowing more about the sorts of behaviors that classroom teachers observe on a daily basis. They can help by taking time out to explain the work that they and their colleagues in the field do in language that is accessible to the layperson.

Sixteen Fallacies That Fooled Us

Educators can help by challenging some of the fallacies from the self-help movement that have infiltrated the learning professions and have become faddish. For example,

- You use only 10 percent or less of your brain.
- You have three brains in one.
- Your brain is like a sponge.
- Stress prevents you from learning.
- You either use it or you lose it.
- Your left brain is logical and your right is creative.
- You have an emotional brain.
- There is a special-needs brain.
- Listening to Mozart makes you more intelligent.
- An enriched learning environment gives your child a better start in life.
- Children can concentrate for only two minutes more than their chronological age.
- The brain cells you get at birth are all you have for life.
- There are critical periods within which specific developments must occur.
- Genes are destiny.
- Your memory is perfect.
- Male and female brains are so different that we ought to teach boys and girls in different ways.

1. You Use Only 10 Percent or Less of Your Brain

For years, the 10 percent myth has circulated in the world of self-help psychology. It is a beguiling thought: If the brain has so much spare capacity, what if we could exploit only 1 or 2 percent more of it? The truth is that functions such as movement, perception, memory, language, and attention are all handled by different areas of the brain. These areas are widely distributed. If you were to lose 90 percent of your brain, how well would you function? If 90 percent is indeed held in reserve, what is it held in reserve for? If the 10 percent myth were true, should there not be better recovery after trauma? There is no area of the brain that can be damaged without some loss or impairment of function, however temporary. The brain is highly integrated. For example, imaging studies of sleep show activity in all areas. The 10 percent myth arose when the self-improvement industry misinterpreted early researchers who said they knew how only at most 10 percent of the brain functions.

2. You Have Three Brains in One

Pick a number! This fallacy derives from Dr. Paul MacLean's (1990) triune brain theory. The theory that our brain is composed of a primitive, or reptilian, center, an emotional and attention center, and a higher-order thinking center was first proposed in the 1940s, and modern researchers would not know anything about it. It has endured because it has a powerful, easily understood metaphorical value and it aligns with Maslow's hierarchy of needs theory (see, for example, Maslow 1982). Educators can grasp it right away. The three brains in one theory is not wrong, it is out of date. Science has left it behind.

3. Your Brain Is Like a Sponge

This idea assumes that you take everything in, you store it somewhere, you have infinite capacity, and you can draw on that capacity at some time in the future. It is true that your brain probably looks and feels like a sponge, but it never acts like one. Among neuroscientists there is a concept known as neural pruning. As you grow, you reorganize your brain to cope with the demands you place on it. Millions of neural connections that are not put to use get pruned away. If you were to attend to every bit of data that reaches your senses, you would not be able to cope with life. To have all your life's accumulated data available is a dysfunction. Selection is part of what the brain does to keep you healthy. Sponges are not selective.

4. Stress Prevents You from Learning

This idea is partly true! The effects of stress on learning, however, depend on the nature and duration of the stress, the individual concerned, and what is being learned. Short-term, moderate stress is good for learning.

Some learning under stress is so "successful" that it is impossible to forget thereafter. Post-traumatic stress disorder (PTSD) is an example of this situation. The old thinking was that "downshifting" occurred during stress, making higher-order thinking impossible. Different and more sophisticated models now prevail.

5. You Either Use It or You Lose It

This statement is true—but with clarification. Active engagement in a task reorganizes the brain, whereas passive stimulation does not do so to anything like the same degree. Learning can and does occur out of conscious awareness, but such learning is less enduring than that occurring through active engagement. A further improvement on our understanding of the "use it or lose it" idea is that the brain is programmed to be experience-dependent and experience-expectant. In other words, at some stages in our development, some types of experiences are more important than others. An adult learning a new language uses different brain structures than does a child learning a first language. The former is dependent and the latter expectant.

6. Your Left Brain Is Logical and Your Right Brain Is Creative

This seductive idea has slipped firmly into popular culture. While there is some localization of brain functions, there is no gene, no synaptic connection, no chemical, no area or region, no hemisphere in the human brain that is exclusively responsible for any specific behavior. Different neural networks within the brain interact with different chemicals to produce responses. Damage the networks or alter the chemicals and you change the responses. Localized damage to one site on either side of the brain can result in permanent or temporary loss of function. This does not mean that that site alone was responsible for the function.

7. You Have an Emotional Brain

There is a view that we have four basic emotions: anger, sadness, fear, and joy. Other emotions derive from a mix of these. Scientists believe it improbable that one brain structure could be responsible for competing emotions. Just as separate but interconnected structures contribute to everyday functions, so it is now thought that different but connected structures contribute to the subtleties of emotional response. Many neuroscientists are skeptical about claims that there is an "emotional intelligence" linked to brain structures.

8. There Is a Special-Needs Brain

There is no such thing as a Muslim brain, a white brain, an Inuit brain, a football fan's brain, a store owner's brain, or a special-needs brain. No individual, particularly not a child, should be labeled with any category of function or dysfunction. It is a wonderful spin-off from brain research that we now know a lot more about very specific cases of dysfunction from which we can begin to generalize. Paula Tallal's work at Rutgers University on dyslexia is a good example (see, for example Nagarajan et al. 1999; Tallal 2000). Such findings can have applications for teaching, but it remains a terrifying thought that we should begin to teach a brain rather than the child who owns it.

9. Listening to Mozart Makes You More Intelligent

No it does not! The Mozart effect is a classic case of the media, with its love of a sexy story and a promise of an instant reward, latching on to one research project—which had a limited cohort and a very tightly defined task—and prematurely sounding off about it. Not once but again and again worldwide. Hidden deep within this myth is genuine, quality research. What is of equal interest is how quickly the research can be selected, distorted, and repackaged when there is sufficient public demand. Playing your slumbering infant Mozart piano sonatas is unlikely to do much more than disturb its, and later your, sleep.

10. An Enriched Learning Environment Gives Your Child a Better Start in Life

There is no substantive scientific evidence to support this statement. The evidence from laboratory research on rats proves that the absence of a normal environment inhibits learning. It does not prove that *extra* stimulation enhances brain growth, learning, or intelligence. Cancel your subscription to *Infant Genius Monthly*, throw away your flash cards, and play together the three of you: baby, you, and the cardboard box.

11. Children Can Concentrate for Only Two Minutes More Than Their Chronological Age

This maxim has become accepted as truth, but there is no science behind it. Scientific findings would not make such an easy generalization. Buy your "hyperactive" teenager a PlayStation 2 and put it to the test. The nature of human attention varies. Concentration times are dependent on the individual, the task, and the context, not on chronological age.

12. The Brain Cells You Get at Birth Are All You Have for Life

Stem cell research and research into neuroplasticity in adults suggest that we can and do grow new brain cells in certain areas of the brain. The hippocampus, an area associated with learning and memory, is one such area.

13. There Are Critical Periods Within Which Specific Developments Must Occur

This was long held to be true, but some aspects are recently being questioned. The preferred terminology now is *sensitive periods*. It is believed that rather than stopping abruptly, developmental periods fade away.

14. Genes Are Destiny

Educators often hear such laments as, "He gets it from his father." These are usually apologies for perceived problems or lack of ability. What the boy sees his father do, how the father talks to and around him, and how the father relates to life's challenges contribute as much to the boy's subsequent behavior and abilities as his genetic legacy. Genes instruct and guide the body as it develops. Environment interacts with genetic inheritance to create a unique brain. Identical twins with the same genes do not have identical brains. The brain alters with use. Adult neuroplasticity is real and remains so right into old age.

15. Your Memory Is Perfect

The claim that your memory may be perfect—or at least a lot better than you realize—is, sadly, wholly untrue. If you had a perfect memory, your life would be hell. Memory is less about recall than it is about reconstitution. Memories do not reside hidden away in specific sites within the brain. Memory relies on a coming together of a number of variables. Change any of those variables, and the memory changes. Memory is by its very nature imperfect! False memory syndrome is real.

16. Male and Female Brains Are So Different That We Ought to Teach Boys and Girls in Different Ways

No justification for teaching boys and girls in different ways comes from brain research. Men and women are different, behave differently, and have some differences in the organization and structure of their brains. This fact does not provide a good rationale for education policy. Many popular texts exaggerate the differences between male and female brains.

In the remaining sections of this book, I try to separate fallacy from fact, locate facts in order to get beyond fads, and arrive at some findings. In doing so I recognize that I raise my head well and truly above the parapet and am in danger of creating my own set of fallacies and fads. Some shorthand is necessary in a book such as this, but by the time you complete it, I hope that the questions on page 17 will have had some sort of answers and the fallacies that I believe lead to fads will have received full and proper correction.

1
PART ONE

Wired
The Development Cycle
of the Learning Brain

Chapter 1

Pre-wiring

What Happens to the Brain in the Womb

This chapter contains the following sections:

A quarter of a million cells every minute. How the brain develops from the moment of conception. Why some brain cells are created but will never be used.

Two controlling forces. How learning becomes a "dance" between genetic inheritance and life experience.

A child inherits its mother's lifestyle. What to do and not do during pregnancy. How a child's learning ability can be affected in the womb.

Emotional rescue. When a parent has a high level of anxiety, it can be passed to the children, resulting in hyperactivity, especially for boys.

Learning and the womb. Is learning possible in the womb? If so, what sort of learning is possible or desirable?

It will answer the following questions:

- At what point in development does each brain start to become unique?
- To what extent do genes shape destiny?
- What factors in a mother's lifestyle will influence her unborn baby's capacity to learn?
- Is a mother's anxiety in pregnancy passed on to her child?
- Can any learning take place before birth?

Introduction

The Human Genome Project is mapping the 100,000 or so genes that constitute humankind. It is estimated that more than half these genes are devoted to producing the brain. Genes are not destiny. Only in a very few cases does a single gene take responsibility for a human disposition. If we are a long way from making a leap from knowledge of brain function to learning behaviors, then we are even further from making the leap from gene to learning behavior. But it will come![1]

The genes provide broad boundaries for human dispositions, not the dispositions themselves. A human being is created from a single fertilized egg. When a child is born, what has taken place over nine months is a highly complex interactive dance of genes, biochemistry, and the environment.

A Quarter of a Million Cells Every Minute

During every minute of the nine months of pregnancy, the brain gains a quarter of a million brain cells (see figure 1.1). The brain is genetically hardwired to produce a staggering total of around one hundred billion neurons and a trillion glial cells, which provide all the support and protection it needs. These cells are capable of forming a network of multi-trillions of connections capable of performing twenty million billion calculations per second. At birth, the architecture for supporting vital functions like seeing, hearing, breathing, touching, smelling, and tasting is largely in place. The potential for executing those second-by-second decisions is there.

The brain's development begins with fertilization. DNA from the mother and father combine to form a new cell. Within twenty-four hours of fertilization, cell division has begun. Three weeks after fertilization, the neural tube forms. The neural tube is the beginning of the central nervous system.

The front end of the tube develops into the brain, and the remainder becomes the spinal cord (see figure 1.1). At around this stage, the cells of the neural tube begin to divide very rapidly. Some of these dividing cells will become neurons (the basic cellular unit in the brain) and others will become glia (a range of cells that provide structure and nourishment to the emerging neural network).

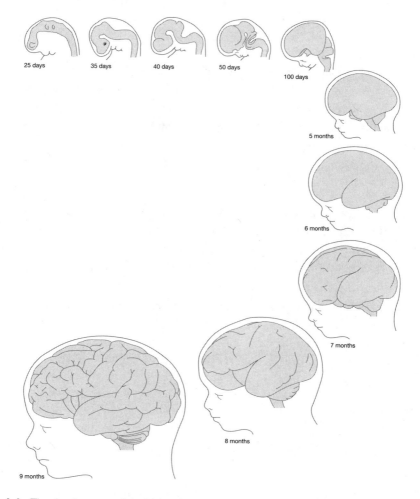

1.1 The development of the human brain from three weeks to nine months, showing the forebrain, midbrain, and brain stem.

As this process of division continues, cells begin to migrate to positions throughout the developing nervous system. Proper migration of neurons is imperative for the development of a healthy brain. Some learning disorders, including dyslexia, apraxia, and autism, may be caused in part by migration problems. Over the next few weeks and months, as the cells continue to divide and move, the walls of the neural tube thicken and form the structures of the cerebral hemispheres, cerebellum, brain stem, and spinal cord. Once the migrating neurons reach their destinations, they begin to send out dendrites and axons.

A number of fibers extend from the cell body of the neuron but only one is an *axon* (a fingerlike extension through which the neuron sends out signals). Axons carry signals away from the cell body and may extend for a few meters. The size and quality of the axon determines how fast the impulse travels—ranging from 1 to 150 mph. Repeated use coats the axon in a protective sheath called *myelin.* This process of myelination makes the transfer of information more efficient so that less neural space is needed.

The neuron sends an electrical signal down its axon to the axon terminals. There is a small gap between the end of the axon and the dendrite of a receiving neuron; this gap is known as the *synapse*—from the Greek word for union. Dendrites receive chemical and electrical signals from other neurons. They emerge from many points on the cell body and form relatively short, complex branches. When axons reach the right dendrites, they form synapses. The synapse is the point where the neurons almost touch and nerve impulses are passed from one neuron to the next via molecules called *neurotransmitters.* Electrical impulses are changed to chemical signals at the synapse (see figure 1.2).

Around the fourth month of pregnancy, synapses begin to form. At this point the brain asserts its uniqueness. A single neuron may have thousands of synapses, meaning that within the nervous system there are many trillions of connections between neurons.

As the brain continues its development, it produces more neurons and glial cells than it will need. A newborn has twice as many brain cells as there are in the adult brain! Then, in a process that is sometimes described as neural Darwinism, half the cells produced die off. We go from about two hundred billion to one hundred billion neurons. There are many reasons

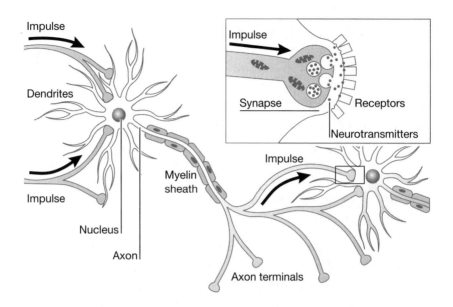

1.2 The major components of the neuron. The cell body, or neuron, sends an electrical signal down a myelinated axon until it reaches a synapse, or gap. Here the signal, if strong or enduring enough, is converted into a chemical called a neurotransmitter that floats across the gap to a receiving dendrite. If the signal is chemically coded, strong, and enduring, it is then passed along to the next neuron.

for this. Some neurons have a temporary function related to development itself; they do not outstay their usefulness. Other neurons are created for insurance purposes—they hang around to guarantee that all the proper connections are in place. When the proper connections for that development stage are all developed, any extra neurons are pruned away. When a baby is born, all the neurons are in place ready to be stimulated through interaction with the surrounding world.

Early on in utero the brain exhibits torque: It turns in the skull. By thirty-four weeks the right hemisphere has begun to twist forward and counterclockwise. The left has twisted back and counterclockwise. The left hemisphere develops later than the right, particularly those areas devoted to language. Later in this book the significance of this asymmetry in the brain will be examined.

Two Controlling Forces

Throughout all of this development, two controlling forces exercise their influence (see figure 1.3). The first is the genes. Inherited from the parents, they direct the development process, telling the cells when to begin their migration and where to travel. The fate of a given cell will depend upon which gene gets activated within its nucleus. For example, in cells of the developing spinal cord are several *hox* genes; if one hox gene is activated in a cell, it goes on to become a motor neuron—which sends signals to muscle fibers. If a different hox gene is activated, the cell will develop into another cell type.

The other controlling force is the womb itself. According to Dr. Lise Eliot, author of *What's Going On in There? How the Brain and Mind Develop in the First Five Years of Life* (2000, 40), "only in the last few decades has research begun revealing exactly how and when a woman's diet, health, emotional state, and exposure to various environmental agents influence fetal formation."

Every insult to the mother's health, every threat to her body's homeostasis, every enduring change in her physical well-being is passed on in some way to her unborn child. The most crucial time is within the first six weeks. Sadly, in some cases, a woman discovers herself to be pregnant after this period has elapsed and perhaps after smoking or drinking to excess. General lifestyle, health before and during pregnancy, drug and alcohol use, high levels of stress, even exposure to radiation, can all have profound effects on the developing embryo.

Research conducted by Dr. Bernie Devlin and reported in *Nature* suggests that the womb environment does contribute to intelligence (Devlin, Daniels, and Roeder 1997). The research, conducted in the Department of Psychiatry at Carnegie Mellon University in Pittsburgh, involved a reanalysis of more than two hundred twin studies. Some of these studies involved twins separated at birth who were given IQ tests when they were adults in their fifties or even their eighties.

Devlin attempted to identify whether there was a "womb effect" on intelligence. He compared the intelligence scores of twins versus sibling pairs and found that twins were much more alike in IQ scores than were

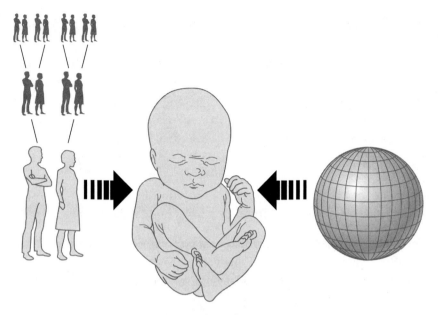

1.3 In children's development there are two controlling forces. One is their inheritance from their parents, which includes genes and lifestyle factors. The other is life experiences, including factors such as sensory stimulation, emotional bonding, nourishment, and the absence of threat to life or health.

siblings born at different times. There's a womb environment for twins and another for siblings, he explains, adding that these are joined by a common home environment to influence IQ. Factors influencing IQ are subtle and, as he says, difficult to pin down, but there are some obvious factors such as diet and alcohol and drug consumption.

In the study, Devlin and his colleagues estimated the impact of genetics on IQ at about 34 percent. The womb environment probably accounts for 20 percent of the IQ similarity between twins and about 5 percent of the covariance in IQ noted among brothers and sisters. The authors say one implication of their study is that interventions aimed at improving the womb environment could lead to a significant increase in the population's IQ.

A Child Inherits Its Mother's Lifestyle

The mother's diet plays a critical role in fetal development. The food the mother eats supplies all the nutrients available for the developing baby. Unwelcome invaders such as illness, radiation, toxins, drugs, or excess of artificial chemicals are likely to be more harmful to the embryo than an impoverished diet (see figure 1.4). However, shortages of certain nutrients can and will lead to problems. For example, proper closure of the neural tube early in development depends upon the presence of folic acid. A deficiency of folic acid in the mother's diet could lead to improper closure of the tube, resulting in birth defects like spina bifida or anencephaly.

Recent research across four European Union countries correlated low birth weight to subsequent learning difficulties. There was also a correlation between low birth weight and behavioral problems: Babies who weighed less than 1.1 kg (2.4 1b.) at birth had a significantly higher incidence of subsequent maladaptive behavior. Recent evidence has also associated below normal birth weights with diseases that arise later in life, such as diabetes, breast cancer, obesity, and heart disease, all of which were previously thought to be the result of lifestyle, genetic predisposition, or both.

Low birth weight can, of course, be caused by a number of factors, many of which are associated with poverty: poor maternal nutrition, ignorance of lifestyle risks, limited access to prenatal care, or exposure to certain hormones. In the case of poor nutrition, problems can arise because the fetus will send the available nutrients to the developing brain, at the expense of the other organs.

According to Dr. Bradley Peterson, associate professor of child psychiatry at the Yale Child Study Center, there are dramatic differences between the brain sizes of children who were born prematurely and those born at full term ("Study finds key areas" 2000). His research compared the brain scans of twenty-five eight-year-olds who had been born prematurely with those of thirty-nine children who were born at full term. The Yale team, whose results were published in the *American Journal of Science*, found that volumes in crucial areas of the brain were lower in those born prematurely.

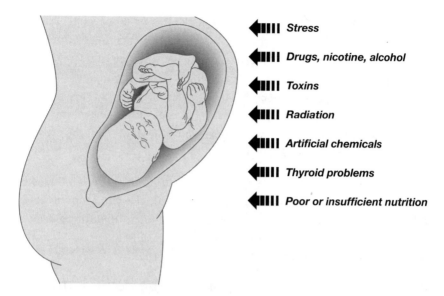

Stress

Drugs, nicotine, alcohol

Toxins

Radiation

Artificial chemicals

Thyroid problems

Poor or insufficient nutrition

1.4   The womb is designed to be "womblike": free from illness, radiation, toxins, drugs, or an excess of artificial chemicals. If a mother is denied key nutrients, her health can suffer, which will in turn lead to difficulties for the unborn child. For example, proper closure of the neural tube early in development depends upon the presence of folic acid.

According to Dr. Peterson, "The differences in brain volume on average were dramatic in all regions, with reductions ranging from 11 percent to 35 percent. Not all children born prematurely showed these abnormalities, but those born at a younger gestational age were most affected. The magnitudes of the abnormalities in fact were directly proportional to how early the children were born, and they were strongly associated with IQ of the children at age eight years" ("Study finds key areas" 2000, 1).

In recent years there has been an increase in the number of children regarded as having special educational needs. This is often attributed to their needs being better recognized, but some scientists think the improvement in survival rates of premature babies is also a factor.

"Premature birth at less than 1,000 grams birth weight (approximately two pounds) is a major cause of developmental disability," says Dr. Laura Ment, professor of pediatrics and neurology at Yale. "Infants in this birth weight range represent almost 1 percent of all births in our country, and the survival rate for these infants is well over 80 percent. But the incidence of handicap is high. . . . By age eight years, over 50 percent are in special education or receiving extensive resource room help. One-fifth have already repeated a grade of school. This study of very low birth weight infants who have been followed since six hours of age provides important insights into the adaptive mechanisms of the developing brain. From these studies, risk factors can be examined and interventions tested" ("Study finds key areas" 2000, 1).

The fetus relies entirely on its mother's hormones in the early stages of pregnancy, so if a hormonal disorder is present, the child may develop problems. For example, according to Dr. Robert Utiger, "Hypothyroidism in pregnant women can adversely affect their child's subsequent performance on neuropsychological tests" (Herzmann et al. 1999).

One in one hundred American women is estimated to suffer from hypothyroidism, which is treatable. It is generally caused by a chronic autoimmune disorder, radioactive iodine therapy, surgery, or age-related changes to the thyroid gland. Diet, ethnicity, and geography are also thought to play a big part in the disorder. Iodine is vital for the production of thyroid hormones. In many developing countries and in communities containing large populations from those countries, iodine deficiency is endemic.

Dr. Utiger proposes systematic screening and also that manufacturers should increase the supplementation of iodine in foods such as salt and vitamin supplements. Intake has declined in some Western countries in recent years because people are worried about consuming too much salt in their diet and because manufacturers have reduced the amount of iodine added to bread and animal feed.

Alcohol in the bloodstream during pregnancy can inhibit cell migration. This is a disaster for the unborn child. The brains of alcoholics are smaller than average; they are lighter and have less neural density. The brains of babies born to alcoholic mothers show exactly the same characteristics. Fetal alcohol syndrome babies have learning and behavior problems at school, have low IQ scores, and are more likely to become alcoholics themselves.

Smoking during pregnancy is one of the biggest threats to the health of the unborn child. The statistics are chilling. Children born to mothers who smoked during pregnancy are 50 percent more likely to suffer from a cognitive impairment. The risk of spontaneous abortion is 1.7 times higher and the risk of congenital abnormality 2.3 times higher. Babies born to smokers are three times more likely to have a disorder of attention. They are also more likely to have low birth weight. Smaller babies have an increased risk of learning and behavioral problems later in life.

Emotional Rescue

Stress for the mother also means stress for the fetus. Stress hormones such as cortisol are released into the bloodstream. Cortisol raises resting heart rate and affects other vital functions as part of the fight-or-flight response. Exposure to excessive cortisol in the womb could cause problems later in life such as hypertension, quicker stress responses, and impaired cognitive abilities. Women who suffer from high levels of anxiety during pregnancy are twice as likely to have a hyperactive child.

According Professor Vivette Glover (*BUPA Health News Journal* 2001), her research suggests a chemical element in the higher risk of hyperactivity, in that stress leads to changes in the mother's hormone levels. Some of these hormones, such as cortisol, can cross the placenta, which may affect fetal brain development. Another theory is that the mother's anxiety reduces the blood flow to the womb and thus to the baby, cutting the amount of oxygen and nutrients it receives.

Animal studies have shown that exposure to excessive stress hormones before birth may lead to premature aging of the brain, with direct effects on the hippocampus, a brain structure important to learning and memory. As discussed later, the stress response is largely set for life in the womb and in the first few months after birth. Our ability to adapt to, and cope with, unforeseen circumstances begins to be laid down before we are born.

Harvard University research led by Dr. Mary Carlson found that the emotional bonding between mother and infant also influences the infant's brain. Infants who were deprived of what would be deemed normal levels of physical contact had abnormal levels of cortisol; those in daycare settings where they received low levels of one-to-one interactions showed abnormal levels on weekdays, but not on weekends, when they were home. Such children had low scores on mental and motor testing. Maternal separation causes loss of brain cells in animals such as laboratory rats. If you want to cause stress in a lab rat, deprive it of maternal grooming and suckling. Although the growing brain normally prunes excess synapses and cells, the neurons in the maternally deprived animals die at twice the normal rate.[2] Stress-reduction techniques, such as meditation, may have a positive effect not just for the mother, but for the developing fetus as well.

Learning and the Womb

I watched a television program called "University of the Womb" with fascination and a slight queasiness. Expectant mothers were being encouraged to teach their unborn child basic mathematics through a combination of light taps and slaps to different parts of their bulging stomachs. An "expert" was encouraging the mothers to sound out the problems as they tapped: "*Three*—slap, slap, slap—plus *two*—tap, tap—is *five,*" followed by five robust and very earnest thumps! I could not bring myself to watch to the end. I was too worried about long division.

Dr. Lise Eliot, a real expert, points out that the womb is designed to be womblike! "There is one feature that best characterizes life in the womb: It is the relative lack of stimulation. The womb, like a sturdy eggshell, is a highly protected environment: dark, warm, confining, and generally quieter than the outside world. This isolation seems to be just the right thing for early brain development" (Eliot 2000, 41). This conflicts with the view that learning as a result of external stimuli can occur in the womb.

A newborn baby will, within hours, respond to its mother's voice over other voices in the immediate environment. It shows recognition signs. The newborn also responds to its mother's native language over other languages it may hear in the immediate environment. This suggests that a fetus may be sensitive to external sounds from within the womb. I met a concert cellist who told me that she had played the cello right up to the week before her daughter was born. At the time she was practicing an Elgar piece for a recital she had committed to. She practiced the piece daily in the months before her daughter's birth. Fifteen years later her adolescent daughter is still moved every time she hears the music, and has been from the earliest she can remember.

Despite the evidence of sensitivity to sound, there is no strong evidence that a baby is able to learn in the womb. Some scientists believe attempts at prenatal learning, such as exposing the fetus to sound, could prove detrimental, especially if the sounds are invasive, too loud, or interrupt the sleep patterns of the developing baby. Sound penetrates the uterus, and there is evidence that newborns can recognize sounds heard before birth, but the mechanisms and long-lasting effects of this phenomenon remain uncertain.

What do you do to become the perfect parent? I guess what you do is become informed, stay self-aware, and relax! Avoid beating yourself up over all the things you do not do and focus on all the things you could do. Lise Eliot (2000, 459–60) puts it better than I ever could:

> In a perfect world, there's obviously a lot parents could do to improve their children's intellectual prospects. The perfect parent, if she [or he] existed, would devote herself full-time to care and teaching of her child. She would begin, even before conception, by shoring up her folic acid reserves and purging her body of any chemical remotely suspect. Once pregnant, she would never touch a drop of alcohol, pump her own gasoline, get less than eight hours sleep, or allow herself to be stressed in any way. She would have an ideal, unmedicated, and uncomplicated delivery, and breastfeed from the moment of birth until the child was potty-trained.

She would spend hours every day playing with him—
singing, cuddling, talking, massaging, exercising, reading,
showing him how all kinds of toys and other fascinating
objects work. She'd start him on piano, tennis, dance,
French, swimming, art, violin, computer, Spanish, and
tumbling lessons at age three, practicing herself, to provide
a good role model. But this isn't a perfect world. Parenting
is hard work. Most of us try the best we can, given the
limits on our time, stamina, and resources. **,**

Chapter **2**

Wired to Fire

Brain Development in the First Five Years

This chapter contains the following sections:

Babies learn from the earliest moments. How and when a baby begins to make sense of information from the outside world.

The first learning style: imitation. About the area of the brain devoted to imitation. An explanation of the earliest learning style and why mother-child interaction takes place in the way it does.

The best time to learn any language. Why talk is so important for a child. Infants store spoken words before they can speak them. Word learning may begin at around eight months.

Expectancy and dependency. An explanation of sensitive periods. Some brain growth is programmed. Some is dependent on experience.

Enriched environments. Why the idea that enriched environments accelerate learning is flawed. A scientific justification for early emphasis on social interaction, play, and exploration.

Get yourself connected. An account of how the brain is organized for learning. Why all meaningful learning is about seeking and securing connections.

It will answer the following questions:

- What crucial development takes place at seven months?

- Was Piaget too conservative in his estimate of what children can understand in infancy?

- What is the best time to learn any language?

- Are there "windows of opportunity" when brain development must occur or that capacity will be lost forever?

- What is the best time for a child to begin formal learning?

- Is there an area of the brain responsible for learning?

Introduction

The brain is the world's most complex, wholly integrated system of interconnected parts. It has phenomenal processing power. Scientists have not come near replicating the brain's unique capacity for managing information. If you are a parent, you have at least one of these complex problem-solving machines lounging in your living room. If you are a teacher, you will have about thirty floating in fluid at an average height of about 4 feet 9 inches above your classroom floor. Without exaggeration, how those brains experience life in the first five years influences how they will do so forever.

Babies, far from being the blank slates we once thought they were, are born with a great deal of understanding. Such understanding can be measured, in part through brain-imaging technologies coupled to advanced computers, and in part through what is now a relatively primitive technology: the video camera. Video allows scientists and pediatricians to observe the subtleties of babies' behavior over extended periods of time and then to replay those recordings, observing specific behaviors and comparing them with others in the sample. Piaget never had the luxury of a video camera. If he had, perhaps he would have formulated his theories differently.

Research on how very young babies make sense of the world will, in time, tell us a great deal about learning and behavior. Disorders of perception and attention may appear earlier than was previously thought and may have real significance in determining our readiness and ability to learn.

Babies Learn from the Earliest Moments

Babies start to see complex objects in the same way as adults at the age of seven months, according to new research. Using a game similar to the video game Pac-Man, called the Kanizsa Square, and a geodesic sensor, which the baby wears like a swim cap, scientists discovered that somewhere around age seven months the brain begins to perceive objects in a different way.

When placed in a particular way, the pieces of the Kanizsa Square create the illusion of a square, to the adult brain at least (see figure 2.1). The scientists wanted to find out when babies start to see the square too. When the babies interpret the image as a square, the geodesic sensor picks up a burst of brain activity known as a gamma oscillation. The researchers reported in *Science* that they found no sign of the brain signals in six-month-old babies, but did detect them in eight-month-olds, indicating that the crucial developmental shift takes place around the seven-month mark (Institute of Cognitive Neuroscience).

Dr. Gergely Csibra, leader of a research team from Birkbeck College, says

> Understanding how an infant brain develops is obviously fascinating and may have implications for the education and care of babies. This new work not only tells us that babies as young as eight months recognize complex objects in the same way an adult does, but also allows us to think of new studies into early infant development. The difference between six- and eight-month-old babies is also intriguing and may show that there is an important development in how the brain organizes information from the outside world at that age. (Müller et al. 2001, 163)

In the opinion of Professor Alison Gopnik, "In the last thirty years we have revolutionized what we think about babies and learning."[1] Scientists like Alison Gopnik and those in the Birkbeck team, now believe that babies evidence powerful learning capacities from birth. A lab at the University of Washington Obstetrics Unit has been set up to enable observations of newborns within minutes of their arrival. In studying babies, scientists look at the pattern of interactions between those babies and the support systems around them—namely parents or caregivers—as well as how information is passed on, interpreted, and responded to.

Babies, from the moment they are born, treat humans preferentially. They respond to faces, structures that are made to resemble faces, voices, and smells. At birth babies can distinguish between different visual stimuli.

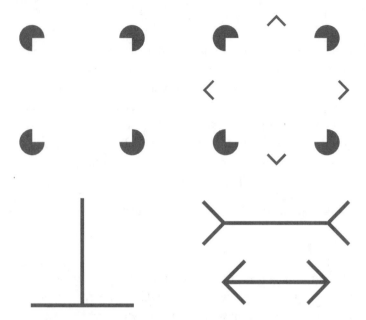

2.1 The Kanizsa Square (above), named after Italian psychologist Gaetano Kanizsa, is not a square but rather contours suggestive of one. The geometric illusions (below the squares) show how we perceive images according to our experience of similar images in real life. The upside-down T looks taller than it is wide, although both lines are the same length. We tend to perceive vertical distances differently than we do horizontal, interpreting them as farther away than their horizontal equivalents. The topmost images are seen to be bigger. Does this explain why the moon, always a half-degree in diameter in the sky, looks bigger when it is close to the horizon (Haber and Levin 1989)?

Newborn babies get bored and look away when they have been shown the same visual stimulus for some time, and they only look again if something new is presented.

Similarly, young babies will listen to their mother's voice longer than a stranger's voice. There is even evidence that babies recognize their mother's voice at birth, from hearing the faint but audible sounds in the womb (DeCasper and Fifer 1980). Babies recognize their mother's smell. They enjoy *kangaroo care*—that is, skin-to-skin contact. They favor their mother's voice over those of others, and they imitate: You stick your tongue out, they stick theirs out; you open your mouth in an exaggerated way, they open theirs. As there are no mirrors in the womb, we can safely assume that the baby has not learned this by watching itself. The baby is somehow linking how it feels on the inside with the emotional responses of others it sees on the outside (Harris 1989).

Babies can count! If you show a baby two cards, each with a large dot placed in the center, then slip a blank card in front and remove it again, the baby stares at the dotted cards again. If you do the same thing again, but this time add a third card with dots, the baby stares at those cards longer. The baby notices the difference, and its curiosity signals that it has noticed the difference.

The First Learning Style: Imitation

Where might a baby learn to imitate? What is the significance of this behavior for theories of learning? There are limited opportunities for babies to learn, other than through what knowledge they may already possess or through interaction with their environment. What is in their environment usually is a parent or parents and other adults in the babies' lives.

Within a few days of birth, babies learn to recognize their mother's face—they will look at a picture of their mother's face longer than a picture of a stranger's face (Field et al. 1984). They enjoy watching their mother make faces. Facial expressions are believed to be universal and cross-cultural. The grimaces and face pulling that come with the "parentese" that adults lapse into at the merest sight of a baby could have many functions, not the least of which is an introduction to learning (see figure 2.2). One of the purposes of imitation is to begin to learn the responses that are necessary to survive in the world of humans, including to behave like other humans do. Across all primates, imitation is an important feature of learning in the neonate phase. Through imitation, neonates explore the functions of their bodies. They begin to distinguish what is internal from what is external, which is part of distinguishing "me" from "you." Babies have no way of knowing whether they are imitating accurately, other than through the encouragement they get and possibly a kinesthetic sense that they are doing the right thing. A link is made: You get this nice, reassuring, faintly smelly shape that makes a noise near you when you do something with your body. The sequence begins to be familiar, you do something you feel inside and the nice, reassuring, smelly thing makes the noise again. It must be right because there it goes again!

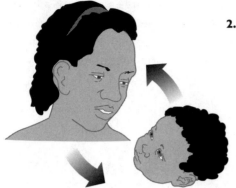

2.2 The interaction between mother and infant shows that you get more of what you reinforce. For some reason "parentese" involves exaggeration and repetition of sounds and gestures. Is a mother preprogrammed to encourage imitation in her child?

There is compelling evidence that observing someone doing an action activates a component of the brain's motor system to be ready to imitate the action. Areas of the brain that are active when doing a task are also active when imagining doing it. So, I watch you do something, such as a physical gesture, and the neurons in my brain alert themselves to "mirror" your gesture, whether or not I necessarily do so. Normally, an area of the prefrontal cortex, usually active when you simply watch a task, suppresses the act of imitation. When this area of the brain is damaged, the individual mirrors and matches behaviors observed.

Research on nonhuman primates shows that the premotor cortex, an area involved in controlling movement, is activated when a monkey "observes someone grasping an object, while the monkey makes no movements itself." The theory of mirror neurons has beguiling promise for educators and points us to the first learning style (Rizzolatti 1990).

What role does imitation play learning? Does it play the same role in older learners? Authors such as Judith Rich Harris (1998) make a compelling case that the peer group has as much or more influence than the parents in shaping a child's behavioral traits. It is within the peer group that most youngsters learn advanced imitation. If you move from one part of the country to another (or from one country to another) when your child is very young, the child will quickly abandon your accent in favor of the local one. The theory that any successful behavior can be broken down into its component parts and modeled is the basis for learning techniques such as neuro-linguistic programming (NLP).

Brain scans show that humans' pattern of neural mirroring is similar to monkeys'. When you or I watch someone make a movement, a part of the brain's motor system is very quickly activated without any corresponding physical movement in the body. Watch two people in conversation in a bar. The more engaged they are with each other, the more imitation occurs. I take a sip of a drink, you quickly follow; I lean back, you do the same; I nod my head, you nod yours. Is this more than showing empathy? Maybe it is part of the system for learning to understand the behavioral patterns of others (Meltzoff 1999; see also Iacoboni 1999).

By age nine months imitation has already become more sophisticated. In an experiment on babies' imitation, the researcher bangs her hand in an exaggerated way on a little box with a hinged door, and the door swings open. This is done several times in front of the baby. A week later, when brought back, the baby bangs its hand on the box. Bring the baby back a month later and it bangs its hand on the box. Some learning has occurred. Some scientists believe that some autistic children lack this fundamental ability to imitate and may be born without it.

Alison Gopnik, a philosopher by training, is concerned with the question of mind. At what stage does a baby realize that there are other minds? Piaget believed that such a level of thought was not possible until well into the school years. Gopnik believes that there is evidence of it from about eighteen months. In experiments at the University of California at Berkeley, Gopnik used Goldfish crackers and broccoli to demonstrate this (Gopnik, Meltzoff, and Kuhl 1999). The experimenter working with the baby "tastes" a Goldfish cracker and makes a face of either delight or revulsion. The experimenter then tries the broccoli and makes the opposite face. The baby is then invited to give the adult some food. At fourteen months, the baby gives either. At eighteen months the baby follows the cue and gives the preferred food. Something happens between fourteen and eighteen months. The baby develops a sense of a mind other than its own (see also Eliot 2000).

The Best Time to Learn Any Language

We do not yet know whether there are ideal times—what neurologists call sensitive periods—for things like learning math and reading, but we do know that they exist for language. Japanese native speakers have difficulty recognizing and getting their tongues around the r and l sounds. When they were much younger—and I mean much younger—they could do so successfully, however. Japanese babies can detect the difference between r and l up until about ten to twelve months. Because they are not hearing these sounds from adults around them, they habituate them out, so that after their first year of life they no longer notice them. Expose children to the sounds of their language through the exaggerated babble of parentese and they become more adept at detecting those particular sounds. Later these sounds form the basic building blocks of words and, even later, sentences.

Peter Jusczk, a scientist at Johns Hopkins University, points out that language input is critical before a child even begins to speak or utter any sort of sound.[2] His evidence suggests that infants use long-term memory to store spoken words before they can speak them. Word learning may begin around eight months, probably earlier than many parents realize.

According to Professor John Stein (2000a), of Oxford University, nearly two-thirds of the differences in British eleven-year-olds' reading ability can be explained by poor auditory and visual transient sensitivity. That is, that the brain is not yet good at tracking the subtle changes in sounds of spoken words or the changing shapes of words written on a page as the eyes move across that page. Developmental dyslexics are known to be less sensitive to changes in sound frequency and intensity. People who are illiterate have different patterns of brain activation than their literate counterparts when asked to do language activities that do not require reading.

We are all born with an equal potential to learn any language. At six months we begin to build the phonemes specific to our native language. Then we get an opportunity to practice manipulating the sounds. With luck we will have a coach who will help us with our manipulations, repeat them, rehearse them, and reward our successes with them. We call this coach a parent. A lot of the evidence shows that poor reading skills can be traced in many cases to poor language learning skills and that as many as 30 percent of children start school with poor language learning skills. Much classroom teaching is language based. Listening to stories helps prepare the brain to be more effective at making its own stories.

The basic unit of language is the phoneme. Learning phonemes starts in the crib or earlier. Children with deficits in phonological awareness in kindergarten are likely to be reading two years or more below grade level by fifth grade. In a project conducted simultaneously in Kansas and in Alaska, the learning performance of and language heard by four-year-olds from welfare, blue-collar, and white-collar families were compared. The children in welfare families had up to fourteen million fewer words of cumulative language experience than the four-year-olds from the other families (Kotulak 1996). When all socioeconomic, class, and ethnicity variables were stripped out, what seemed to have made the difference to learning performance was the extent to which the child had encountered language in the first four years of life.

The best three pieces of advice I can give parents to help their child become a confident reader are

➤➤❶ Provide a caring home environment with lots of, but not too much, sensory stimulation.

➤➤❷ Check your child's eyesight, hearing, and motor skills.

➤➤❸ Speak positively and often to, with, and around your child.

It is in the first few years of life that babies become explorers and part-time furniture bumpers. They become mobile. This allows them to move toward desired objects. They can manipulate their bodies to travel toward objects or people that catch their attention. This is a period of phenomenal neural growth. The provision of a safe space in which to explore becomes important. So, too, does the opportunity to practice and to imitate. Babies learn that some things—objects—do not move unless perhaps you propel them, and so are not as much fun to imitate as things that do move. Other humans, large and small, are fair game for this. Big humans—adults and older siblings—are instructors in this game. Mobility necessitates a bigger brain. This is true for birds, it is true for reptiles, it is true for mammals. With increased mobility comes more flexibility in behavior. Where there is more flexibility, there is need for more brain power to accommodate it.

Expectancy and Dependency

Brain development in the early years is both experience expectant and experience dependent. This means that certain things are preprogrammed to happen and other things happen or not depending on external stimulation. An example of experience dependency comes from Professor Nick Rawlins of the University of Oxford.[3] Songbirds' brains change during the breeding season. The acquisition of singing is correlated to the breeding season. When birds do not need to sing, the centers within the brain controlling singing shrink. Hippocampal volume in songbirds is also seasonal and experience dependent. (The hippocampus is an area of the brain where maps of space are represented in some way.) Marsh tits store seeds and retrieve them, blue tits do not. Birds that store seeds, like marsh tits and magpies, have bigger hippocampi than birds like blue tits and jackdaws that do not. Male Argentinean cowbirds visit lots of nests—so they get a large hippocampus to help them remember where the nests are. The female sits on only one nest—it loses out in hippocampal volume. The brain reflects the demands placed upon it.

There are what scientists call *sensitive periods.* These are windows of opportunity when the brain is primed to be exposed to certain developmental experiences. There are ideal times for the brain to be exposed, through the sensory systems, to sound, shape and color, movement, tastes, and smells. Missing the window causes problems later in life. The brain remains open to receiving these experiences for a limited period then begins to lose that sensitivity. The first five years of life contain most but not all of the sensitive periods. This is when the "use it or lose it" adage is most applicable.

Donald Hebb points out that brain cells are activated by sensory stimuli and by thought, and the more a particular pathway is activated, the more likely it will continue to be activated. Prime the connection between brain cells by repeated experience and the cells adapt and become better at responding to that experience. Then the surrounding cells are recruited into the process so that the brain becomes better and better at noticing subtle differences. Columns of neurons assemble themselves for this purpose (see figure 2.3). The brain is now rewiring itself in response to the experience—that is, becoming experience expectant. It expects and wants to become good at identifying sounds, seeing shapes, and making

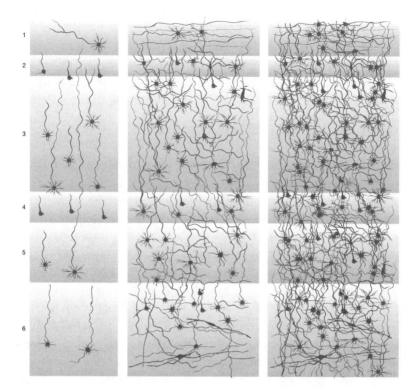

2.3 A cross-section of the cerebral cortex representing the organization of neuronal columns in six layers. Illustrated on the left are typical neurons with cell bodies, axons, and dendrites. The center panel shows how the cell bodies are distributed. On the right are shown the neuron fibers and axons. Note how some axons run throughout the layers.

sense of what is around. As the process continues, something called *neural trimming* occurs. If an expected experience does not occur and then does not occur again, eventually the brain goes somewhere else. In other words, the brain cells that were ready to respond to that particular experience migrate to another function: "If I'm not wanted around here, I'll go somewhere where I am wanted!" The study of sensitive periods is important for scientists, parents, and educators alike.

For scientists, sensitive periods show how the brain develops and organizes itself in response to the outside world. No two environments are exactly alike, and no two brains are exactly alike. Over time, difference adds to difference and each brain becomes unique. This is what is meant by "ontogeny reflects phylogeny."[4] The brain you develop is a reflection of the uses to which you have put it.

For parents, understanding sensitive periods helps in vigilance over their child's health. The best action a parent can take is to monitor the outward signs of the sensory systems at work. A protracted ear infection, which goes undiagnosed at eighteen months and causes a short-term hearing loss, could lead to reading problems later in life. All reading has its base in the processing of sounds. A difficulty in segmenting sounds as a result of a hearing problem will not be overcome by use of a different reading program.

For teachers, understanding the true nature and purpose of sensitive periods takes them further and further away from the idea of "hot-housing." In a classic case of misusing laboratory research with animals, we now have a lobby for hothousing children. The theory goes that because laboratory rats put in enriched environments showed neural enhancements, this makes the case for enriched environments per se.

Enriched Environments

At the Salk Institute of Neuroscience, researchers discovered in 1997 that laboratory rats in an enriched environment grew 15 percent more neurons in the hippocampus—which, as previously mentioned, is an area of the brain that contributes to visual and spatial memory—compared to those in the control group. The enriched rats also performed better in maze and intelligence testing. Among their conclusions was that the mechanism for controlling the production and destruction of neural cells is variable, not fixed (Gage 1997). This is one study among many that investigates enriched environments. An enriched environment for a rat in a lab is not one with magazines, sun loungers, a guests-only bar, and a whirlpool. An enriched environment contains pipes and tubes to crawl through and around, paper to rummage under, flaps to nudge open, and maybe a maze to navigate. In other words, it is a normal environment for a rat! Scientists acknowledge that enrichment studies prove the detriment of extreme deprivation, not the value of enriched environments. There is no evidence that adding more and more stimulation gives you more and more return in terms of neural capital. But take it away, and you very quickly get losses.

For policymakers this concept is important. A hint of sanity was brought by Sarah-Jayne Blakemore, author of a report to the Parliamentary Office of Science and Technology, London, entitled "Early Years Learning" (2000). She concluded

> Research suggests that children under the age of four or five may not have fully developed the social and cognitive skills that facilitate learning from formal instruction. Such research has led some to question the value of formal education at an early age and to suggest that a focus on social interaction, play and exploration might be more valuable.

And later,

> There is no convincing evidence that special enriching environments are advantageous to the development of the child.

The answer to the question, Should I hothouse my child? is no.

Talk to, around, and with your child from the earliest days. Use rich language and lots of repetition. Encourage learning behaviors—noticing, naming, describing, speculating, and questioning. Encourage physical exploration and robust play. Use lots of imitation. Put away your flash cards! Be prepared to be surprised!

The best form of enrichment has to be the security of a positive and supportive relationship with a consistent adult. Harsh words, abuse of trust, and dramatic changes in mood are profoundly harmful to a developing brain.

Abuse in childhood irreparably alters neural development. Work at the McLean Hospital and at Harvard Medical School attempted to find out if childhood abuse might impair the development of the limbic system. The teams were working with adults who, years earlier, had shown up on checklists as having suffered some sort of abuse in childhood. A significant number of these abused people showed abnormalities in an area of the cerebellum that released norepinephrine and dopamine, chemicals related to motivation and reward. Many had a smaller corpus callosum—particularly boys who had been neglected and girls who had suffered sexual abuse. In some there was reduced integration between the right and left hemispheres. Many of these individuals showed symptoms of borderline personality disorder, first placing someone on a pedestal then, as a result of some slight hurt, seeing them as a vindictive enemy, shifting all the while from paranoia to uncontrollable rage. As this happened, brain activity shifted from left- to right-dominant states, each with different accompanying emotional perceptions and memories.

What was happening? The researchers suggest that early exposure to stress had generated molecular effects that had changed the way in which the developing brain coped with threat. To cope with a world of pervasive threat, the brain needs to mobilize survival responses quickly, to prepare for violence without qualm, to be ever vigilant, and to be capable of enduring pain and recovering quickly. Thus the brain adapts to a state that will help it survive throughout the reproductive years—but this state is fraught with long-term health risks. Overactivation of stress responses will increase risks of obesity, diabetes, hypertension, and psychiatric problems. It will also age the brain more quickly and impair memory function. The brain, always highly adaptable, is sculpted to exhibit various antisocial behaviors.

In the early years of a child's life, the cells in the brain proliferate at a phenomenal rate. Such neural activity begins to stabilize around puberty. Understanding what goes on is important for parents and educators.

Get Yourself Connected

Professor Susan Greenfield (1999, 28–29) describes the organization of the human brain as like the building of a house. This is the simplest and best analogy I have come across. Both work up from the smallest unit of function. Bricks are individually made from basic materials like clay, sand, water, and cement. The rooms and floors within the house are built from bricks, ties, and beams comprising interconnecting walls. Rooms and floors have obvious functions—living, sleeping, resting, and eating spaces—and also less obvious functions—systems for heat, light, water, waste disposal, and communication. The house itself has a unique identity and is both functional—"a machine for living in"—and aesthetic. In many respects, the house is organized in a hierarchy of interdependent systems and structures, and so is the brain.

From bottom up, the brain is organized via the basic unit of the brain cell, or neuron. The brain cell is shaped by genes and by the presence of chemicals. Brain cells combine through electrical and chemical bonds to form circuits. The circuits organize themselves into networks. The networks form large-scale neuronal assemblies. These support specialized brain regions (see figure 2.4). The specialized regions are supported by whole-brain systems, some of which have overlapping functions. The whole is organized into a unique entity. Other brains look similar—but each is truly unique. This is the equivalent of consciousness. Sometimes the house functions well, but occasionally it malfunctions. In such circumstances, we can usually do something about the malfunction, but every now and again, we have to live with the flaws. The brain itself has meaning only when it interacts with others around it. A house is similar. You do not understand it entirely through its occupants or its bricks or the type of mortar holding the bricks together or its wiring. You need a holistic view. You build your house, and then you live in it. Build a good one.

As previously mentioned, a synapse is the physical structure that makes an electrochemical connection between two brain cells. Like many things in life, it is the coming together that makes the difference. The synapse is the mechanism by which brain cells connect. Synaptic density refers to the number of synapses per unit volume of brain tissue. Very early on in life, a baby's brain has greater synaptic density than an adult's. Millions

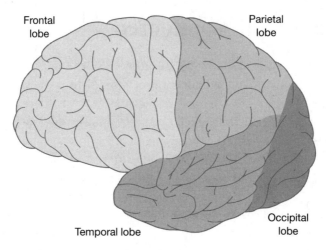

Frontal lobe

Parietal lobe

Occipital lobe

Temporal lobe

2.4 The major regions of the brain. The cerebral cortex has four lobes, each of which contributes to specialized functions. The frontal lobe is involved with planning, disinhibition, decision making, and some voluntary movement. The parietal lobe contains sites for speech, touch sensitivity, and perception. The occipital lobe contains the primary visual area. The temporal lobe is involved with hearing, speech, smell, and aspects of memory.

of connections are being made with each minute that passes, in a process known as *synaptogenesis.* Then, in a process typical of the brain development of different animals, frequently used connections are strengthened and infrequently used connections are eliminated: Use it or lose it.

It is worth remembering that the process of synaptogenesis varies by species, by individual, by brain region, and by type of neuron. The cells in a baby's brain are not all the same, they do not develop on the same time line, nor do they develop to the same extent. The same is true of neural pruning. *Pruning* occurs when brain cells that are insufficiently activated die off. Compare the process to going to a student dance and not being asked to dance. You hang around for a bit, prepare yourself as best you can, make yourself available to the best—and eventually any—offer, and finally go home sheepishly to look for some other distraction. Not a great deal is known about the process of proliferation and pruning of human brain cells during development because brain tissue can be studied only at autopsy. We do, however, now know more about the development of vision than about any other mental faculty. What has been learned in the last forty years of research has shown us the general pattern of how the brain wires itself.

The brain devotes more of its area to sight than to all the other senses combined. Researchers have identified at least thirty-two distinct, tightly organized areas devoted to vision in each hemisphere of the cortex. Each area is highly specialized, serving a different function of visual recognition. Some areas are devoted to recognizing vertical lines, some to recognizing lines one degree off vertical, some to recognizing horizontal lines, and so on. Well-established evidence exists that the eyesight of human babies is enhanced by a very rapid increase in the number of synaptic connections in the first two or three months (Huttenlocher 1979, 1987, 1993). It then peaks and plateaus between eight and ten months, before declining and stabilizing at around age ten years. If you are a parent of a newborn, keep in close contact with your pediatrician and monitor your child's eyesight, particularly in the first ten months.

The way the brain becomes wired shapes our personality and plays no small part in determining our future. For Salk Institute researchers, this means recognizing the importance of shaping: As we build networks—patterns of synaptic patterns—when very young, we build the framework that shapes how we learn as we get older. Such shaping determines to a significant extent what we learn: It will create both an opportunity and a constraint. The broader and more diverse our experiences when very young, the greater the chances are that, later in life, we will be able to handle open, ambiguous, uncertain, and novel situations (Quartz and Sejnowski 1997).

The early years of life are like the early years of living in a new house. Whether you build an addition is dictated by life needs. How you allocate rooms, decorate them, heat them, and organize furniture in them is dependent on how you will use them. As you become more settled, the urge to redecorate, to extend, to build anew declines. You are now living in what has been built. All that an infant sees, hears, touches, smells, or tastes shapes synaptic connections. The more the experience is repeated, the more enduring the connection becomes. With experiences that never or rarely occur, those connections never arrive or are never laid down. With insufficient electrical or chemical activity, proficiency in a second language or an ear for perfect pitch or an eye for artistic detail or a perfect left-handed pass never develop, and eventually the possibility of developing them is gone forever.

Chapter 3

Wired for Desire
The Brain and the Onset of Puberty

This chapter contains the following sections:

Brain development and adolescence. How the brain develops unevenly. Some areas of the brain develop earlier than others. More information is provided about language learning and development of coordination.

Passion's slaves. Why most adolescents, particularly boys, are not good at reading emotions. The sources of emotional response in the brain.

Pay attention. Attention—what it is, and how to get it and keep it. Two responses to threat. Why your mouth dries up just as you are about to give that talk.

A forgotten secret of learning. The brain circuitry of motivation and how it is linked with emotion. Why the best learning involves a degree of risk.

Learning addicts. How the brain not only recognizes winning and losing, but also responds to these experiences differentially. The brain can become addicted to highs. What sort of highs?

It will answer the following questions:

- ⇥ What does brain science tell us about ability tracking?
- ⇥ Is it possible to teach emotional intelligence?
- ⇥ Can I control my own fears? If so, how?
- ⇥ What's the link between emotion and attention?
- ⇥ How might learning become addictive?

Introduction

Picture the scene. You dare not go into the bedroom in daylight. You are not allowed to look at what is on the walls or to pick anything off the floor. You creep carefully, for it is asleep. Deep inside its nether regions a creature who was once your son or daughter lurks. It used to pick up its bedroom, it used to help with the shopping. Once upon a time it did the dishes. Now it has discovered mood swings! You have entered the adolescent bedroom. Hormones becalmed through childhood are suddenly raging with a vengeance. You pick up the tab.

If you are a parent of an adolescent, do not worry. Help, in the form of reassurance, has arrived. A growing body of research suggests that the mood swings, the antisocial behaviors, the tantrums, and the sulks may not be exclusively hormonal but may have their origin in preprogrammed changes in the adolescent brain. Three separate studies have attempted to map the development of the adolescent brain. The findings are of real significance for parents and those educators who teach youngsters between the ages of five and sixteen.

Little is yet known about individual differences in the brain. Research tends to focus more on similarity than on difference. At some point in the future we will have adequate tools to give us differentiated profiles of children's learning potential, their learning dispositions, and their thinking preferences. At the moment, we are a long way off. We do know, however, that differences exist and that some of those differences involve the maturation and development of the brain in and around the adolescent years.

Brain Development and Adolescence

Science points to a brain characterized by its uniqueness, but we remain with a one-size-fits-all education system. Crucial choices influencing a child's future are made on the basis of chronological suitability, with the moments of landmark choices occurring when the brain is at its most susceptible to change—around puberty. The brain, in its immature phases, develops not in a neat chronological continuum, but in spurts and plateaus, spurts and plateaus. The pattern of spurts and plateaus varies by brain, and by function and region within the brain. No Child Left Behind deems it expedient to make life-changing decisions about a child's learning potential based on paper-and-pencil tests notorious for measuring a narrow range of abilities. Brain profiling might allow similar decisions in the future to be timed by readiness rather than chronological age. Brain profiling would lead us into a genuine education for inclusion.

Starting at about age eleven, the brain undergoes major reorganization in areas associated with managing impulsivity, social interactions, and risk evaluation. Debra Yurgelen Todd, director of neuroscience, cognitive psychology, and brain imaging at the National Institutes of Health in Boston, is of the view that schools ought to pay more attention to the schooling of emotions, stating, "As important as teaching math, science, or reading is teaching social behaviors." She points out that "the neurobiology of development has not been systematically examined in healthy children and adolescents." Her work looks specifically at the adolescent brain in development.[1]

It has been assumed for many years that by the time a child begins school, all the hardwiring of the brain has occurred and all that remains to occur is the programming of the system. Yet research shows otherwise through a series of time-delayed images of developing brains from ages three through fifteen.[2] The images show that the period around puberty is critical for the pruning of neural connections in the prefrontal cortex. The prefrontal cortex contributes to what are sometimes described as *executive functions*—evaluation of outcomes and of risk, impulse inhibition, interpretation of social cues—and is not fully developed until well after puberty. Adolescents in Yurgelen Todd's study were very poor at reading the emotions on the faces of individuals whose photographs they were shown. In many instances they made completely wrong interpretations, confusing anger with joy, sadness with fear. Their brains had not yet been wired to interpret emotions through experience with a range of social interactions.

In a project at Buffalo University, seventeen boys and eighteen girls between the ages of eight and eleven years were asked to perform two different types of face-recognition tasks (Everhart et al. 2001). For the first task, a face-recognition memory task, the teens had to identify target faces that appeared on a series of slides. EEG equipment was used to measure electrical changes in their brain waves in the left and right hemispheres. The second task concentrated on identifying facial expressions from alternatives offered on a series of slides. This time there was no EEG measurement, but the researchers measured the accuracy and speed of the teens' responses.

Although boys and girls were equally good at both tasks, they used different, though sometimes overlapping, parts of their brains to process the information. The boys showed more activity in their right brain, while the girls showed more in their left. The researchers believe it is possible that boys process faces at a global level, an ability more associated with the right hemisphere of the brain. Conversely, girls may process faces at a more localized level—an ability associated with the brain's left hemisphere. What if this were true? Would girls have an advantage in "reading" people and interpreting subtle changes in mood and behavior? Is it possible that male and female brains are organized differently before adulthood? This work suggests so (see figure 3.1).

3.1 Is it possible that the brains of males and females are organized differently before adulthood? Work on face recognition shows that boys and girls use different parts of the brain when looking at faces.

Research conducted at the same time on the West Coast found further valuable evidence that the adolescent brain develops in spurts and plateaus. Using Magnetic Resonance Imaging (MRI) scans from children of normal health aged between three and fifteen years, Dr. Paul Thompson and his colleagues at UCLA found that children's brains develop in a specific pattern (Thompson et al. 2001; see also figure 3.2). The researchers scanned the children's brains at intervals ranging from two weeks to four years, which allowed them to follow changes in the brains with maturation. They found that the brain did not grow at a constant rate. Contrary to their expectations, they found that there are dynamic waves of growth in the brain, with striking, spatially complex patterns of growth and tissue loss. They identified a spurt of growth in the front of the brain from ages three to six. Between the ages of six and thirteen, the researchers found that the pattern of rapid growth moves from the front to the back, toward the areas of the brain that are specialized for language skills. The researchers also found that growth rates in an area of the brain linked to language were slow between the ages of three and six but speeded up from six to fifteen years, when fine tuning of language usually occurs. The research team suggested that the most efficient time to learn a second language would be in this period of dynamic growth.

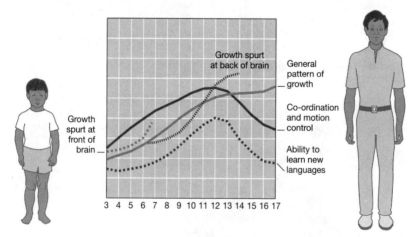

3.2 A growth spurt occurs in the front of the brain from ages three to six. Between six and thirteen, there is rapid growth in the areas of the brain that are specialized for language skills, which grow relatively slowly before then. The ability to learn new languages declines rapidly after twelve years of age. Coordination ability declines between ages thirteen and fifteen, when about 50 percent of the brain tissue that controls motor skills is pruned away.

The UCLA team emphasizes that the results do not mean that one cannot learn a language at older ages, but simply that doing so is a great deal easier during those prepubescent years. Dr. Thompson points out that these imaging results are supported by a number of surgical studies of people suffering from brain injuries or tumors. These studies have shown that if the language cortex is removed before puberty, the brain is plastic enough to compensate for the loss. If the language cortex is removed after puberty, however, people find it very difficult to reclaim their language skills.

The Thompson team also found that development of fine and large motor control, and coordination of voluntary movement, began to decline around ages thirteen to fifteen, when about 50 percent of the brain tissue that controls motor skills is pruned away.

In a report produced for the UK-based Economic and Social Research Council Uta Frith and Sarah-Jayne Blakemore (2000) commented on the significance for educators of such research:

> These findings will need to be replicated and related
> to changes in learning. They may have implications for
> teaching. For instance, language learning and activities that
> require motor skills, such as playing an instrument or a
> sport, may have a critical period in which it is particularly
> easy to acquire these skills. Thus, brain imaging could
> in theory give a biological underpinning to concepts of
> critical/sensitive periods. In particular, it may be possible
> that research using diffusion tensor imaging will tell us
> about the development of myelination, connectivity, etc.,
> and that this may relate to optimal windows for learning
> performance.

The corpus callosum—200 million nerve fibers crossing a structure four inches long and one inch high—also completes its maturation in the late adolescent years. The corpus callosum acts like a relay station, sending electrical signals between the two hemispheres of the cortex. Its successful development and integration is part of the wiring that occurs in the adolescent brain, somewhere in the age range of sixteen to about twenty-five years (see figure 3.3).

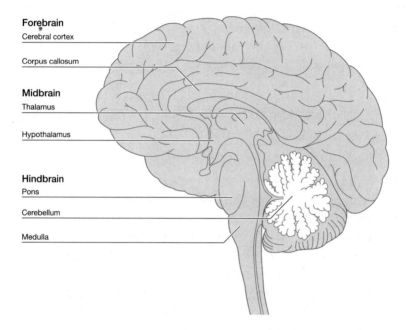

3.3 The major structures of the human brain showing forebrain, midbrain and brain stem. The brain is shown longitudinally with the front of the brain to the left. The major structures emerge from the spinal cord and include medulla, pons and cerebellum, all part of the brain stem. The midbrain contains the limbic and hippocampal areas. The forebrain, which is very prominent in humans, contains the cerebral cortex (which with the basal ganglia is called the cerebrum), the corpus callosum, thalamus and hypothalamus. The corpus callosum lies centrally between the right and left hemispheres and under the cerebral cortex.

It is also in the period up to and around puberty that the emotional skills that will play such an important part in shaping our lives are fine tuned. The frontal lobes will not be fully developed until late adolescence and early adulthood. The frontal lobes play an important part in emotional regulation. If you were to fail to develop the ability to recognize emotional responses in yourself and others, life would be hard for you.

Passion's Slaves

Is it possible to develop emotional intelligence? Daniel Goleman authored a worldwide bestseller, *Emotional Intelligence* (1995), in which he argues that a core set of emotional sensitivities can not only be identified but also developed. This work is welcome, not for its understanding of the emotional circuitry of the brain, but because it opens a debate about identifying and developing a range of understandings appropriate to a wide variety of human experience. To attempt to measure emotional intelligence is a valuable endeavor, but we are a long way from accomplishing it. Measuring emotional intelligence is nowhere near an exact science and never will be. The brain does not have a single center that controls all emotions. Emotional intelligence presumes that there is a correct emotional response to certain situations, when in fact a variety of emotional responses could be valid. Deficits in emotional intelligence could become yet another label if we are not careful. Harvard psychologist Jerome Kagan, whose child-development research Goleman draws on in talking about the nature of shy and gregarious kids, warns that emotional intelligence has the same blind spots as IQ. Furthermore, people are different: Some people handle anger well, but can't handle fear. Some people can't take joy.

Fear, anger, joy, and sadness are the four emotions that some cognitive psychologists believe make up the different threads from which a tapestry of emotions is woven. Each individual eventually settles on, and retains for life, a unique emotional tapestry. Some argue that surprise, disgust, and guilt are additional separate emotions; others argue that they are woven from a mix of the four basic threads.

What would your life become if you lost the ability to recognize and respond to basic emotions? As a result of illness, a young English woman recently had her amygdala removed in both hemispheres. The job of the amygdala is to alert us to dangerous, novel, or interesting situations, and to direct our internal readiness and reaction systems to respond appropriately. Researchers at Cambridge University are monitoring her progress. She has no cognitive damage and performs well on intellectual tests. Yet she finds it impossible to recognize emotions such as fear and anger in others' voices. She has an intellectual understanding of these emotions but no ability to comprehend or respond appropriately to them in real life.

Our emotions determine what we give attention to. Our emotions shape what we remember and how we remember it. Our emotions dictate our future behavioral responses. Educators need a better understanding of the role of emotions in human development. Too many of the prevailing models are dependent on common sense and hearsay. A more informed understanding of the role of emotions in learning and their manifestation in the brain will help us design better learning models.

I grew up in a small town in Scotland in the 1960s and early 1970s. If you, like me, suffered badly from teenage angst, you will appreciate that a crucial part of that teenage angst was loyalty at a tribal level to certain types of music—even specific artists. At that time it was commonplace to buy your clothing from the back pages of the *New Musical Express*. This journal specialized in flared denims called loons, often split at the knee and sometimes two-tone. It offered cheesecloth shirts, kaftans, and afghan coats. People who bought this journal and wore these clothes liked artists such as Neil Young, Joni Mitchell, and James Taylor. They smelled of joss sticks and patchouli oil. I avoided them. I wore tartan shirts, suspenders, Levi's, and boots that I bought from an emporium in the next town. I liked Slade and anything noisy. To this day I can sing the repertoire at the slightest hint of interest. To be honest, I can sing most of the other songs from that period too. If I do so, I am washed in nostalgia. The sights, smells, sounds, confused emotions, and feelings of embarrassment become instantly real. Why?

I had always assumed I was "passion's slave," except that my passions were rather banal. Now I discover that perhaps my brain, like that of every other adolescent, was altering in ways that actually made it better at remembering these things. The sights, smells, tastes, sounds, and feelings of adolescence are encoded to make them more accessible years later. Work done on autobiographical memory and "the lifetime retrieval curve" by Professor Martin Conway (2002) describes a "reminiscence bump" (see figure 3.4). The reminiscence bump begins in the mid-teens and lasts until the mid-twenties. In this phase of our lives, we recall more memories. The shape of the bump is the same for different cultures, although the type of things remembered varies and so does the time frame of the bump. In the United States the memories tend to be autonomous and emotional. People remember more about their own experiences as individuals. Interestingly, in China the memories tend to be more social.

In the United States the earliest childhood memories tend to cluster around forty months. In China it is nearer to sixty months. Memories differ because the prevailing culture shapes our concept of self. Who I am is partly dependent on who I need to be. Different cultures have different definitions of what success looks and feels like. Another reason we remember more around our formative years is that around this time we wrestle with our concept of self. It is a highly emotional period.

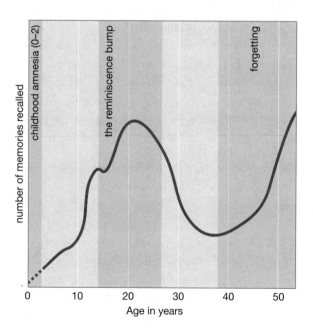

3.4 Autobiographical memory and the life span retrieval curve. Our memories seem to be more distinct and more numerous around a period beginning just before puberty and lasting for some years after.

Anything with a significant emotional resonance is tagged for later recall. Thus, experiences with a high level of emotional resonance are easier to recall than other memories. They remain unusually stable over time because they have a completely different encoding and decoding system than other memories. If you want something to be remembered, suffuse it with emotion.

The limbic system is a primitive center deep within the brain that links bodily with intellectual responses. In this sense it takes primitive and instinctual drives and integrates the capacity to manage and make sense of those drives. It was first introduced by Dr. Paul MacLean in 1967, when he talked about three "types" of brain (see MacLean 1990). MacLean argued that the brain's structures reflected its evolution and that we had retained the parts of our ancestors' brain that were of use. The "reptilian" brain acted as a control center for everyday life, monitoring survival functions: respiration, heart rate, temperature control, automatic movement, arousal, rest. Sitting on top of this knob at the base of the brain was the limbic system, which coordinated survival responses and was responsible for emotional arousal and memory. Added on top was the neocortex, a late developer responsible for higher-order functions such as planning and abstract thinking. Neuroscientists no longer talk in terms of a triune, or three-part, brain and have not done so for many years. The present generation of brain scientists may not even know what it means. Nor is the term *limbic system* used in the same way. For educators and others, however, the triune concept still offers a compelling metaphor for brain organization.

The limbic system has anterior and posterior lobes. The anterior is actively engaged in emotional responses and the posterior with related memory and evaluation functions. It is, however, part of an integrated system so, for example, the memory of an experience can be state dependent. Our recall improves when we are back in the same state. To remember something really well, attach it to an emotional state. But, if there is too much emotion, you get a dysfunctional response. If there is too little, the memory is more difficult to retrieve. The developmental period to and around adolescence is a period of high emotional resonance. Something about the process of emotional tagging improves recall.

There are many more pathways from the limbic system to the cortex than there are in the reverse direction. It seems we are designed to get information that has been emotionally tagged as part of a response system. This may be part of the reason we often react instinctively and before careful thought. A useful metaphor is that of taking the high road or the low road. Emotional tags make that choice for you, as described in the following section.

Pay Attention

Sometimes we are so busy concentrating on the details we do not notice the big picture. In an experiment at Harvard University, Professor Daniel J. Simons (2000) showed how we are often blind to change, especially if we are focused on detail. In the experiment, students submitted registration forms at a library reception desk. The desk assistant bent down and was replaced by another, physically dissimilar assistant. One bent down, and another popped up. Everything else remained as before and the assistant assumed the part his predecessor played. How many people noticed the change? Seventy-five percent of Professor Simons's subjects did not notice the swap.

Dr. Candace Pert says that the emotions help us decide what to remember and what to forget:

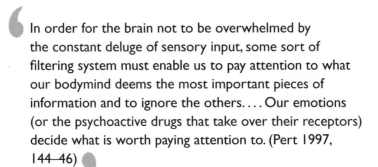

In order for the brain not to be overwhelmed by the constant deluge of sensory input, some sort of filtering system must enable us to pay attention to what our bodymind deems the most important pieces of information and to ignore the others.... Our emotions (or the psychoactive drugs that take over their receptors) decide what is worth paying attention to. (Pert 1997, 144–46)

If the students had been involved in some sort of emotional tryst with one or other of the receptionists, you can bet they would have noticed the change. If the day before they had had a major argument with one of them, they would have noticed. But remove emotional resonance, and we are in the land of the bland.

The high-road choice, referred to previously, involves a different set of systems from the low-road choice (see figure 3.5). The high road uses a "relatively slow, analytic, reflective (primarily cortical) system to explore the objective, factual elements of a situation, to compare them with related memories of past experience, and then to rationally respond" (Sylwester 1999, 65; see also LeDoux 1998). The high-road system is useless in an emergency. It will not get you into trouble but sometimes, when an immediate response is required, it will not get you out of it either.

The low-road choice is more primitive, more survival focused and more likely to bypass analysis and higher-order thought. It is shaped by instinct and primed by basic emotion. It is the rapid response system activated when you are confronted by a predator. It is a whole-body response, fast but exhausting. It gets you away from immediate danger. The high-road choice is reflective; the low-road choice is reflexive. One is slow, the other fast. Your low-road, or reflexive, system is also the default mode: "In confusion go to this." "If uncertain, or in data overload, activate

3 .5 High-road and low-road responses to an everyday stimulus. One's response to a spider is different, depending on whether you are a collector or a phobic. The former is a high-road response, and the latter a low-road response. Isn't education about increasing the high-road choices available to our children?

the low-road response." Going into default mode is what happens when you metaphorically "see red." With a sudden rush of blood to the head, you respond with a learned behavior acquired in a formative phase. For example, you are driving a car. When you learned to drive, the car horn was in the center of the steering wheel. Years later you are in a different car where the horn is down at the side of the steering column. Someone cuts you off in an intersection. What do you do? In a sudden rage you may find yourself beating the center of the steering column with the flat of your hand or, worse, you give him a quick flick of your windshield wipers! Why? Learned, or default, behaviors assert themselves when you are under stress.

Fear always evokes a low-road response. Some children have a fear of school. It is really difficult to remove conditioned fears once we have learned to be afraid of something. Again, there are good survival reasons for this. There is a biological basis to most phobias. Many others are learned responses that have become difficult to break. Useful, survival-oriented phobias include a fear of anything that might pose danger: open spaces where predators proliferate; closed spaces where escape from predators is impossible; shapes that seem to slither or crawl; creatures that leap at you; objects that may fall on you; objects that you may fall off; things that brush your face and threaten your air passages.

All these experiences are potentially low road. When they happen you mobilize. For example, you visit the reptile house at the zoo with your two young children. Inside it is cool, damp, and gloomy. Not a good start. As you stand, separated from the inch-thick bulletproof plate glass by a rope attached to posts, you notice that on the other side of the glass a lizard-like thing of some size is having lunch. Lunch is being dropped in and, as it eats, there is a lot of tugging and wrenching near the glass. So the three of you watch, transfixed, separated from the lizard by posts, rope, five feet of space and an inch of glass. Your mind wanders into reverie until, catching a glimpse of itself reflected by your dark sweater against the glass and fearing a rival, the lizard pounces, only to be stopped by the glass barrier. What is your response? Is it high or low road? High road would be, "Oh, I wonder if it poses any sort of threat? What do you think, children?" Low road does not involve any conscious thought; it is a leap backwards with a gulp of breath and your hands raised to defend yourself.

The difference explains how the system works to our advantage. More and more, neuroscientists are telling us that emotions are "the result of multiple brain and body systems that are distributed over the whole person" and that "we cannot separate emotion from cognition or cognition from the body" (Ratey 2001, 223). Motor and emotion systems are in close proximity within the brain. The emotions are expressed throughout the body in physiological changes, some of which are subtle and many others, like survival responses, are less so. Some are learned—a disparaging frown, for instance—and some are hardwired into the brain: laughter, blushing, smiling, and the startle response.

The mechanics of the high- and low-road response systems tell us about emotion and learning. To understand human motivation, you need to know about the limbic system and, more specifically, the amygdala (see figure 3.6). The amygdala could be described as the Trojan mouse of motivation: Upon this small site, all else depends. It plays a powerful part in labeling or tagging an experience as significant. Once an experience has been tagged, we respond thereafter in very different ways.

The amygdala is a part of the limbic system, which I described previously. It is very small, the size of a thumbnail, almond shaped, and composed of a dozen or so neural clusters. Each of these clusters links with different structures elsewhere in the brain and utilizes different chemical messengers to facilitate connections. The amygdala is involved in regulation of arousal, sleep, immune responses, movement, reproduction, and memory. The amygdala seems particularly involved in aggression, fear, and fear's younger siblings, anxiety and worry. The amygdala's closest friends are the frontal lobes. The frontal lobes are involved in managing impulsivity, long-term planning, discrimination and fine judgment, and goal setting. The amygdala and the frontal lobes seem to hang out together; they have good connections. There are more connections from the limbic system up into the cortex than in the reverse direction, and there are more connections from the frontal lobes into the amygdala than from any other part of the brain. The two are an act.

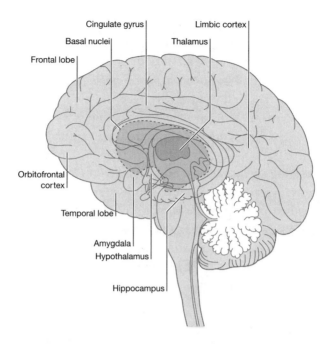

Cingulate gyrus
Limbic cortex
Basal nuclei
Thalamus
Frontal lobe
Orbitofrontal cortex
Temporal lobe
Amygdala
Hypothalamus
Hippocampus

3.6 The amygdala (shown in cross-section to illustrate its proximity to the frontal lobes) is close to and in front of the hippocampus. There are more connections from the limbic system (which includes the amygdala) up into the cortex than going the other direction, and more connections from the frontal lobes into the amygdala than from any other part of the brain.

Imagine you find yourself in a novel situation that has, for you, an element of threat. The threat is not to your life, but it has the modern-day equivalence: You are on a training course and you are going to be asked to speak. What happens? From the amygdala, communications go two ways. The first way goes directly to the senses and to the thalamus. The thalamus is a structure in the brain that routes sensory information such as vision, hearing, and touch. You go on alert. The second goes to the internal response system via the hypothalamus. At the same time, whoosh, the amygdala sends information directly to the brain stem, which regulates breathing, heart rate, body temperature, and blood pressure. At the thought of having to talk in front of your peers, your amygdala has gone on red alert!

Your response has an internal and an external aspect initiated through the same system. Internally, adrenaline starts to flow, blood pressure rises, breathing gets faster, heart rate goes up, and you are mobilized for response. Externally you blush, your body posture stiffens, you become more fidgety, and you perspire. Now, if you have had a previous embarrassing experience of speaking that your brain has tagged as such, these responses happen more quickly. In this case another brain structure, known as the basal nuclei, gets a message from its near neighbor in the limbic system, the amygdala, that something out of the ordinary is going on, and it gets involved. One of the things it does is to release a chemical messenger called acetylcholine, which travels up into the cortex. The chemical speeds up the firing pattern between neurons, and the system moves to overload. You get a sinking feeling in your gut and your mouth feels dry. This guarantees that the experience will be remembered.

A Forgotten Secret of Learning

Motivation has been described as a process that ties emotion to action—emotion in motion. The word *motivate* has origins in the Latin word meaning to move; so does the word *emotion*. My contention, quite simply, would be that motion and emotion are two forgotten secrets of learning. Many levels of the brain become involved in the experience of motivation. According to Zohar and Marshall (2000), leading researchers on spirituality and the brain, the human brain rewires itself when it is interested, passionate, or creative. Motivate yourself, and your brain responds accordingly. High-road and low-road systems are both involved in true motivation. How quickly might you react if your child was about to cross a busy street with a car only yards away and closing fast? You cannot answer. The speed of your low-road, reflexive-response system would astonish you. To be properly motivated, we need to tag an experience or a prospect with a strong enough tag. For the tag to have value to us at both high and low levels, it must have emotional significance. I always tell teachers to sell benefits not features to their students, and to sell those benefits at the personal level. Doing so engages the extended amygdala, the route to the primary pleasure center.

Research into the human brain and reward learning is growing. Work has been done on addictions as well as into the effect on the brain of perceived financial reward (see Blakemore and Frith 2000). In animal research, the amygdala, basal ganglia, and prefrontal cortex, which comprise the dopamine reward system, are all involved when animals are bribed with food or, indeed, mild drugs. Research done with monkeys showed how connections between brain cells were dramatically enhanced when a reward system was built into a task. In the cortex are regions of the brain responsible for touch. Using scanning technology, these cells were mapped as the monkeys played with a slowly revolving wheel. Then an incentive was added. When the monkeys responded to a pattern and speed of spinning by pressing a buzzer, they were rewarded with food. As they became expert, the neurons devoted to recall of the task proliferated. Neural networks close by were also recruited. The incentive had played its part in enhancing the recall. The task mattered to the monkey; therefore, it was tagged as significant, neural investment was made, and the process was remembered. This is proof positive that motivation matters in learning.

The cingulate gyrus is the main link thereafter: It is the main conduit between motivation and reward. It has the sensory mechanisms to receive processed visual, auditory, kinesthetic, gustatory, and olfactory information while also getting information about the internal readiness of the body. It assembles the information and transmits it to different areas of the brain. Thus, the basal ganglia are contacted for motor reaction, the brain stem for physiological arousal, and the hippocampus for appropriate memory.

Prompted by the amygdala, the cingulate gyrus is the main conduit between emotion and reward. It constantly takes in data about levels of physical readiness, arousal, and past experience and then, on this basis tags experiences as significant or otherwise. Thus, decisions get made very quickly about appropriate levels of response.

The amygdala and cingulate gyrus are actively involved in learning that is meaningful. Meaningful learning engages powerful emotions because it involves risk. What appears to a skilled learner to be mundane—Will

I get this wrong?—can for others be highly intimidating. Ask yourself what you remember most distinctly about school. I'd guess that, on the whole, your recollections are probably positive. Could this indicate that you had successes there? To be interested in, and still reading, this book shows a level of comfort with things academic that is not necessarily shared by the general population. When I ask general audiences what they remember most distinctly about school, the overwhelming, and sad, response is negative.

Adults talk at length about being humiliated, intimidated, overlooked, or forgotten. In formal learning, why would a learner take the risk of saying "I don't know" if the consequence is humiliation, intimidation, or neglect? Participation in a formal learning environment is like a visit to life's bookmaker. You have to make the choice whether to go for the big money. To do so requires a large personal stake. You risk losing, the losses will be emotional not financial, and the scars will remain. Those students who develop the healthy risk taking that is meaningful learning become hooked for life. Those who take a big loss early on do not come back in the shop. How can we make sense of risk-taking behavior?

There are three motivators for taking a risk. If a benefit is self-evident (or made to appear so), if we can connect to that benefit on a personal level, and if we feel we can achieve it, then we may take the risk. The thinking that accompanies this process switches from present to future and back again—future to present—again and again. If the desired outcome seems big, bright, and attractive enough, it may be sufficiently compelling for us to move from the present. The present position has attractions of certainty and security. If the present seems uncertain, insecure, and sufficiently unattractive, then we also feel compelled to move. The movement itself may carry enough promise for us to do it anyway. We may carry memories of similar risks that were pleasurable enough that we want to revisit them. The behaviors may themselves generate a vague pleasurable state that is sufficiently reinforcing. So, we have three motivators for risk taking: a compelling future, an undesirable present, or a vague pleasure in the experience itself.

Learning Addicts

Scientists such as Antonio Damasio (1994) have shown that the frontal areas of the brain, and specifically the ventral prefrontal regions, may be an important link between intellectualizing risk and the emotions surrounding risk. Gamblers who have damage to these areas of the brain do not exhibit any appreciation of the possible consequences and remain locked in pleasure seeking.

Gambling changes hormone levels in the body and as such can become an addiction. Heart rates and cortisol levels were higher in gamblers playing with their own money than in those playing for points. A team from the University of Bremen studied the physical changes that took place in men playing blackjack. The gamblers reported feeling surges of euphoria when they placed bets. Dr. Gerhard Meyer suggests that this experience echoes the euphoria of drug takers, which results from a surge of the neurotransmitters dopamine and serotonin in the brain: "The theory behind addiction is that if you consume an [addictive] substance, more dopamine is released than normal, and this is what happens when people consume drugs or alcohol. When people gamble, they say they feel this euphoria through a behavioral surrogate. Cortisol may contribute to such mood alterations" (Meyer et al. 2000). In a similar experiment, neural responses to reward were measured while gamblers played poker for money (Elliott, Friston, and Dolan 2000). The scientists correlated brain activity to how well the poker players were doing. If a player lost, the hippocampus was more active. If a player won, the midbrain became more active. As a player won more and more, the pleasure centers in the brain became more active. These included centers associated with control of movement, control of excitement, and higher thought. If a player happened to lose more and more, there were very different responses in the same brain areas. At the time of writing, research is underway with individuals who are addicted to shopping. They are a self-selecting group who volunteered in part as a way of overcoming credit card problems. The outcomes are awaited with interest.

So what? This work shows that the brain not only recognizes winning and losing, but it also responds to the experience differentially and in a way that is dependent on the advantage or disadvantage experienced. If it is possible to get a high from gambling, why should it not be possible to get a high from learning? Perhaps the reason that 99.9 percent of the population never experiences a learning high is because they are never persuaded to take real risks. Passive learning does not engage any sort of emotion other than perhaps apathy. Learning that is individualized and has emotional resonance elicits a dopamine response, and it sticks. We become addicted to the high of negotiating and overcoming personal risk. Reinforce it enough and we get learning addicts (see figure 3.7).

3.7 The brain responds differentially to the thought of winning. Many schools focus on failure and many learners in those schools opt out of the gamble of learning. They expect failure. How can we do more in our schools to sell the benefits? How can we create a generation of learning addicts?

The nucleus accumbens is also involved in tagging information that has a positive emotional value. It is a "pleasure seeker" located deep within the brain. It can be roused to action very quickly, and it remembers. It says to itself and to other areas of the brain, "I enjoyed this, I'd like to enjoy it again." It too is linked to the amygdala. Heavy smokers activate the nucleus accumbens every time they light up. If you stimulate the nucleus accumbens of rats, it helps them learn more quickly. Tag the experience with pleasure! A child who suffers from a deficiency in the brain's reward system may overcompensate by indulging in substances or behaviors that are in themselves rewarding. Reward deficiency syndrome states that a lack of internal rewards leads a person to "self-medicate" in this way.

Curiously enough, some researchers would say that apathy seems to be a specific malfunction of the motivation circuits of the brain. It is a neurological condition masked by other related problems. I would like to go into this in more detail, but it will have to wait until I can get around to it!

Joseph LeDoux (1998, 127) says that at the neural level, "each emotional input consists of a set of inputs, an appraisal mechanism, and a set of outputs." The appraisal mechanisms are either programmed by nature—natural triggers—or are acquired through experience—learned triggers. Triggers can be positive or negative—and all shades in between—with different neural systems devoted to them. Hence, there is no one emotional brain, but rather a series of emotional response systems. Antonio Damasio (2000) suggests that people learn appropriate emotional responses through everyday experience. Then the decision-making process about behavioral responses is facilitated by a somatic marker that narrows the range of alternatives. When this marker works well, we can read facial expressions, body language, and contextual cues and make good choices. If there is damage to the prefrontal region of your brain, you may be less skilled at making choices. Patients with damage to this area—including the gamblers—had flatter emotional ranges and were prone to making bad life choices because they were no longer guided by their emotions. Both LeDoux and Damasio suggest that conscious thought is primed by an underlying emotional sensing, which can occur outside of conscious awareness. Intuition nudges the choices we make. In the next chapter we will find out more about intuition and learning.

Chapter **4**

Wired to Inspire
The Completion of Brain Development

This chapter contains the following sections:

Thinking is hard work. Thinking burns energy. When we think, different neural structures are called on to assist. Knowing which neural structures can help in designing effective learning.

The tuition of intuition. Thinking independently is not a given. Much of our thinking is determined by factors outside of conscious awareness. Intuition, an integral part of creativity, is foreclosed by Western education.

Mathematics and the brain. Two types of mathematical thinking have been exposed by brain scientists. Why they may have great value for math teachers.

We are all musical! Science proves we all have musical ability. How music can aid learning. Why Mozart will not make you a better thinker.

Doing "good looking." The ability to "look" with different parts of the brain can be developed. How to use visual stimuli more effectively in classrooms.

Mental rehearsals of success. This section proves that you can develop muscles by thought. How to develop the mental rehearsal muscles of children.

It will answer the following questions:

- Does thinking tire you out?
- Can I learn something without being aware that I am doing so?
- How do I help my child improve at math?
- Why are some people more musically gifted than others?
- Does a trained artist look at a painting with the same parts of the brain as an amateur?
- Can I improve my performance in a sport just by thinking about it?

Introduction

What is going on in your brain when you learn to play the piano or read or do math or paint? Is there a part of the brain for algebra and a separate part for geometry? Do you use different parts of the brain for learning a foreign language? What about using different parts of the brain for different languages? One of the most exciting possibilities offered to educators by neuroscience is the hope that soon we will not only be able to identify how the brain is used for specific learning functions but also be able to modify and improve the brain structures used. It is highly unlikely that the same neural structures activate the different sorts of intellectual engagement required by various disciplines. The sort of thinking required for artistic creativity is not the same as that required for algebraic calculation. So what do we know about the different sorts of thinking and brain activity?

According to Professor Robert Sternberg the essence of intelligent thought would "seem to be in knowing when to act quickly, and knowing when to think and act slowly" (cited in Gleick 1999, 114; see also Sternberg 1988, 1996). Is there a best way to think? If so, can it be taught? We are often advised to think "hard" about something or to give it "serious thought." But what might thinking hard mean? What happens in the brain? Is thinking tiring? Can thinking hard actually cause fatigue?

Thinking is Hard Work

A team from the University of Virginia carried out research on how thinking consumes energy in rats (see, for example, Gold 2003; Salinas and Gold 2005). They found that having to think hard drains glucose from a key part of the brain. The effect was more dramatic in older rats, whose brains also took longer to recover. As they explain, glucose is the brain's fuel. Young rats are usually able to supply all the glucose that a particular area of the brain needs until the task becomes very demanding. Older rats have much more difficulty supplying their brains with glucose, even on tasks where no glucose use is seen in young rats. This correlates with a big deficit in performance. A lack of fuel affects the ability to think and remember.

Glucose is the main source of energy for the brain. It has long been thought that, unless a person is starving, the brain always receives an ample supply of glucose. The Virginia team measured glucose levels in the brains of rats as they navigated through a maze. They found that in a brain area concerned with visual and spatial memory, the demand for glucose was so high that levels fell by 30 percent. In contrast, levels stayed constant in other brain areas that played no role in spatial memory.

In a follow-up study, the researchers showed that in older rats glucose levels in the active brain areas dropped by 48 percent during the maze task. They also found that in the older animals glucose supply did not return to normal until thirty minutes after the task was completed. In young rats recovery was immediate.

The researchers found they could boost the rats' performance by giving them glucose injections. One of the implications of this research is that the contents and timing of meals may need to be coordinated to have the most beneficial effects on thinking and learning. School breakfast programs in schools help overcome some of the metabolic starvation brought on by poor fueling habits.

Would playing a game such as chess exercise and thus develop the brain? If so, what structures in the brain would benefit? If you are about to checkmate an opponent, you are thinking hard and doing so against the clock. All your knowledge and experience are brought to the moment. You are perceiving colors, shapes, and combinations of possible moves on the board and separating them from activity in the periphery of your senses. You are assigning values to the pieces. You retrieve the rules. You consider consequences and recognize and retrieve familiar patterns. Your mind shifts between reflection and speculation, back and forward, back and forward.

In a 1994 research project, ten chess players played each other under competition conditions while being monitored by positron emission tomography (PET)—a method for detecting chemical changes within the brain (Nichelli et al. 1994). It was found that glucose uptake was increased in very different neural structures simultaneously (see figure 4.1). The results suggested that the brain was working hard to perform the game. Separating colors and identifying shapes activated areas toward the back of the brain on both sides that are known to be associated with visual processing. Remembering the rules and sequences of plays activated two areas on the left side of the brain, a small structure deep within the brain associated with indexing memories, and a structure in an area near the left ear associated with memory storage. Forward planning and specifically checkmating activated both the prefrontal cortex (vital for planning and fine judgment) and the visual cortex (for mental rehearsal of the look of the moves).

A structured intellectual activity such as chess offers an opportunity to integrate very different functional specialties within the brain in an experience shared with others. It also requires the successful player to think globally and locally simultaneously. He or she must focus on the upcoming move but not lose sight of the chain of consequences. As such, it provides a cameo of some sound learning principles: simultaneous global and local thinking, reflection and speculation, structured challenge, agreed on measures of performance, shared experience upon which to draw, and open-ended outcomes.

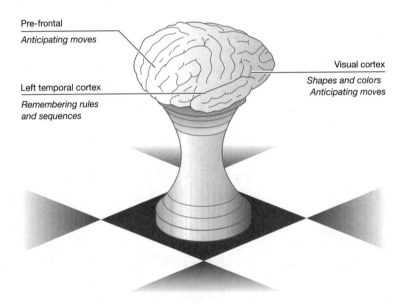

Pre-frontal
Anticipating moves

Visual cortex
Shapes and colors
Anticipating moves

Left temporal cortex
Remembering rules
and sequences

4.1 Thinking reorganizes the brain. Thinking can be locally or globally focused. Both types of thinking are desirable. Chess players exhibit both. Visual processing areas centered at the back of the brain identify shapes and colors. Structures in the left temporal lobe are used for remembering rules and sequences of moves. Anticipating moves activates both the prefrontal and visual cortexes.

The Tuition of Intuition

Can you think without being aware you are doing so? Is effort a necessary part of thinking? If we can have intuitive knowledge, does this mean that we can learn without awareness?

Our unconscious thought processes support conscious thought. When I lift a cup to my mouth, I do not have to attend to the separate movements of all the muscles in my right hand and arm, nor do I have to look at the cup to guide it safely to my mouth, nor do I have to take deliberate care to open my mouth before I start to drink. After I initiate the process, there is little conscious decision making involved. The necessary behaviors are being initiated at a level outside of conscious awareness. They have been learned and rehearsed over time until they are now part of me. What other behavioral responses of which I am no longer consciously aware might be part of me?

Repeated exposure to a phenomenon develops a favorable view of it even if we are not conscious of this attitude. This is known as the *positive effect.* Independent of what I want at a conscious level, my thinking is being shaped by familiarity. For example, subjects were asked to rank invented words and photographs of faces on characteristics such as Which word might best mean goodness? or, Which face do you like the most? In both cases and again and again, there was a strong correlation between frequency of exposure and positive effect. The more they had seen the fake word or the photograph, the more they were attracted to it. This means that much of our thinking is primed by familiarity. Thought is not as independent as we might think!

It is possible through participating in an activity to learn embedded rules and codes of conduct without being consciously aware of doing so. If you have a telephone number with ten digits, you will tend to remember it in chunks. This chunking is effective to such a degree that if you buy something over the phone and the vendor chunks your telephone number differently when repeating it back, you may not recognize it immediately. At no time did you consciously sit down and practice your telephone number. You assimilated it through exposure. Research on implicit learning shows you have the capability of learning procedures, rules, patterns of play, and complex sequences without focusing your attention on doing so. When players practiced a simple reaction time task, their pattern of brain activation changed. Without being consciously aware of any pattern embedded in what they were being asked to do, the players rehearsed the reaction time task repeatedly. There was, in fact, a complex sequence hidden within the activity. After extended rehearsal, a very slight alteration in the sequence of the game resulted in immediate and corresponding blood flow changes in the brain. There was more activity in the left premotor area, left anterior cingulate, and right ventral striatum. Activation was reduced in the right dorsolateral prefrontal and parietal areas. Without the players being aware of it, learning had occurred. The brain had become more efficient at dealing with the embedded pattern. The researchers believe that the ventral striatum is responsive to new information, and the right prefrontal area is associated with the maintenance of known information. They also believe that you can engage in an activity that requires simultaneously understanding context and developing new skills without being consciously aware of doing so.

Schools are good at teaching bits of information. They are not so good at making connections between them. The Western curriculum tends to be packaged up in discrete bits attended to for given periods of time within an established chronological window. The brain is better at making connections than learning isolated pieces of information; without the conscious engagement of its owner, it will seek to find connections. Albert Einstein noted that the relationship between two entities is more important than the entities themselves. If humans are connection seekers, if we seek the connections consciously and unconsciously, and if conscious seeking is the exception rather than the rule, teachers ought to be acutely conscious of the embedded learning that occurs on an everyday basis within and outside of their classrooms. Learning itself is all about seeking and securing connections. Finding and emphasizing the connections is what schools should be doing.

Mathematics and the Brain

Dyscalculia, or difficulty with numbers, affects between 3 percent and 6 percent of the population in the West. Their trauma is as painful as that experienced by dyslexics. Imagine being unable to make change, tell the time, or catch the correct bus. Math involves symbols as well as letters, and a plus sign + looks very similar to the letter x for many people. The language of math is also potentially confusing, and if young learners latch on to their first interpretation of a phrase or word, then they may develop longstanding misinterpretations. Professor Brian Butterworth of University College, London, author of *What Counts: How Every Brain Is Hardwired for Math* (1999), has shown that children with dyscalculia are troubled by even the simplest numerical tasks, such as selecting the larger of two numbers or counting the number of objects in a display (see figure 4.2). His research suggests there is a genetic basis for the problem. When someone says, "I'm no good at math; I get it from my dad," there might be a grain of truth in the statement. He also suggests that in some cases difficulty with math arises from bad teaching. Being taught in a way that gives flawed understanding, then being asked to move on and build on top of that flawed understanding, leads to alienation.

Some of the world's leading researchers into mathematical thinking believe that infants display a sense of number. They can count, do elementary addition and subtraction, and understand relationships between quantities. What is more, many animals show the same abilities! Professor Butterworth maintains that the brain has evolved special circuits for numbers and that math is built on a "specific innate basis whereas

4.2 What is the total of the three dice? How did you arrive at the total? Did you add the dots? Did you also have to count the dice? We all add the dots. We do not count the dice. Children with dyscalculia may have difficulty making such decisions in mathematical problem solving.

reading is not" (D'Arcangelo 2001). Although the experts would say that research on dyscalculia is about twenty years behind that on dyslexia, diagnostic tests for dyscalculia are in development and should be available to educators soon.

A dyscalculic child would be more likely to

- show difficulty in learning simple number concepts.

- have an impaired sense of number size.

- be poor at estimation.

- have problems navigating up and down number lines, especially in twos, threes, or more.

- have difficulty comprehending new terms and concepts—for example, units in tens, hundreds, or thousands.

- have difficulty linking facts to procedures—for example, subtract 2 from 7.

- show functional impairment of the parietal lobe.

- have generally normal cognitive and language abilities but occasionally have other masking learning difficulties.

How does the brain deal with different types of mathematical reasoning? Some recent research might help improve the teaching of children with dyscalculia. A team of French and American researchers, led by cognitive neuroscientist Stanislaus Dehaene of the National Institute of Health and Medical Research in Paris and cognitive psychologist Elizabeth Spelke of the Massachusetts Institute of Technology, say they have established that two very different brain functions are involved in mathematical reasoning (Cromie 2001; Dehaene 1997).

Previous studies of people with brain injury have hinted that different areas of the brain may be used for different types of mathematical activities: a nonverbal visual and spatial sense of quantity, versus symbols related to language. Mathematicians themselves have suggested that this might be so. Albert Einstein said numerical ideas came to him more or less as images that he could combine at will, whereas others have said they rely on verbal representations of numbers when thinking about problems.

Volunteers who were fluent in two languages—English and Russian—were asked to solve a series of problems after first being taught the necessary math. One group was taught in Russian, the other in English. The first discovery was that exact calculation required more time than estimation. In addition, if the volunteers who learned in English were tested in Russian, or vice versa, they needed as much as a second more to complete exact calculations. (Does 53 plus 68 equal 121 or 127?) When they were tested on estimation (is 53 plus 68 closer to 120 or 150?), there was no language effect. Thus, the brain appears to be solving the tasks in two very different ways. Despite the seeming similarity of the tasks, the difference was marked.

The volunteers were then tested on more complex mathematical operations, such as addition in a base other than ten and the approximation of logarithms and square roots. The difference remained. PET scans showed which parts of the brain were operating in each kind of task (see figure 4.3). Exact calculations lit up the volunteers' left frontal lobes, an area of the brain known to make associations between words. Estimation activated the left and right parietal lobes, responsible for visual and spatial representations. The parietal lobes are also responsible for finger control—and counting on the fingers is something children almost everywhere do early on in learning arithmetic.

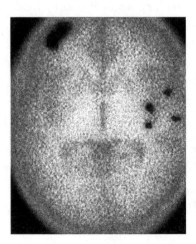 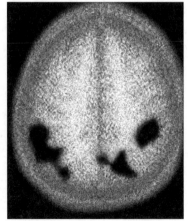

4.3 The scan on the left shows how the left frontal lobe, an area of the brain known to make associations between words, was active when subjects were asked to make exact calculations. Estimation involved the left and right parietal areas (right photo).

In explaining the findings, Dr. Dehaene pointed out that many studies have indicated that education probably has a much greater effect on skill in mathematics than any initial difference in innate ability. The findings will not, therefore, predict which children will naturally be better at math. The results could however lead to improved teaching methods. A practical idea would be to encourage children to talk themselves and others through their work more frequently. Teachers should make every effort to use visual and spatial representations as well as oral explanations when teaching math.

Imaging studies on adults show that the intraparietal area—located in the brain area above each ear and involved in visual-spatial processing—is responsible for "number sense." Damage to this area leads to dyscalculia. Dr. Dehaene is of the view that the parietal lobe is actively involved in our ability to make sense of numbers throughout development (Dehaene, Dehaene-Lambertz, and Cohen 1998; Dehaene et al. 1999). As we engage with the world of numbers throughout our school years, the nonverbal representation system known as the quantity system is repeatedly linked to other systems for numbers that are visual (symbols) or verbal (words) or both. Rote learning is predominantly verbal. Approximation is predominantly quantity-based. What would happen if one had an impairment in areas of the brain responsible for quantity, visual-spatial, or verbal systems? The result would be difficulty with numbers. A genetic weakness could cause such a problem. So could brain trauma. In a less obvious way, if the neural structures connecting the processing areas are poorly developed, there may be a loss of fluency. If I am overly reliant on one strategy, then I could suffer as a consequence. Learning multiplication tables by rote is fine, but not if I am unable to connect each outcome to a sense of quantity.

Brian Butterworth (1999) confirms that the brain uses different memory systems for the storage of mathematical information—including facts and procedures—than is used for ordinary, everyday information. Declarative and procedural memory rely on the temporal and frontal lobes. Math facts and procedures seem more reliant on the parietal lobe. So, as we have seen, any damage to this area has a profound effect. It is vital for math teachers to help children understand the process of what they are doing. Learning number patterns by rote is like learning a narrative poem: It activates language centers rather than number centers in the brain. Knowing number facts does not necessarily make you better at manipulating number systems. Knowing how to manipulate number systems makes you better at number facts. It seems there is a neurological basis for this distinction. In addition to practice in manipulating numbers, articulating the methodology behind problem solving is important. Reflective rehearsal allows the math procedures to be stored in long-term memory. Reflectivity thus leads to reflexive responses: The more a person does something in a considered way and has opportunities to reflect on doing so, the more reflexive it becomes. Next time, the process is automatic. It has been learned.

One scientist climbed the slippery slope of explaining the effect of technology on a child's brain by claiming that computer games are damaging to brain development. Professor Ryuta Kawashima and his team at Tohoku University in Japan compared the brain activity of children playing Nintendo with children doing a simple, repetitive mental arithmetic exercise. The team claimed that the game stimulated those parts of the brain associated with vision and with movement, whereas solving the arithmetic problem stimulated activity in both left and right hemispheres of the frontal lobe. Kawashima took the unusual step for a neuroscientist of extrapolating about ideal learning conditions based on his findings: "There is a problem we will have with a new generation of children who play computer games that we have never seen before. The implications are very serious for an increasingly violent society and these students will be doing more and more bad things if they are playing games and not doing other things like reading aloud or learning arithmetic" (*London Observer*, August 19, 2001, 7).

We Are All Musical!

Should you wish to, you can buy a boxed set of CDs entitled *Baroque a Bye Baby* (by Roland Roberts, distributed by National Childbirth Trust, London). It includes classical pieces that the publishers claim will develop your baby's brain. Simply tuck in the child, turn up the volume, and away you go—neural structures activated aplenty! How useful a practice might this be? Does playing classical music to very young children enhance their capacity for learning? Is there such a thing as a Mozart effect? Is there any benefit to the brain in learning to play a musical instrument? If so, what instrument, to what level, and when should a child start to learn? If I am a musician, how is my brain different from my next door neighbor's?

According to Professor Gordon Shaw and colleagues at UC Irvine, originators of the Mozart effect research, "training a child in music at three or four years of age improves the way in which their brain recognizes patterns in space and time" (Rauscher, Shaw, and Ky 1993, 661; see also Rauscher, Shaw, and Ky 1995). A great deal of accumulated evidence supports the all-around advantages of early training in music. To follow a discipline of smooth, controlled, voluntary, cross-lateral movement, involving both hands—and possibly feet—while simultaneously tracking the notes on a page so as to anticipate the sounds to come is a great all-around workout for the brain. To do so regularly and for pleasure is a wonderful thing. Some would have us believe this makes you more intelligent. Professor Norman Weinberger is of the view that "millions of neurons can be activated in a single musical experience." He adds, "Music has an uncanny manner of activating neurons for purposes of relaxing muscle tension, changing pulse, and producing long-range memories which are directly related to the number of neurons activated in the experience" (Weinberger and McKenna 1988). Music offers educators a means of energizing or relaxing students, conveying content information, priming certain types of cognitive performance, and enhancing phonological awareness.

What is the Mozart effect? *Mozart effect* is a term that has been corrupted through a global game of Chinese whispers. Professor Shaw and his team found in a controlled study that undergraduates undertaking mathematical tasks involving spatial and rotational symmetry showed significant performance improvements when played the Mozart Piano Sonata for Two Pianos in D for ten minutes prior to the task. They did not postulate all-around improvements in intelligence scores as a result of listening to Mozart. Two conclusions can be drawn. First, when research is compelling and accessible to the general media, its message can be corrupted. Second, scientists are reluctant to generalize, so when quality findings emerge they are always tied tightly to the particular context investigated. Engagement with music may lead to some specific improvements in cognitive performance. For example, some musicians, as a result of their training, would appear to have a larger left cranial temporal region. This difference may help with some aspects of verbal memory. This does not make them more intelligent.

"Adults with music training in their childhood demonstrate better verbal memory," says Dr. Agnes Chan of the Chinese University of Hong Kong, who conducted research with sixty female college students, thirty of whom had at least six years' training on one Western musical instrument (such as violin or piano) before the age of twelve (Chan, Ho, and Cheung 1998, 128). The other thirty had received no musical training. The students were read some words and asked to remember them—a very common clinical test for memory. Dr. Chan describes the outcomes: "We found that people who have had music training can remember about 17 percent more information than those who have not had any music training (128).

It is believed that this extra ability to remember spoken words is based in a specific part of the brain that is enlarged in musicians. As Dr. Chan explains, "Musicians have asymmetrical left cranial temporal regions of the brain. That is, that part of the brain is relatively larger in musicians than in non-musicians. Some data has suggested that that part of the brain is involved in processing heard information. If that part of the brain is relatively larger, it may be better developed and so this explains very nicely our results" (128).

The brains of trained musicians do, in fact, differ from those of the rest of us. The corpus callosum is larger and so too is the primary motor cortex and the cerebellum. Perhaps the structured and distributed practice required to be accomplished in any musical instrument, combined with the need for smooth and controlled voluntary cross-lateral movement, leads to these changes. In other words, you have to use your left and right hands simultaneously while thinking about what you are about to do and coordinating it with symbols written in front of your eyes (see figure 4.4). No mean feat! The part of the brain that processes sound (the auditory cortex) in highly skilled musicians is enlarged by about 25 percent compared with control subjects who have never played an instrument. The amount of enlargement was correlated with the age at which musicians began to practice, suggesting that the reorganization of the auditory cortex is use-dependent (Pantev et al. 1998).

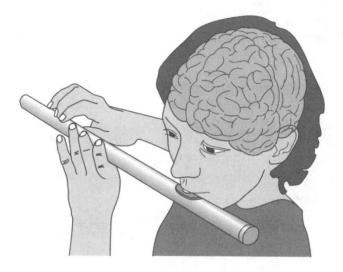

4.4 While playing an instrument such as the flute, the motor and supplementary motor cortexes on the left and right are active. The cerebellum is engaged in eye tracking and anticipating movement. The auditory cortex is listening to the sounds played. The frontal cortex is engaged in planning the combination of physical movements needed to create the desired pattern of sounds.

Practicing an instrument alters brain structure. Non-piano-playing adults practiced a five-finger exercise on the piano for two hours a day over the course of five days. The area of the brain responsible for finger movements enlarged and become more active in these subjects compared with control subjects who had not learned the piano exercise. This demonstrates that in just five days the adult brain can adapt according to how it is used (Pascual-Leone et al. 1995).

Do you consider yourself musical? At what point in your life would you have enough evidence to know? What would it be like if we were all musical? Auditions for my Sunday school choir took place under formidable circumstances. The director would line us all up and then listen to us one at a time as we sang. As we were only ten years old at the time, the audition was highly stressful—especially for the one or two of us who were encouraged to mime rather than actually sing when the choir eventually performed. A common belief about music is that only a few of us are musically inclined and that being musical is a gift. Brain research suggests otherwise! Most of our capabilities are not even known to us. They occur in the brain on an unconscious level, so although someone like me will indulge the Sunday school teacher and believe that I have no musical ability, I can never be certain—and isn't that a great thing?

Stefan Koelsch and his research team from Leipzig found a definite pattern of key recognition in the brain. Adults who had no musical education and had never attempted to play a musical instrument were given a series of chords that infrequently contained a chord that did not fit the key implied by the chord sequence. They did not know about chords or key structures and had scant musical knowledge.

When all the chords belonged to the same key, their brains showed no special response. When one of the chords did not fit the key that was implied and unconsciously abstracted in their brains, there was a marked changed in brain activation. Puzzled by this, the team repeated the experiment several times with the same results. The brain response occurred even though the subjects had no musical training. Their conclusion was that the brain itself seems to make musical sense out of sounds automatically, without prompting and at a level beyond conscious awareness (Weinberger 2000). We are all musical!

Kodaly music training uses folk songs and emphasizes melodic and rhythmic elements. In 1975 a yearlong study on music and reading was begun with an experimental group who received extensive music instruction: forty minutes per day, five days a week, for seven months. A control group of similar age, IQ, and socioeconomic status received no musical training. The children were tested on reading ability at the start of the school year then again at the end of the year. After training, the music group exhibited significantly higher reading scores than did the control group, scoring in the 88th percentile versus the 72nd percentile. The effects were also long-lasting. The music group remained better readers.

Reading requires phonological awareness. The reader must recognize the visual symbol, relate this symbol to a sound, and then get good enough so that the process is automatic. Researchers believe that musical understanding improves recognition of sound changes—the phonemic stage of reading. A recent study by Lamb and Gregory investigated the relationship between musical sound discrimination and reading ability in first-grade children. After a range of different sounding out and sound recognition tests, they found a high degree of correlation between how well children could read both standard and phonic material and how well they could discriminate pitch. Timbre awareness was not related to reading, showing the specificity of the findings. Recognizing change of pitch in the sounds that make up words is thought to be the most important factor in word discrimination. Musical training and listening to music develop pitch discrimination (Hurwitz et al. 1975; see also Frith 1985; Lamb and Gregory 1993).

Doing "Good Looking"

Does an artist use the same areas of the brain when looking at a Jackson Pollock as I do? I am without any sort of artistic training and am no more than an average painter. Some recent research does suggest that artists' brains function differently than those of non-artists. Researchers scanned the brain of one of Britain's leading painters, Humphrey Ocean. They asked Mr. Ocean to sketch while inside a brain scanner and compared the results with scans of non-artists doing the same task, to identify the regions of the brain that were most active during the creative process. The results showed that non-artists tended to use the rear of the brain more. This region is associated with taking in and processing visual information. But Mr. Ocean used the frontal cortex more, the region associated with complex thinking and emotions.

Our brain has limited visual processing capacity and yet multiple objects in our visual field are constantly competing with each other. Some researchers have shown that visual clutter actually suppresses the brain's responsiveness. The theory is that in focusing its attention on just one stimulus, the brain suppresses nearby stimuli to enhance information processing of the desired stimulus (Kastner and De Weerd 1998). These findings conflict with educators who want to create surroundings and texts that are visually rich and often complex.

Subjects in an MRI scanner focused both their eyes and their attention on the lower left corner of a computer screen, while colorfully patterned squares flashed in the upper right quadrant. The images appeared under two conditions: one at a time or four simultaneously. As expected, the stimuli evoked weaker responses in the brain when presented simultaneously versus sequentially, confirming that multiple stimuli do, in fact, suppress each other. The amount of mutual suppression increased progressively along a circuit that processes object vision, which runs forward and downward from the back of the brain. Neurons at the beginning of this circuit respond to only a very small portion of the visual field, while neurons near the end respond to almost all of what the eyes see. So neurons at the beginning of the circuit simply could not view the multiple stimuli and were thus spared the suppressive effects. Spacing the images farther apart also decreased suppressive interactions.

4.5 Although visual stimuli are immensely attractive to the centers of the brain that specialize in recall, they need to be an active rather than a passive feature of a learning environment.

Spatially directed attention enhances the brain's visual processing ability by preventing suppression of nearby stimuli. What is the significance for educators? Assuming that learners will necessarily assimilate information presented at the periphery of vision is unwise. A visual such as a learning poster needs to have attention directed to it to activate learning. A good illustration in a book needs to have attention directed to it for best recall. It makes a lot of sense to have visual material that is interactive and requires directed attention (see figure 4.5). Also, some neurons in object vision see the big picture; others are designed to focus on detail. Some learners may be content with digital and small-chunk learning but others will need analog and big picture learning. We may have to teach "looking for learning" lessons, in which we show the class how to access and retain visual information, how to take notes visually and spatially, and how to review for an exam using visual tools such as memory maps and learning posters.

Mental Rehearsals of Success

I was watching the final of the women's high jump at the World Athletics Championships in Edmonton, Canada, live on television. I saw a pattern of behaviors reminiscent of one of the polar bears that for many years had been a feature at Bristol Zoo. An unnatural pacing up and down, backwards and forwards, again and again: in the case of the bear, all day long; in the case of the athletes, before their turn to jump. What for the bear may have been a release from anxiety and boredom, was, in fact, more purposeful for the athletes.

As I watched I realized they were mentally rehearsing their stride pattern and their approach to the bar. One athlete in particular, a South African, fixed her gaze on her imagined stride pattern and with her right hand simulated the movement she wanted her body to make in order to successfully clear the bar. With her head cocked to one side her eyes "bounced" the stride around the front of the bar—one, two, three, four, five—then spring, hand curving round as she maneuvered her body over the bar. Pause, then again, the same routine.

What was the point? In my day the PE teacher encouraged us to run full-tilt straight at the bar, execute a scissors kick, then land on our rears in six inches of builders' sand—and various other less savory stuff—and we then spent the next five minutes trying to remove the sand from our underpants. A sports psychologist would say that the body follows the mind. A neuroscientist would say that mental rehearsal is closely related to better motor performance. Experimental psychology has shown the value of mental rehearsal in advance of performance. It can improve muscle strength, physical movement, reaction times, speed, and timing. Extended rehearsal of tasks in one's head leads to physiological changes in recovery time and heart and respiration rates. In 1994 research showed that motor imagery is closely related to motor preparation. In other words, becoming ready to ski the downhill course by mentally representing it in sequence engages many of the same structures in the brain, particularly in the motor cortex, as actually skiing the course (Jeannerod 1994). Similar effects have been found in experiments that involve imagining grasping 3D objects or simulating the movement of a joystick.

In November 2001 Guang Yue, an exercise physiologist at the Cleveland Clinic Foundation in Ohio, and his colleagues published findings suggesting that you could strengthen your muscles just by imagining yourself exercising. This "Homer Simpson" approach to exercise will undoubtedly appeal to many. It also offers real benefits to those recovering from an injury or a stroke who might be too weak to resume physical activity. Guang Yue and his team asked ten volunteers to imagine flexing their biceps as hard as they could for as long as they could five times a week. Their brain activity was recorded and so was electrical activity at the motor neurons of the arm muscles. The training lasted three months. After the first two weeks, the participants showed an amazing 13.5 percent increase in upper arm strength, which they maintained until the training stopped. The authors interpreted the results as follows: Muscles move in response to impulses from nearby motor neurons, the firing of which depends on the strength of electrical impulses from the brain. Thus, you can increase muscle strength solely by sending a stronger signal from the brain to the motor neurons (Yue, Bilodeau et al. 1997; Yue, Liu et al. in press; Yue, Ranganathan et al. 1999; see also http://www.lerner.ccf.org/bme/yue).

The skill of mentally rehearsing successful learning behaviors has to be a very powerful endowment to give to any learner. What do your students think of when they hear the word *test*? Do they rehearse patterns of success or do they tend to mentally represent failure? Here is an area where direct intervention is possible. Encourage your students to capture the "look" of moments of success and then to rehearse that look again and again. Have them practice a successful test-taking technique in their head. Guide them through a mental rehearsal of coming into the room well prepared and relaxed, feeling confident, sitting down, looking around and relaxing in the familiar surroundings, laying out materials, reviewing the test and reading all the questions, deciding which to answer and in which order, allocating time to the various sections, and beginning each answer with a quick visual plan. All of this can be rehearsed in the head so that it is in place in moments of high anxiety.

Chapter **5**

Wired to Misfire
Learning from Dysfunction

This chapter contains the following sections:

How the brain recovers from damage. How the brain reorganizes itself to compensate for localized damage. The concepts of adaptability and plasticity.

Addiction and the brain. An explanation of addictive behaviors, in particular addiction to nicotine. The concept of disinhibition of desire and the role of the nucleus accumbens.

Attention-deficit/hyperactivity disorder. Making sense of a confused picture. How deficiencies in attention affect short- and long-term memory. Some possible strategies for helping children with ADHD.

The roots of aggression. Case studies showing links between aggressive behavior and damage to the prefrontal lobes.

Reading problems. Some neurological explanations of reading difficulties.

Movement problems. How poor motor control contributes to learning difficulties. How physical movement can be harnessed to help children learn.

It will answer the following questions:

- How does a brain cope with trauma? Is full recovery ever possible?

- What happens in the brain when you become addicted? Can you become addicted to non-chemical experiences, such as gambling? What about shopping?

- Is ADHD real?

- Is there something about the brain of an aggressive person that marks it as different?

- What are the major causes of reading problems in children?

- Why will the children in my class not sit still?

Introduction

The case of Martha Curtis, a young musician who suffered epileptic seizures, showed us what happens in the brain during a seizure. Neurologist Hans Luders was able to conduct an MRI scan during a seizure. As described by John Ratey (2001, 189-90), it "began as a local electrical disturbance in the right temporal lobe, then spread, eventually taking over her entire brain in a global thunderstorm." The seizures became so severe and so frequent that they could no longer be controlled effectively by drugs and surgery was required. The area targeted for surgery was the right temporal lobe, the area most important in remembering music.

As Ratey (2001) describes it, as soon as Martha got out of intensive care, she picked up her violin and played a very difficult Bach piece "beautifully." Sadly, the surgeons had not been aggressive enough. The seizures returned. She underwent a second operation and then a third. By the end of the third operation, the neurosurgeons estimated they had removed 20 percent of the right temporal lobe.

Could she still play? She could, and as well as ever. The surgeons concluded that, as a result of measles at age three years, her brain had suffered slight damage and had adapted. For her to become such an accomplished instrumentalist, the centers that would normally be highly active in musical memory must have been rewired and, of necessity, other sites within the brain had adapted to the complex musical tasks. Martha is still an accomplished soloist and a living testimony to the plasticity of the human brain.

How the Brain Recovers from Damage

When scientists talk of the human brain they use adjectives like integrated, complex, adaptive, parallel, holistic, and plastic. In a brief study of the indexes of five general books about the workings of the human brain, the word *plastic* appeared more than any other. What is the significance of this word?

Plasticity is the idea that the brain can reorganize itself to compensate for localized damage. The younger the individual, the more adaptable the brain. The more bilaterally organized the brain, the more it can cope with trauma. Infants who have the left hemisphere completely removed before six months of age are by age four indistinguishable in language function (Plunkett 2000). Being plastic also means that when a function is lost or inhibited in some way, other parts of the brain can take over that function. Knowing this helps us understand more about learning difficulties.

Another word often used in relation to studies of the brain is *homeostasis*. The brain receives information from the external world through the senses and from the internal world through the workings of the body. The brain tries to achieve a constant state and adjusts to maintain constancy, a condition called homeostasis. The idea that we self-regulate and adjust to a norm is important in looking at behaviors and, in particular, addictive behaviors.

Addiction and the Brain

Research into addiction is a major, perhaps the major, neurological research industry. There is, quite rightly, great professional caution about premature theorizing. Governments, pharmaceutical companies, alcohol and tobacco manufacturers, law enforcement officers, and candy and toy manufacturers would all love a silver bullet theory of addiction. There is not one. What we can say is that addictive behaviors are a complex coming together of inherited and learned variables. Sensitive windows exist for introducing chemicals to the brain, during which there are consequences for the brain's reward system that can lead to what is described as a disinhibition of desire (see figure 5.1). Pile on top of this all the socioeconomic and family variables, moral opprobrium, laws, norms regarding what is antisocial behaviors, and organized (and even disorganized) crime and you can see that the neurologists are the ones who offer the most hope of a clean explanation. They have focused their attention on the nucleus accumbens.

5.1 Addictive behaviors are a complex coming together of inherited and learned variables, with sensitive windows for the reward system. Add to this societal factors and inhibition of desire is a difficult pattern of behavior to develop. A key role for parents and educators is to foster young people's ability to manage impulsivity and disinhibition.

The nucleus accumbens is a cluster of cells that is highly active in motivation and reward. Located in the forebrain, it has direct links to the limbic system. It is saturated in neurotransmitters associated with pleasure, such as dopamine. Many drugs act directly on the nucleus accumbens. These include highly addictive drugs such as cocaine; prescription drugs such as Ritalin and others used to treat ADHD; everyday drugs such as chocolate, coffee, and tea; and occasional drugs such as running, bungee jumping, and completing the *New York Times* crossword. Damage to the functioning of the nucleus accumbens results in a failure of disinhibition. If, for whatever reason, you have an imbalance of chemicals in your nucleus accumbens, homeostasis prompts you to restore the balance. Seeking pleasure or reward, often through novelty, becomes part of your homeostatic response. At this level it is not a conscious choice.

Scientists researching the addictive effects of nicotine have found that in the West, the vast majority of smokers start during their teenage years. They found that girls were the most vulnerable to addiction and to brain alterations, which can lead to depression. Some studies suggest that starting to smoke early in life can increase the chances of suffering depression in adulthood.

Research shows that the adolescent brain responds more intensely to nicotine than does the adult brain. A team at Duke University injected rats with nicotine every day for more than two weeks to simulate a typical smoker's intake.[1] In every rat the number of chemical receptors dedicated to nicotine increased. This is one way of measuring addiction. In adolescent rats the increase in the number of nicotine receptors was double that of the adult rats.

A follow-up study showed that adolescent exposure to nicotine contributed to subsequent and permanent behavioral problems—especially for females. After two weeks of nicotine injections, female adult rats were more sluggish, less interested in their environment, and less interested in looking after their young than adult rats that had no exposure to nicotine.

A possible explanation is that the nicotine acted as a suppressant and reduced the amounts of dopamine and norepinephrine the rats' brains produced. Levels of these chemicals are lower in humans who are suffering from depression. Another is that nicotine retards cell division in the hippocampus, an area of the brain that contributes to visual and spatial memory and continues growing into adulthood in females but not in males.

The public face of addiction is that it is bound up with self-interest, pleasure seeking, and reward. Might children who misbehave be addicted to misbehavior? What about attention-deficit/hyperactivity disorder? Is there such a thing as ADHD? Are there links between ADHD and what we know about addictive behavior? ADHD arouses considerable debate among scientists, clinicians, and educators alike, who adopt positions ranging from moral outrage and outright denial to precise clinical diagnosis.

Attention-Deficit/Hyperactivity Disorder (ADHD)

Of the worldwide prescriptions for Ritalin, a drug that elevates dopamine levels and is used to treat ADHD, 95 percent are written in the United States. More than three million American children between the ages of five and sixteen are diagnosed with ADHD. The behavior patterns that typify ADHD usually arise between the ages of three and five. Yet the age of onset can vary widely; some children do not develop symptoms until late childhood or even early adolescence.

Boys are at least three times as likely as girls to be diagnosed with the disorder; indeed, some studies have found that boys outnumber girls by nine to one, possibly because boys are genetically more prone to disorders of the nervous system. Many studies estimate that between 2 and 9.5 percent of all school-age children worldwide have ADHD (Barkley 1997, 1998b).

Opinion varies as to what constitutes ADHD and how, if at all, it should be treated. Many experts are of the view that it is a recognizable neurological condition, that it has been around longer than its label, and that it is treatable through both chemical and non-chemical interventions. Others argue that it is a consequence of poor parenting, inappropriate diet, or a culture that promises immediate gratification.

In making sense of a confused picture, there seems agreement between those in the neurological camp that ADHD is a deficiency affecting all or some of the components of our attention and reward and memory systems. In this respect, there are many parallels with addiction. Four components comprise the human attention system: arousal, motor orientation, novelty detection and reward, and executive organization. Deficiencies in attention affect both short- and long-term memory.

One school of thought takes the view that ADHD has its basis in deficiencies in the motivation systems around pleasure and pain and that it is best understood as a reward deficiency syndrome, a form of addiction to thrill seeking. Those with the condition become besotted with novelty, not because of some moral weakness, but because of an imbalance of chemicals associated with reward—dopamine, serotonin, and endorphins—in their brains. Like alcoholics who feel they must drink, people with ADHD "seek the intensity of the present because their attention and reward systems are fueled by the pursuit of immediate pleasures" (Ratey 2001, 126). Activities involving a high degree of novelty provide a temporary surge of dopamine in the brain.

Other researchers have found that children with ADHD are less capable of planning motor responses in anticipation of an event and are insensitive to feedback about their responses. For example, in a commonly used test of reaction time, children with ADHD are less able than other children to ready themselves to press one of several keys when they see a warning light. They also do not slow down after making mistakes in such tests in order to improve their accuracy.

Some very experienced researchers, including Russell Barkley, director of psychology and professor of psychiatry and neurology at the University of Massachusetts Medical Center, is even more specific. Barkley (1998a) argues that ADHD arises as "a developmental failure in the brain circuitry that underlies inhibition and self-control." He believes that "loss of self-control in turn impairs other important brain functions crucial for maintaining attention, including the ability to defer immediate rewards for later, greater gain."

Barkley believes that this "abstinence aversion" is largely a consequence of an inherited genetic disorder. Scientists have discovered that brain areas regulating attention are significantly smaller than average in children with ADHD. In a 1996 study, F. Xavier Castellanos and colleagues at the National Institute of Mental Health found that the right prefrontal cortex and two parts of the basal ganglia called the caudate nucleus and the globus pallidus are significantly smaller than normal in children with ADHD (Castellanos et al. 2001). The right prefrontal cortex is involved in monitoring one's behavior, resisting distractions, and developing an awareness of self and time. The caudate nucleus and the globus pallidus help to switch off automatic responses to allow more careful deliberation by the cortex and to coordinate neurological input among various regions of the cortex.

There is a growing body of evidence that ADHD is caused not by chemicals in the diet, poor parenting, or electronic games but by genetics. Research done at the University of Oslo and the University of Southampton with

526 identical twins, who inherit exactly the same genes, and 389 fraternal twins, who are no more alike genetically than siblings born years apart, found that ADHD has a heritability approaching 80 percent (see, for example, Gjone and Stevenson 1997). A high percentage of the differences in attention, hyperactivity, and impulsivity between people with ADHD and those without the disorder can be explained by the genes they inherit.

Furthermore, U.S. statistics show that the siblings of children with ADHD are between five and seven times more likely to develop the syndrome than are children from unaffected families. And the children of a parent who has ADHD have up to a 50 percent likelihood of experiencing the same difficulties. Nongenetic factors also contribute to ADHD, including premature birth, maternal alcohol and tobacco use, exposure to high levels of lead in early childhood, and brain injuries—especially those that involve the prefrontal cortex. But, even together, these factors account for only between 20 and 30 percent of ADHD cases among boys; among girls, they account for an even smaller percentage.

When scientists compare the symptoms of ADHD with those of frontal lobe damage, they find remarkable consistency (see figure 5.2). Both individuals with ADHD and those with frontal lobe damage are easily distracted, show highly erratic attention, have poor social inhibition, often intrude, and self-talk inappropriately.

The frontal lobes, which do not fully develop until early adulthood, are highly involved in social inhibition. Some scientists think that the frontal lobes mature more slowly in some than in others, perhaps accounting for developmental ADHD. Frontal lobe function is maintained by dopamine. Scientists such as Barkley are of the opinion that defects in genes responsible for the secretion of dopamine in the brain may contribute to ADHD behaviors. Dopamine is secreted by neurons in specific parts of the brain to inhibit or modulate the activity of other neurons, particularly those involved in emotion and movement. Some impressive studies specifically implicate genes that encode, or serve as the blueprint for, dopamine receptors and transporters; these genes are very active in the prefrontal cortex and basal ganglia. These are areas of the brain that are directly involved in managing impulsive responses, resisting distractions, and setting goals.

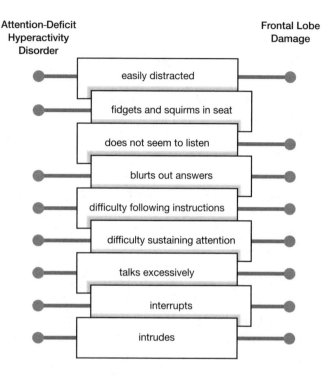

5.2 A comparison of the symptoms of ADHD with those of frontal lobe damage shows notable overlap.

Barkley has a very interesting and useful hypothesis as to what happens next. He believes that children with ADHD do not fully internalize the executive functions of self-control.

To develop self-control in children who exhibit ADHD, parents and teachers should be aware of what leads to their behaviors. To exercise self-control children need

① a functional working memory.

② the ability to "talk themselves through" things in their heads.

③ the ability to control emotions, motivation, and mood.

④ the ability to learn from observed experience.

1. Memory

Children who are unable to direct their attention to an activity for an age-appropriate length of time have problems with short-term memory. Children need to be able to hold information in their heads while working on a task, particularly when the original stimulus has gone. If they cannot do this, then information will not be transferred to long-term memory. Life for such children is constantly in the present. Remembering is crucial for learning chains of consequence, setting goals for the future, learning through reflection, and anticipating the future. Remembering is also important for imitation and learning through observation and rehearsal. All these functions are drastically limited in children with ADHD.

2. Self-Talk

A normal part of growing up is learning to talk yourself through something in your head. When children are young they perform this *executive function* aloud; for example, talking themselves through a task. This is natural and good for learning. It is also more prevalent in girls than in boys. As children grow up, the thoughts are internalized and become part of their thinking skills. Children with ADHD lack the restraint to internalize their thinking and continue to externalize their thoughts. Tourette's syndrome is an extreme manifestation of this problem. Before the age of six, most children talk aloud to themselves when reminding themselves how to perform a particular task or trying to cope with a problem. Talking aloud evolves into private muttering, and by the age of ten becomes silent (Berk 1994). Researchers at Illinois State University reported in 1991 that the internalization of self-directed speech is delayed in boys with ADHD.

3. Managing Impulsivity

Children need to learn through practice to adjust their behavior according to the circumstances. In order to learn and practice this adaptability, children must be able to regulate their own emotional responses. Managing the moment of impulse is, for some, an intelligent behavior of the highest order. Individuals with frontal lobe damage due to accidents frequently have problems doing this. In many cases, they are unable to discern the motivations of others. They often fall into a cycle of impulsivity, recklessness, and aggression. In order to complete a learning task, a child may have to manage or delay an emotional response to a potential distraction. This requires strong internal resources. A child with ADHD does not yet have such internal resources.

4. Safe Rehearsal

Children with ADHD have to work very hard to learn from others. They need to observe the behaviors of those around them, then break those behaviors down into rules. They then need to reconstitute these rules into new actions. To do so is complex, demanding, and time-consuming. It is what motivation and goal setting are all about. Children work toward goals without having to learn all the steps by rote. The necessary behaviors become learned responses through rehearsal. For rehearsal to be safe, it needs to be done privately and again and again. With practice, responses become reflexive and ingrained. As children get older, and by means of safe rehearsal, they ought to become better at chaining together behaviors across longer and longer intervals to secure a goal. Initial studies suggest that children with ADHD are less capable of safe rehearsal and reconstitution than are other children.

Children with ADHD are often prescribed drugs such as Ritalin. Prescriptions in the UK have gone up by more than forty-five times in the six-year period from 1991 (2,000 prescriptions) to 1997 (92,000). Ritalin and other psychostimulants act by inhibiting the dopamine transporter, thus increasing the time that dopamine has to bind to its receptors on other neurons. This boosts the child's capacity to regulate impulsive responses, which, in turn, helps him or her resist distractions, hold information longer in short-term memory, and rehearse goal setting. Drugs such as Ritalin have been found to improve the behavior of between 70 and 90 percent of children with ADHD older than five years. As a result of better self-control, these children attract less censure from adults and peers and therefore begin to be liked more.

Surely our first strategy as parents or teachers of children with ADHD is to create structure in the lives of these children, who, through no fault of their own, have poor experience of coping with structure. Here are some ways to do this:

▼ Define the benefits of completing a task rather than the task's features.

▼ Break the task down into achievable chunks.

▼ Model practicing self-talk, aloud at first then more and more quietly.

▼ Provide lots of rehearsal to embed information in short-term memory.

▼ Practice time lines.

▼ Practice goal setting continuously and insist that the child articulate each goal to you.

▼ Gradually extend the goals.

▼ Praise very specific, perhaps small, improvements.

The Roots of Aggression

It is naïve to assume that all aggressive behavior can be traced to an impairment in functioning somewhere within the brain. The causes of aggressive behavior in humans are many and varied, a fact that needs to be acknowledged. However, systems within the brain do operate with greater or lesser effect to manage impulsivity and allow time to think through a more considered response.

Aggressive people often have underactive frontal lobes, the areas of the brain that restrain impulsive action and inform reasoned thought. Damage to the frontal lobes can lead to irresponsible behavior. Inability to manage impulses can lead to a cycle of recklessness and aggression. Some recent research suggests that damage to the part of the brain that learns moral and social rules—the prefrontal cortex—could cause children to grow up into irresponsible adults and even exhibit criminal behavior.

Phineas Gage was a railway worker who, in 1848, suffered terrible but not fatal injuries when a rod with which he was tamping down some dynamite caused an explosion. This metal rod was driven with such brutal force that it went clean through his prefrontal cortex (see figure 5.3). Before the accident Gage had been industrious, dependable, and well liked, but afterwards he became a drifter who was profane, unreliable, impulsive, and inconsiderate to his family. His intellectual capacities nevertheless remained intact. He could articulate answers to complex questions, he could reason, and he understood cause and effect. But after his accident his moral behavior was distressing to family and friends. The man had changed beyond recognition. He survived for many years through exhibiting himself, his wound, and the tamping rod in circuses throughout America. Eventually he died alone, penniless, an alcoholic.

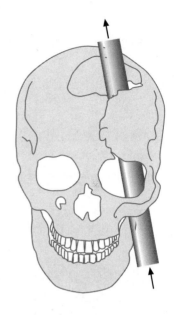

5.3 Phineas Gage has become a cause célèbre in neuroscience. His skull is preserved in the Smithsonian Museum and clearly shows the serious damage caused by the tamping rod.

In more recent times, neuroscientists from the University of Iowa published in *Nature Neuroscience* the case studies of two individuals who had suffered damage to the prefrontal cortex as babies (Anderson et al. 1999). One was a girl aged twenty who had been hit by a car at fifteen months. The other was a man aged twenty-three who had undergone brain surgery at three months. In each case the children apparently made full recoveries and enjoyed advantaged upbringings. They were nurtured in middle-class families by educated parents. On reaching puberty, however, their behavior began to change. Whereas before they had been well behaved, considerate of others, and seemingly content, now they lied, behaved selfishly, and were lazy and disruptive. In school they started fights and stole money. They also became sexually reckless, becoming parents of children that they neglected. In both cases, their cognitive functions, such as reading and writing, were unaffected. What was affected was their ability to realize the social consequences of misbehavior and to carry out moral reasoning.

One of the most interesting findings from this case study is that these two, who sustained brain injuries as children, are different from people injured as adults. The adults understand moral and social rules but appear unable to apply them to their own lives. Those brain injured at an early age seem unable to learn the rules in the first place, having as adults the moral reasoning skills of ten-year-olds. They are also more likely to exhibit psychopathic behavior, such as stealing and being violent. Another intriguing finding is that individuals with such damage do not learn lessons from being punished after misbehaving. This finding could call into question the effectiveness of applying criminal penalties to this group. Two is a very small sample, but it is hard to find documented cases where brain damage has such restricted effects.

Very low or very high levels of serotonin in the brain can also contribute to aggression. Without modifiers to dampen the bonfires of impulsive responses, we become prone to impulsivity, recklessness, and aggression. Serotonin imbalance can be treated with SSRIs (selective serotonin reuptake inhibitors) such as Prozac. High levels of testosterone can also lead to aggression. When there are unusually low levels of serotonin alongside high levels of testosterone, the combination is potentially dangerous. Dion Sanders is a young man currently serving a life sentence without parole in a U.S. prison in Ohio for the murder of his grandparents. His crime was particularly violent, but he claimed not to have knowledge of just how violent. He agreed to allow a spinal tap for analysis of the levels of neurotransmitters in his system. Scientists discovered a rare combination of low levels of serotonin alongside high levels of testosterone in Sanders. His death sentence was commuted to life in prison.

Reading Problems

Both learning to speak and learning to read require acquisition of phonological skills that depend on sensitive auditory perception of frequency and amplitude changes in speech sounds. Girls and boys appear to differ in the way they acquire and develop language. Girls usually say their first words and speak in sentences earlier than do boys. Some studies have found that women speak in longer, more complex sentences than men. Also, boys outnumber girls in remedial reading classes. Stuttering and other speech and language defects also occur more frequently among males.

The brain is not designed to be literate—which is a socially constructed phenomenon—but it is designed for language. Becoming literate does, however, have consequences for the structure of the brain. If I were to give two pieces of advice to a parent concerned about promoting his or her child's literacy, the first would be to monitor the child's health and the second would be to talk to, with, and around the child frequently and positively. I used a saying earlier, "You build your house, and then you live in it." This is especially true of the brain and language. If it is possible to rewire a brain, and I think it is, then the early acquisition of language has to be the most potent force for doing so. Television, video, and computers do not make good babysitters. In less than 2,000 years mothers in some Western countries have gone from spending twenty-four hours in the company of their young children to, in some cases, spending two or three hours of quality time. The result is a lot less language exchange.

Longitudinal research conducted in Kansas and in Alaska attempted to quantify socioeconomic-based differences in exposure to language. Todd Risley and Betty Hart led a project that compared children from different family backgrounds: welfare, blue collar, and white collar (cited in Kotulak 1996). They found a startling pattern of difference in exposure to language. By the age of four, children in the welfare families had as much as thirteen million fewer words of cumulative language experience compared to their peers in the blue- and white-collar families.

An experiment conducted in Portugal compared literate and illiterate elderly women matched for social background (Castro-Caldas et al. 1998). The women were asked to listen to and repeat simulated words and real words. The brain areas that showed activity were the same in both groups for real words but differed for the nonsense words. In the brains of the literate women, the nonsense words were treated like familiar and real words and processed in the language areas of the brain, whereas in the illiterate women, different brain areas related to memory retrieval were activated. At a level beyond consciousness, the brain was showing recognition patterns through the areas activated. When there was no recognition (in the illiterate women), lots of resources were directed toward finding and securing a match from memory. Becoming literate enabled those women to make more efficient use of their brains. The corpus callosum, a structure within the brain that directs signals across the two hemispheres of the cortex, tends to be thinner and has less neural density in people who are illiterate.

Dyslexia is a real phenomenon. In recent years research has shown that it is a developmental disorder with genetic origins. It is also culturally shaped insofar as different languages place different demands on brain function. What is interesting about this is the idea that people of different cultures have differences in the shape and organization of their brains, especially those who are active users of language within that culture. No single physical cause has yet been recognized as the "signature" of dyslexia, but a number of scientists have observed a pattern of brain abnormalities in the processing of language. One of the features that distinguishes the brains of dyslexics is the degree to which a language area in the brain is asymmetric. During reading tasks, the auditory cortex and Wernicke's area, in the left temporal lobe, which would normally show high levels of activity in organizing sounds into words and also in retrieving those words from memory, is less active in dyslexics generally (see figure 5.4).

The English language has a great number of irregularities in grammatical construction and in the rules of spelling. To become a skilled reader of English requires different patterns of brain activation than becoming a skilled reader of Italian. English dyslexics have a harder time learning to read. Paulesu and Mehler (1998) showed that both groups used the same structures in the left hemisphere. But Italian readers made heavier use of the superior temporal gyrus, which is involved in translating sounds into letters. English readers made heavier use of the inferior basal temporal areas and anterior regions of the frontal gyrus, which are areas involved in interpreting word meaning. Why should there be any difference? What significance might the difference have?

Because English has many spelling irregularities and more exceptions to its grammatical rules than Italian does, English readers devote more effort to decoding meaning and less to linking sounds to letters. Although, in the experiment reported, no irregular words were presented, the English readers engaged more areas associated with word identity than with

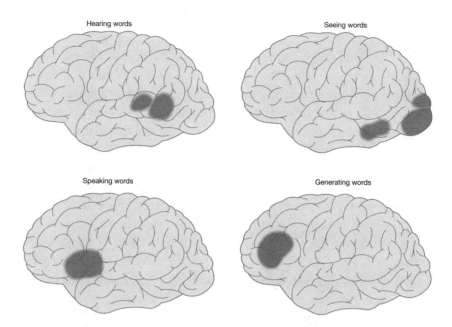

5.4 As illustrated using PET scans, different areas of the brain are activated by a reading task. Activity in the primary auditory cortex and in Wernicke's area is increased when hearing words. Seeing words activates the visual cortex. Speaking words activates the primary motor cortex. Generating words activates Broca's area.

sound-letter decoding. A knowledge of irregular words—"we went" instead of "we goed"—is necessary for reading them successfully. Differences in brain structures are subtle, but they do reflect the uses to which different brains are put. Does this mean that different methods are required for teaching Italian than for teaching English?

Most classroom instruction is orally based. Children who are equipped with poor mechanisms for recognizing, separating, remembering, and replicating sounds struggle in a classroom. Children with poor phonemic awareness become slow readers. Children in the bottom 20 percent in phonological awareness at age five are likely to be two and a half years behind in their reading age by the time they are ten years old (Torgesen 1999, 2000; Torgesen et al. 2001; Torgesen and Mathes 2000). The left hemispheres of people with dyslexia appear to be particularly suscep-tible to abnormalities such as ectopias (structures occurring in abnormal positions). These arise before birth and can be related to autoimmune disorders. For children with these inherited abnormalities, normal learning of speech-sound and sound-to-letter decoding is very difficult.

Problems can be compounded by poor verbal short-term memory and poor eye tracking. According to Professor John Stein, professor of neurology at Oxford University, "more than half of dyslexic children may have eye control problems" (2000b; see figure 5.5). Some can be helped with eye patches or tinted eyeglass lenses or colored overlays for reading material. As I write, state-of-the-art "eye wobble" diagnostic eyeglasses are in trial. Adapted from cockpit control systems where pilots direct missiles with their eyes, the kit uses a tiny video camera attached to the eyeglass frame and linked to a computer to assess eye tracking. A child with eye wobble is unlikely to be able to move his or her eyes steadily along a line of text. Remedial eye exercises can then be prescribed. Early diagnosis is crucial. Simple tests already exist to pinpoint youngsters with dyslexia by the time they start school.

Changing the reading program does not help these children. New teaching methods might. *Fast ForWord for Language* (FFW-L, 1998) is a series of computer-based training programs to help dyslexics and those with genuine reading difficulties. Fast ForWord is designed to improve the brain's capacity for identifying, separating, remembering, and replicating sounds. The computer is used to replicate ideal learning conditions, something it can do better than humans can. According to the developers of Fast ForWord, effective computer-aided learning for a reading disability

- is intensive
- is distributed
- is frequent
- requires a motor response
- reinforces correct responses
- is gradual
- progressively works toward a targeted goal

When reading the eyes do not move in a straight flowing line.

5.5 When reading, the eyes do not move in a straight, flowing line but in a series of small jumps known as saccades. Children with poor eye tracking can experience some improvement through tracking exercises.

The phoneme is the smallest unit of sound in a language that carries word meaning (that is, we recognize *pat* and *bat* as different words because *p* and *b* are phonemes). If, as a result of an injury or inherited disorder, the child's brain is poorly equipped to discriminate sound changes at the beginning and ending of a sound, then we have a reading problem stored for the future. Games within the *Fast ForWord for Language* package are designed to remediate this problem by altering word sounds to exaggerate the beginning and ending and stretch out the middle. The child sits in front of a computer screen wearing headphones and completes sound, phoneme, and word exercises. "Old McDonald's Flying Farm" is a sound exercise where children click the mouse when they notice a different phoneme hidden among many acoustically modified to sound similar. "Phonic Match" requires them to distinguish between, and remember, similar real and nonsense words. "Block Commander" builds listening and attention skills through a game in which there are carefully chosen and increasingly challenging acoustically controlled commands.

Another very different form of intervention is the use of carefully constructed physical exercises to improve eye tracking. The cerebellum, in the back of the brain, contributes to balance, eye tracking, and anticipatory movement. Exercises such as balancing on a wobble board, using Hula-Hoop plastic toy hoops, cross-crawling, lying on your tummy on top of a large inflatable ball, and rocking back and forth have all been shown to improve the reading, writing, and spelling of a group of fifty children aged six to eighteen (Dr David Reynolds, Exeter University, personal communication). For the group as a whole, reading skills progressed at a rate 67 percent faster than that of a control group. Progress in writing was 32 percent higher, and in spelling, 42 percent.

Movement Problems

Apraxia is a word with which you are probably not familiar. It is one more to add to a growing list of words that describe specific learning difficulties. *Praxis* has its origins in Greek and means to do. Apraxia is a difficulty with voluntary movement and coordination that occurs in adults following brain injury. *Developmental apraxia* describes similar difficulties observed in children.

The cerebellum plays a leading role in movement and learning motor skills. As a child practices crawling, the gross motor movements are rehearsed, adjusted, repeated, and improved. Adjustments become finer and finer, the movements quicker and more precise. Children who have even the slightest damage to the cerebellum do not make this same steady progress. Impairments in the cerebellum can lead to difficulties in coordinating movement, catching a ball, tapping out a rhythm, balancing on a beam, skipping, or playing a percussion instrument.

In her book *Developmental Dyspraxia* (1999), Madeleine Portwood, a UK-based educational psychologist, suggests that about 6 percent of all youngsters are sufficiently apraxic to require intervention. The ratio of boys to girls with the condition is about four to one. In countries where there is a greater emphasis on physical movement and gross motor skill development as part of early education, the incidence of apraxia is reportedly 1 percent. Portwood is very careful to point out that all children have different developmental trajectories and that being disorganized, forgetful, and clumsy is part of growing up! Accurate diagnosis of apraxia is difficult and requires a variety of tests.

Among the observable behaviors of youngsters around school age are those to do with social skills, gross and fine motor skills, reasoning ability, and language skills. A child who is apraxic may be naïve about social codes and indulge in intentional spoiling, aggressiveness toward others, physical roughness, and an inability to defer gratification. This combination of difficulties allied to physical awkwardness may lead the child to be excluded from group games and become even more isolated. Children with apraxia are more accident prone than their classmates. When they attempt to throw a ball one-handed, the other hand makes a similar movement; while sitting at a desk they swing their legs and fidget. Although they know how to assemble a jigsaw puzzle, they cannot master the delicate sequence of movements necessary to do so. Problems with sequencing, concepts of cause and effect, understanding time, and following instructions may also arise as a result of poor neurological functioning. The brain's internal messaging system works but more slowly than normal.

In motor memory, the frontal cortex anticipates and plans for a movement, then recruits the basal ganglia and the hippocampus for memory of similar movements performed in the past (see figure 5.6). Next the cerebellum and motor control strip are activated to ensure smooth execution of the movement. Early introduction to coordinated motor movements that are deliberate, smooth, and controlled enhances all-around cognitive functioning. Again and again, studies have shown that learning a musical instrument, dance, the movement rules of a sport, or choral singing improves levels of hemispheric integration, enabling the brain to become better at communicating with itself. In other words, use it or lose it, and start doing so early! Intervention through physical activity is important. Distributed practice with structured motor movements can help.

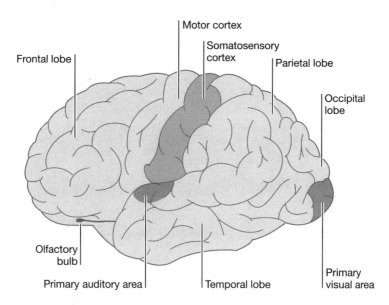

5.6 The motor control strip and the cerebellum control voluntary movement. Early introduction to coordinated motor movements that are deliberate, smooth and controlled contributes to improvements in all-round cognitive functioning.

Chapter **6**

Wired to Retire
Aging and the Brain

This chapter contains the following sections:

Hardening of the attitudes. How to avoid cognitive loss with aging. How learning can reduce cell death in the brain by as much as 45 percent.

The network's down. A summary of what happens with degenerative conditions such as Alzheimer's disease.

Stay active. The importance of physical activity to the brain. How stress in old age has a disproportionate effect on intellectual performance. The effects of heart disease.

Hold on to what you've got. Why procedural learning resists memory loss more than other types of memory.

Sagging, wrinkling, shrinking. As we age the brain shrinks, particularly in males. What are the consequences of this process?

It will answer the following questions:

- What is the effect of new learning on the brain of an elderly person?

- Can anything be done to delay the progression of Alzheimer's disease?

- How does stress affect memory in old age?

- How is it that an elderly lady who cannot remember her own name can nevertheless remember how to knit?

- Why is it that the brain shrinks with age in males but not in females?

Introduction

British actor and comedian Norman Wisdom is hugely popular in Albania. There is something about this small, socially awkward, physically inept underdog that appeals to Albanians. When the English national soccer team played a World Cup qualifier in the Albanian capital Tirane, the aging actor got the biggest cheer of the night when he came on to the field before the game. Norman Wisdom, now an octogenarian, was recently knighted for his services to the entertainment industry. When he was interviewed about the honor he said, "As you get older three things go, the first is your memory and I can't remember the other two."

Can an understanding of aging and the brain tell us anything about learning? Yes. A great deal of effort and money goes into research into aging and the brain worldwide. This is particularly true of illnesses causing dementia. Scientists have not produced many careful studies of how environment affects dementia, but those who have offer some insights into learning.

Hardening of the Attitudes

Studies into aging and memory suffer from the cohort problem: The life experience of a group of people who are now in their seventies is radically different from that of a similar sample who are now in their thirties. In order to measure age-related changes in memory, it is best to compare Mrs. Smith now with Mrs. Smith when she was thirty, but such comparative data are rare. The comparative data that do exist suggests memory in people who are elderly now seems to be better than it was in elderly people seventy years ago.

If you want to stay healthy and live a long life, then stay fit and intellectually challenged. "The only guaranteed antidote to Alzheimer's is to extend the number of years we actively participate in education," claims an Oxford University neurologist.[1] He suggests that the sustained cognitive challenge that some elderly people still put into their lives keeps them healthy. The challenge of learning encourages cell growth and reduces neural atrophy.

Research by Dr. Matthew During and his team from Thomas Jefferson University in Philadelphia shows that a stimulating environment combined with early and continued learning both protects the brain from disease and increases its ability to regrow damaged cells. "We've shown that a learning environment can encourage cell growth and also reduce cell death by about 45 percent," he says ("Stimulating environment" 1999).

During and his colleagues performed experiments in which rats lived for several weeks in either standard housing or "enrichment housing" filled with running wheels, tunnels, balls, and choices of food. The researchers then treated the rats with a seizure-inducing neurotoxin. They found that rats housed in the enriched environment were almost completely protected against seizures. The rate of neural atrophy (cell death) in the hippocampal areas of the brains of rats in the standard housing was 45 percent higher than for those in the enriched environments. The hippocampus contributes to learning via long-term memory.

During believes these findings suggest that an enriched environment can turn on protective genes in the brain. Through this mechanism, he explains, the brain becomes more resilient and more resistant to aging and disease.

Some people worry that as we age we lose our ability to remember things. Some loss of memory function is natural but it should not occur to a significant and noticeable degree before about seventy years of age. Long-term memory seems to suffer little, while working memory—that dealing with day-to-day momentary things—is much more affected. As we age, the weight of the brain decreases. Parts of the hippocampus atrophy, but there is no significant global neural decay. Some people believe these changes occur because the basal forebrain becomes less efficient and so produces less acetylcholine.

As Professor Nick Rawlins of Oxford University puts it, not all memory capacities are affected in the same way by aging.[2] He points out some of the differences:

- Skill learning can be preserved while explicit learning decays.
- Recognition stays longer than recall.
- People remember the context or the source of the memory—it becomes part of them.

Implicit memory is spared when explicit is lost.

Stress seems to affect older people's memory. When pushed hard in simple memory activities, their recall drops. When given time and more relaxed circumstances, recall is restored.

The Network's Down

Contrary to popular belief, no more than 10 to 15 percent of people aged sixty-five plus suffer from senile dementia. Professor Robert Sapolsky (personal communication, January 2000) describes the effects of Alzheimer's on memory function like this: Memory is not lost in Alzheimer's, it simply takes more effort to get the memory out. We require more and more priming cues and immediate cuing to retrieve the memory.

The brain does not have enough neurons for each cell to be able to recognize just one stimulus. Rather, cells work in assemblies called networks. Aging affects these networks, causing some to be lost. A useful analogy is trying to telephone conference on cellular phones when one or two of those phones stray out of signal: Messages are incomplete, partly or poorly sent or received, or missing altogether (see figure 6.1).

As we age we also lose some function in the frontal lobes—through neural atrophy and reduction in blood flow and glucose metabolism—and become

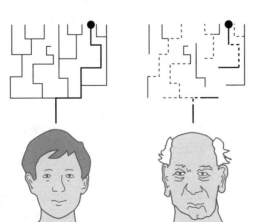

6.1 When the neural network goes down, the memories do not disappear. They just require stronger and more varied cuing to assemble their elements.

less efficient at remembering the order and timing of events. Decline in dopamine production means that neurons become less efficient at receiving messages. Dopamine is the brain's natural reward system. Its loss might be a partial cause of the "narrowing of horizons" that occurs in old age. Or perhaps the narrowing of horizons in old age might cause the loss of dopamine.

Harvard Medical School Professor Marilyn Albert says our memory changes as we age.[3] The biggest change is that we can absorb less information per hour. If learning is spread out by giving twenty-minute breaks, the ability to retain information improves. Naturally, in a person with Alzheimer's, the brain does not normally transfer the learning to long-term memory. One of the keys to the preservation of memory as we age is to enhance blood flow through exercise.

Stay Active

Inactivity can contribute to, and arise from, depression. Some elderly people find themselves locked into this vicious cycle as a result of some profound change in their lives: the death of a partner, the isolation of a sheltered care home, retirement. There is strong evidence that depression causes stress, which can lead to shrinkage of the hippocampus in the elderly. A group of sixty volunteers between ages sixty and eighty-five participated in memory tasks of finding their way through a human maze and recalling photos they had seen twenty-four hours earlier. A third of the volunteers had chronically high levels of cortisol (a stress hormone) in their brains, a problem that seems to be fairly common in older people. The size of the hippocampus averaged 14 percent smaller in this group ("Cortisol levels" 1998). Cortisol also interferes with the function of neurotransmitters, the chemicals that brain cells use to communicate with each other. This makes it difficult to think or access long-term memories. That is why some people get befuddled and confused in a severe crisis: Their mind goes blank because "the lines are down."

Professor Robert Sapolsky's (2000) research with animals showed that an excess of stress-related hormones may cause other problems for the elderly, including fatigue, thinning muscles, adult-onset diabetes, hypertension, osteoporosis, and immune suppression. Professor Sapolsky

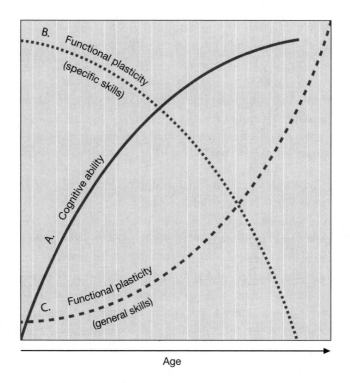

6.2 Line A shows how cognitive ability increases from birth through adulthood and begins to flatten out in old age. Line B shows how functional plasticity for specific skills diminishes from birth through adulthood. Line C shows how functional plasticity for general skills increases from birth through adulthood.

concluded that aged organisms not only have trouble turning off the stress response when the stressor is removed, they also secrete more stress-related hormones in their normal, non-stressed state. Elderly individuals of all sorts tend to have the stress response turned on even when nothing stressful is happening.

As we age the speed at which we store new information slows. Our capacity to deal with changes in routine suffers, and so does our ability to transfer information to memory (see figure 6.2). Elderly people who have a lifetime of using effective learning methods such as categorizing, storing, retrieving, and transferring behind them tend to retain memory better. Their memory is less susceptible than average to impaired function because it has been used more efficiently over an extended period of time.

It is a good idea as we age to monitor our lifestyle. Smoking combined with obesity will not only cause heart disease but also contribute to a decline in learning performance. As Professor Merrill Elias of Boston University School of Medicine, who led the research into risk factors for loss of mental ability, points out, "We want people to function at the highest possible level and for the longest possible time. Individuals are going to have a reduced quality of life if they cannot learn and remember" ("Obesity and smoking" 1998).

Professor Elias's group tested 1,799 volunteers involved in the Framingham Heart Study, which has tracked the cardiovascular health of a group of residents in a community near Boston for about fifty years based on four risk factors: smoking, obesity, high blood pressure, and diabetes. As part of their research the team administered tests of learning and memory, attention, concentration, and word fluency. Their results showed that the more risk factors for heart disease a person has, the greater his or her risk of developing memory and learning impairments. People with one of four risk factors at the time of testing were, on average, 23 percent more likely to be poor performers than those with no risk factors. With each additional risk factor, the volunteer's risk of decreased mental function increased another 23 percent. As reported in the U.S. journal *Health Psychology*, the 140 participants, studied over twenty years, all showed a decline in mental ability. But the higher the participant's blood pressure, the faster the decline.

Hold On to What You've Got

How is it that a frail old lady suffering from dementia and unable to remember her son's name, that he lives with his new wife fifty miles away, or that her partner predeceased her four years previously can nevertheless crochet and knit? How is it that memory for names, faces, places, facts, and everyday trivia seems so fragile but the memory for rehearsed motor movement seems so stubborn? How can it be that a physical movement or an involuntary gesture can precipitate a chain of associated memories?

Acquiring a physical skill is known as procedural learning and it is different—even dissociated—from acquiring factual knowledge (Bechara,

Damasio et al. 1999; Bechara, Tranel et al. 1996). Recent imaging studies would seem to confirm this. Individuals with amnesia are often unable to learn and retain new facts, but they can often acquire new physical skills and in many cases are able to access physical things they could do before their brain damage. Amnesic patients are also able to acquire new skills, despite not remembering how or when they were taught the skills. How is such a phenomenon to be explained?

It comes down to an area of the brain known as the basal ganglia. The basal ganglia are often intact after trauma has damaged other sites within the brain. In such cases, the brain remains capable of procedural learning, demonstration of that learning, and access to previously rehearsed skills. Individuals whose basal ganglia are damaged due to Parkinson's disease can remember facts and episodic information but have difficulty learning new skills. This suggests that a separate set of systems operates for remembering procedural skills than for acquiring and retaining factual knowledge. A dissociation thus exists between declarative and procedural learning.

This leads to a key question for educators. Factual learning and physical learning occur separately: Why? Might there be efficiencies in combining both modes in order to access and retain new information? If historical dates were learned through a combination of procedural and declarative memory, would that multiply the chances of recalling the information? Observing effective classroom practice over many years has pointed me to the answer: a resounding yes!

Sagging, Wrinkling, Shrinking

If you are a mother, did you become forgetful during pregnancy? You can't remember? You are forgiven; you probably had other things on your mind and, besides, your brain was smaller at the time. Research at the Royal Postgraduate Medical School in London showed that women's brains shrink by 3 to 5 percent during pregnancy. In tests, more than 70 percent of women had difficulty learning new information during their ninth month of pregnancy. During pregnancy, women's performance on spatial and verbal tests was 15 to 20 percent poorer. Six months later, the brain, and the scores, had returned to normal. (There was however no conclusive evidence that the partner's brain also shrinks during the hours of labor.)

Finally, as if there was not enough sagging, wrinkling, and shrinking involved with aging, it appears that one's brain shrinks with age, too, and that the male brain shrinks faster than the female brain. Men are more prone than women to memory loss as they age, perhaps because of brain shrinkage.

Human brains reach their full size in adolescence and begin shrinking after age twenty. As the brain gets smaller, the amount of fluid between the brain and skull increases. Between the ages of sixty-five and ninety-five, the fluid in men's brains increased by 30 percent, but women's brains saw only a 1 percent increase. People who have high cholesterol, who have one or more alcoholic drinks a day, and who smoke speed the shrinking process. As a general rule, according to Dr. C. Edward Coffey, a neuropsychiatrist at Henry Ford Behavioral Services in Michigan, the brain shrinks by about 10 percent every ten years (Coffey et al. 1998). The brain shrinkage and fluid increase were seen mostly in the frontal and temporal lobes, which control thinking, planning, and memory. Dr. Coffey, who used MRI to measure the brains of 330 healthy men and women, also found that women are better at retaining verbal memories, while men are better at retaining nonverbal skills, such as map reading or putting a puzzle together. He also noted varying rates of shrinkage, particularly among individuals over the age of sixty, although an explanation for this is proving elusive.

2
PART TWO
Ready, Wire, Fire
A Model for the Learning Brain

Chapter **7**

Physiology
How Do We Maintain the Brain?

This chapter contains the following sections:

The brain marches on its stomach. How girls' diet can lower their exam performance. Why iron intake is so important. The importance of school breakfast programs. What happens when you wolf your food.

The water solution. Does drinking water help you concentrate? Surprising findings about how the temperature of drinking water affects performance.

Sleep, learning, and the brain. Why sleep is vital to learning. What happens to the brain in sleep. Sleep delay syndrome in adolescent boys.

Movement, play and learning. Evidence that movement and play alter brain structure advantageously. Why movement is an integral part of the best learning. Why schools should make a stronger case for structured play.

You've got to laugh about it. The link between laughter and learning. The world's funniest joke. The therapeutic value of laughter.

Sing when you are winning. How singing improves your resistance to illness. The feel-good factor behind singing and why doing it together is best.

It will answer the following questions:

- Will skipping breakfast impair my thinking?
- Is there any real evidence that drinking water improves children's classroom learning?
- How does sleep improve all-round memory and recall?
- What scientific evidence supports the case for structured play in elementary classrooms?
- Is there any evidence that laughter helps learning?
- Why do I feel better when I have been singing?

Introduction

In excess of a hundred different neurotransmitters have been identified in the brain, and others are continually being discovered. It seems that each one probably plays some role in shaping behaviors. In general, a neurotransmitter is classified by whether it excites or inhibits—in various degrees—the nerve impulses in target neurons. The little electrical signals sent by neurons down their axons arrive at the synapse, or junction, but are not able to cross the junction until the correct neurotransmitters are in place and ready to connect to receptors.

A biochemical mating game occurs between the neurotransmitters and the receptors in target neurons. The neurotransmitter wants to meet the correct receptor on the receiving neuron, but there are lots of them. With the right chemical match, the neurotransmitter sticks. This extraordinary mating game of neurotransmitter and receptor influences every aspect of your behavior. And it is influenced by what you eat.

The Brain Marches on Its Stomach

A brain marches on its stomach. Neurotransmitters are made from the amino acids contained in dietary proteins. Proteins are the building blocks of the animal kingdom, and amino acids are the building blocks of proteins. When your body digests protein, it uses those amino acids to manufacture the 50,000 different proteins it needs. It will convert protein into neurotransmitters and chromosomes, hormones and enzymes, antibodies and muscles, hair and nails.

Your body's 50,000 proteins are made from combinations of just twenty-two different amino acids. Eight of these are considered essential nutrients for humans because they can be obtained only from food. The others can usually be synthesized from the eight and are called "nonessential," although they are equally vital to life. If your amino acid levels are low, then a competition takes place. Brain cells compete with body cells, which have an advantage because they can take up essential amino acids more easily from your bloodstream. Neurotransmitters are synthesized within your neurons, so their production depends on which amino acids actually

7.1 Children's lifestyles, exercise, and diet play roles in shaping the brain they will have as adults. Balance is important in all things: physical and intellectual challenge, nutrition, hydration, sleep, and fun.

get into your brain. Lifestyle factors can make a tremendous difference in children's academic success (see figure 7.1).

A study funded by the Durham Local Education Authority, the Dyslexia Research Trust, Oxford University, and the Dyspraxia Foundation is testing the hypothesis that disorders of fatty acid metabolism may be a factor in predisposing children to dyslexia, apraxia, and ADHD. In this study, 120 underachieving children are being given a supplement called Eye Q that contains refined fish oil, evening primrose, and vitamin E. This supplement contains high levels of the unsaturated omega-3 fatty acids that the brain needs for proper myelination. Results have yet to be published.

Another British study has found that one in four schoolgirls is damaging her IQ by dieting and depriving herself of iron (Nelson, Bakaliou, and Trivedi 1994; Ash and Nelson 1998). "We were surprised that a very small drop in iron levels caused a fall in IQ," explained Dr. Michael Nelson, senior lecturer in nutrition at King's College, London. "We conclude that poor iron status is common among British adolescent girls, and diet and iron status play an important role in determining IQ, independent of factors such as menstrual status or social class. By supplementing their diets with extra iron, it is quite probable that cognitive function would improve" (Nelson, Bakaliou, and Trivedi 1994).

The researchers surveyed 595 girls ages eleven to eighteen, from a cross-section of racial groups, who were attending three comprehensive schools in north London. The girls provided blood samples that were analyzed for hemoglobin and packed cell volume. The investigators found that there was a highly significant difference in IQ correlating with blood iron levels: iron-deficient anemic girls (those with the lowest levels of iron in their blood), versus iron-deficient, versus iron-replete.

Skipping breakfast also leads to deterioration in academic performance. During the resulting metabolic starvation, focused attention, recall, and complex mental tasks become increasingly difficult. Many schools organize breakfast programs for low-income children. Breakfast foods are low-cost, high-return investments for schools. Children behave better and learn better on full stomachs. Some research has suggested that children who eat a bowl of cereal on the morning of an exam may perform better than children who eat no, or an inappropriate, breakfast.

Research at Northumbria University suggests that supplements of ginseng and ginkgo biloba help improve performance on memory tasks ("Herbal remedies" 2000). Yet research from the same university, published in July 2001, showed that chewing gum during an exam also helped improve performance. When a group who chewed gum was compared against a group who did not, they showed slightly better performance. A group with no gum who was asked to simulate chewing for the period of the exam also showed a slight boost in performance. The hypothesis is that the movement of the jaw contributes to improved oxygen circulation in the head and the release of saliva, which is associated with a relaxed state!

Research on memory and diet at Swansea University found that students who skipped breakfast made more errors in memorizing word lists (Benton 1997; Benton and Parker 1998; Benton, Slater, and Donohue in press). In other evidence of the importance of nutrition, Dr. Green at Unilever found that weight-loss diets produced impaired functions of memory and that the coincident preoccupation with food avoidance was a contributory factor. Babies' brains may be permanently impaired by malnutrition during sensitive periods.

Obesity is a growing problem in the West. New evidence suggests that it takes ten minutes after the body has taken in enough food for the feeling of fullness to register in the brain. A study carried out at the University of Florida found that the delay in realizing that one is full can lead over-weight people to have an extra portion of pie without realizing they have actually had more than enough. The time the brain takes to respond to glucose ingestion is longer in obese people than in people of a normal weight (Maszuda et al. 1999). These findings are helping to improve the diagnosis and treatment of obesity and other eating disorders.

Brain activity was studied in eighteen participants who fasted for twelve hours then underwent continuous brain scanning for forty-eight minutes. Using fMRI (functional magnetic resonance imaging) the researchers re-corded brain activity in response to internal and external stimuli such as eating and drinking. Ten minutes after the scanning began, participants drank a water solution containing dextrose, a type of sugar. The research-ers detected two peaks in brain response afterwards. The first occurred about ninety seconds after intake and was, the scientists said, related to swallowing and other aspects of the eating process. The second, more important, and sustained peak, began about ten minutes after ingestion and was the brain's signal that it was physically full.

The peak lasted about two minutes and corresponded directly with an increase in sugar and insulin levels in the blood. Brain changes also occurred in the hypothalamus, a portion of the brain responsible for regulating body temperature and metabolism. These findings may help to develop new drugs to treat obesity and obesity-related diabetes (Liu et al. 2000).

 The hypothalamus has been known for many years as being related to the regulation of eating. But this is the first study in humans able to directly demonstrate that it undergoes dynamic and physiological changes as a result. (Liu et al. 2000)

These findings reinforce your mother's advice, which she got from her mother, not to wolf your food. Eating slowly may provide more time for the feeling of fullness to register, especially in the obese, whose fullness signals are slower and weaker. In the United States more than 15 percent of children and teenagers, and nearly 33 percent of adults, are obese, and the numbers are rising (National Health and Nutrition Examination Survey 2000).

The Water Solution

If you visit www.urbanlegends.com, one of the myths you will find there is that you must drink at least two quarts of water daily. The site goes on to explain that this information can be traced to a 1945 statement from the U.S. Academy of Sciences on recommended daily allowances. The last sentence of this recommendation says that most of the water is contained in prepared foods. This sentence has somehow gotten lost. Yet many schools report that allowing children to bring in sports bottles that they can refill during the day has contributed to improvements in learning performance. While this anecdotal evidence should not necessarily be taken at face value, it is worth exploring further.

Where do I begin? According to a leaflet given to me on a transatlantic crossing I need five cups of water for an eleven-hour flight. According to the popular press I need two quarts a day. According to my mother, I need three or more. David Oliviera of the Department of Renal Medicine at St. George's Hospital in London is of the view that

> the minimum volume of urine required by the kidneys to excrete waste products of metabolism is about half a liter per day. Since we lose another half liter via sweat, breathing, and feces, the net intake required to maintain water balance is about one liter a day under normal conditions. Drinking more than this simply results in more dilute urine—the same absolute amount of toxins will still be excreted.

So if you want your learners to have dilute urine, pile on the water! Yet dehydration, irregular intake of fluids, and fueling up with sugary drinks often laced with additives and preservatives may prove a deadly cocktail for the young learners in a classroom. Here are the benefits of appropriate intake of fresh water identified by the International Bottled Water Organization:

- The brain is 75 percent water, so even moderate dehydration can cause headaches and dizziness.
- Water is required for expiration.
- Water helps regulates body temperature.
- Water carries nutrients and oxygen to all the cells in the body.
- Blood is 92 percent water.
- Water moistens the air we inhale.
- Water protects and cushions vital organs.
- Water helps to convert food into energy.
- Water helps the body absorb nutrients.
- Water removes waste.
- Our bones are 22 percent water.
- Our muscles are 75 percent water.
- Water cushions joints.

Some have argued that being allowed to drink water as and when needed might in itself be a positive thing. Perhaps having a physical break from focused attention in the classroom by visiting the drinking fountain may also be a good thing. Simply having water present may also have therapeutic value. It does seem that the presence of individual sports-type bottles with fresh water allows learners to individualize their water intake. This self-regulation may be at the heart of the successes schools report. The practical experience of many schools sits alongside recent research that suggests drinking water in the right circumstances is very important.

Experimental psychologist Dr. Peter Rogers and his colleagues from the University of Bristol carried out tests on sixty volunteers ("Water" 2001). The volunteers were asked to rate how thirsty they felt. Their reactions were then tested by getting them to press a button in response to prompts on a computer screen. The volunteers either drank nothing before the test or had a cupful of tap water, chilled to 50°F. People who were thirsty at the beginning of the test and took a drink performed 10 percent better than those who drank nothing. But the performance of those who were not thirsty to start with dropped by 15 percent after a drink.

Dr. Rogers believes that drinking too much water might affect the ability to drive or perform intellectually demanding tasks. He also thinks that the temperature of the drinks might explain part of the effect. The body has to divert physiological resources to deal with the local cooling effect in the gut, which may be responsible for the effect on performance. The water served was moderately cold, and Rogers also speculated that perhaps colder or hotter would have a greater detrimental impact on performance.

Sleep, Learning, and the Brain

Is there a correlation between academic performance and sleep patterns? According to Dr. Larry Cahill of the University of California at Irvine, the best form of learning is accompanied by some emotional arousal and directed attention and is followed by REM sleep (Cahill and McGaugh 1998; see also Hamann, Cahill, and Squire 1997). So, does sleep improve memory? Can the right sort of sleep pattern make you a better learner? Should I give you time to "sleep on it" before you answer these questions? The scientific community seems split on the findings regarding sleep, learning, and memory.[1]

When we sleep, the production of norepinephrine and serotonin is switched off. During the day these chemicals play a part in regulating our logical and consequential thinking, reminding us of time, duration, and location. When we are asleep, anything goes. Judgments of time and location are distorted. Logic disappears, and we drift through ninety- to one hundred-minute cycles of rapid eye movement (REM) sleep (see figure 7.2). REM is a phase of sleep characterized by very quick flickering of the eyes and high levels of brain activity. Typically, REM sleep occurs four times throughout the night and is interspersed with non-REM (NREM) sleep.

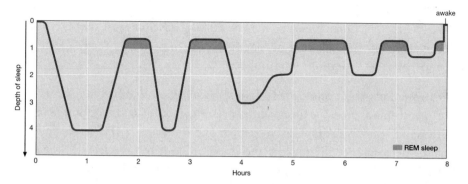

7.2 The stages of rapid eye movement (REM) sleep. We spend 20 to 30 percent of each night in REM sleep, dreaming an average of two hours a night. Within thirty to forty-five minutes of falling asleep, a deep sleep phase occurs. Then a shallower phase of REM sleep occurs. Toward the end of the night, the REM phases become more frequent with shorter periods of deep sleep in between.

Pierre Maquet of the University of Liège in Belgium suggests that the most likely hypothesis is that the function of REM sleep is one of consolidation: "The memory probably isn't actually formed in REM sleep. It's already there, but it seems that the memory is consolidated during REM sleep. Before, it's fragile; after, it's more robust" (Maquet et al. 1996, 163). His team conducted PET scans of participants while they completed a simple keyboarding task and later while they slept. They found that brain activity during REM sleep was similar to that recorded during keyboarding.

Professor Horne at the Sleep Research Laboratory of Loughborough University found that sleep deprivation leads to impairment of activity within the prefrontal cortex, reduction in logical thought, impaired choice of words, and reduction in behavioral flexibility. He concludes, "All the functions of our body have circadian rhythms [a twenty-four-hour cycle]" ("Sleepless in Loughborough").

According to Daniel Kripke, Professor of Psychiatry at UC San Diego, many teenagers, particularly boys in late adolescence, suffer from what is known as sleep delay syndrome.[2] In this syndrome, the sleepy phase of the body clock shifts around so that such teenagers have difficulty falling sleep and waking up and feel tired all day (especially in the afternoons). Thus, the earlier that school, college, or work begins, the less sleep they get. This condition can begin in puberty and worsens in the late teens. What happens is that the REM phase of the sleep cycle is truncated. What we are left with is a teenager who may be moody, irascible, and slightly ill-tempered. Some 2.5 percent of American boys in their late teens appear to be suffering from this condition!

Professor Robert Stickgold at Harvard Medical School conducted research into procedural memory for performance of computer tasks (Hobson and Stickgold 1994; Stickgold, Pace-Schott, and Hobson 1994). The participants' performance improved after about an hour of practice and then began to plateau. Only after six or more hours of subsequent sleep were there additional marked improvements in performance. But not all phases of sleep have the same value to memory and to learning. To find out exactly what was going on, participants were observed in a sleep laboratory. Consolidation was optimized when two types of sleep—REM and slow wave—occurred during the course of the night. Professor Stickgold concludes that a good sleep is important after intensive studying or training, because it is during extended deep sleep, with oscillations between REM and slow wave in roughly ninety-minute cycles, that consolidation of procedural memory occurs.

Others go further in their claims for the significance of brain activity during sleep. Professor Jan Born and colleagues at Lübeck University in Germany say that the same structures that are active in the brain during learning are reactivated during sleep. Undoubtedly, they conclude, sleep helps to consolidate memories. They do, however, add a cautionary note that the mechanisms which cause these effects are not close to being identified. The group's research points to slow-wave sleep as essential for learning, with REM sleep having an additive effect (Mason et al. 1973; Späth-Schwalbe et al. 1992).

Anyone who has had a baby knows that sleep deprivation is the oldest and cheapest form of torture. Missing out on sleep often is dangerous as well. Not only does it lead to impairment and death of hippocampal cells, but also to accidents caused by sleepy drivers and machine operators. Researchers at Harvard Medical School found that cheating on sleep for only a few nights increases brain levels of cortisol. Inadequate sleep also deprives the brain of the time it needs to reestablish its energy. One survey indicated that about two-thirds of the population fails to get enough sleep. In very young children, lack of sufficient, uninterrupted sleep causes behavior problems. A study of five hundred children under five years of age found that those who slept less than ten hours a day, including naps, were 25 percent more likely to misbehave. They would throw temper tantrums, act aggressively toward others, be more vocal in their attention seeking, and be more demanding of adult attention. Children who slept twelve or more hours a day were much less likely to behave in this way.

Perceived morning sleepiness varies by country. The following table shows the percentage of thirteen-year-olds who reported being sleepy at least four mornings per week.[3]

Country	Percentage
Norway	45
Finland	40
USA	38
Scotland	35
England	22

All animals operate on rhythms of biological regulation. Humans have highs and lows for different types of physiological and intellectual functioning, and we have downtime through sleep. There is no simple reason why sleep is necessary. It does not rest the brain; in fact, some parts of the brain are more active in sleep than when we are awake. Circadian rhythms, basically twenty-four-hour cycles, apply to many of our bodily functions (see figure 7.3). Our body clocks are inaccurate—they tend to get later—and can be influenced by things like artificial light. Older people have different sleep patterns than people in their teens and early twenties. The levels of neurotransmitters and brain receptors vary by time of day. Some of us are indeed early birds and some are night owls!

Natural births peak at around 5.00 a.m. There are two peaks for induced labor: one hour before midday and one hour after. The death rate from natural causes is highest at 4.00 a.m. There is much coming and going in that one-hour window in the early hours of the morning. There are bodily changes too: more cortisol in our bodies at the beginning and end of sleep, more growth hormone early in the sleep period. My suggestion would be treat yourself to sleeping in!

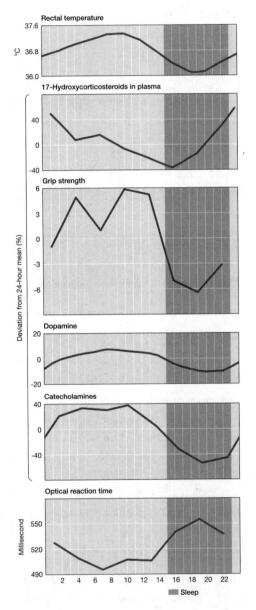

7.3 Circadian rhythms affect many physiological and intellectual functions. Seen here are body temperature and grip strength changes; optical reaction times; and alterations in the chemicals cortisol, dopamine, and catecholamine. Notice the flat period followed by a rise toward the end of the sleep phase.

Movement, Play, and Learning

How important is play to your child or to the children you teach in your school? British anthropologists Iona and Peter Opie spent years observing children's play. They hypothesized that play, perhaps more than any other aspect of a child's life, was where children learned from their peers. They also commented that if children could be transported back to any previous century, they would probably be more at home with the games being played than with any other aspect of society (Opie and Opie 1969). This was written in 1969. Have things changed?

Perhaps some of the games children play in the playgrounds and streets of the twenty-first century differ from those of their parents and grandparents, but many games nevertheless retain echoes of things past. The purpose of play is, I believe, consistent and may well go beyond the transmission of rules and learning of social interactions. When young children are absorbed in play, it becomes more important to them at that moment than any other aspect of their lives. I remember my mother's vain attempts to call me in from the field in the midst of some nail-biting finale to a soccer match. Play can be exhilarating, energy consuming, and an integral part of being human. Young children use as much as 15 percent of their total available energy in play. This figure represents a very high commitment to one activity for a primate in its developing stage. What is the purpose? Behavioral scientists make a compelling case that not only does play improve the physique of the youngster in preparation for the rigors of an adult life and help with practicing the skills related to hunting, social grouping, and mating, but it also causes bigger, and thus better, brains.

Research published in 2001 suggested that in primates, the amount the brain grows between birth and maturity reflects the amount of play in which each species engages (Bekoff 2001; see also Iwaniuk, Nelson, and Pellis 2001). Evolutionary scientist Robert Barton believes this correlation has to do with preparation for learning and probably, "with the importance of environmental input to the neocortex and to the cerebellum during development" (quoted in Furlow 2001, 30). The process of synaptogenesis involves the overproduction of neural connections in sensitive periods of a primate's development. In other words, the human brain produces more connections than it needs, but only for a small window of time. During this window the extent to which connections are laid down depends on the duration and level of stimulation the brain receives. Animals, young humans specifically, can sculpt the overall circuitry of the brain through play. Play lays down the neural pathways needed later in life. Neuroscientist Dr. Steven Siviy studied how play affected the chemicals in the brain and, in particular, proteins associated with the stimulation and growth of nerve cells. He found that play activated lots of different areas of the brain and had a role not only in learning but in creativity as well (cited in Furlow 2001).

Young children who are imaginative in their pretend play are better able to cope with stress later in life, according to another contemporary U.S.-based research project (Russ, Robins, and Christiano 1999). Creative five- and six-year-olds often are better problem solvers by the time they are nine and ten. "Good early play skills predicted the ability to be creative and generate alternative solutions to everyday problems," the authors reported.

The children in the study were given three types of creativity tests: an Affect in Fantasy Task, an Alternate Uses Test, and a Story Telling Measure. In the first test the children were asked to make up a play using two puppets and three blocks. The Alternate Uses Test measured divergent thinking—thinking that explores various solutions to a problem. In the Story Telling Measure, the children were asked to make up a story to go along with a picture book for younger children. The processes learned in pretend play were discovered to be important because they relate to adaptive functioning (creative abilities, coping abilities). To foster creativity in children, the researchers suggest

►| allowing time to indulge in play

►| participating with children as they play

►| praising and rewarding children for their creativity and imagination

►| helping children if they need suggestions for creative play

Play excites different parts of the brain. Children's play can simultaneously excite auditory, visual, motor, and spatial functions. When young children are encouraged to explore through their senses, separate areas

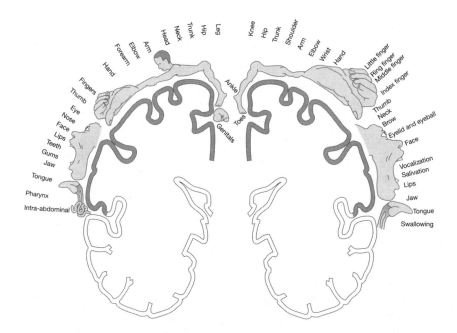

7.4 The homunculus, or "little man," is a graphic illustration of the sensitivity and function of the motor and sensory areas of the cerebral cortex. The motor cortex is located like a hair band across the top of the head between the ears. The diagram represents the region of the body that moves following stimulation of that part of the cortex. Notice how very sensitive areas like the hands, mouth, and lips have relatively more cortical space devoted to them.

of the motor cortex and sensory-motor cortex are activated. The motor and sensory-motor strip runs across the top of the left and right sides of the brain like a hair band (see figure 7.4). In the human brain, larger areas of the cortex are devoted to parts of the body that engage in detailed movements, such as the thumb and forefinger and the muscles of the mouth and tongue.

Research with adults has shown that exercises requiring delicate finger movements will, within days, be rewarded with more sensory real estate being devoted to those functions (Elbert and Pantev 1995). In rats large areas of the sensory strip are devoted to the manipulation of the whiskers. The rats use their whiskers to explore and find out about their world. Children explore and find out about their world through play. Through sensory interaction the structure of the motor and sensory-motor strip changes.

The best learning is like play. Play involves lots of rehearsal and repetition. Children do the same things again and again. It can, and most often does, involve stepped levels of challenge and risk. There is engagement at an emotional level and later at different social levels. Play is not something the contemporary Western child is given opportunities for or learns as a right. With more and more children being driven to and picked up from neighborhood schools, sitting in front of televisions or computer screens, and losing the skills of cooperative play their grandparents learned, maybe it is time to start teaching children how to play.

There is increasing pressure to get more and more academic content knowledge into shorter and shorter periods of time as accountability and standardized testing pressures increase. One of the experiences getting squeezed out is structured physical exercise. Yet, much research of worth points to the benefits of regular physical exercise in improving academic performance. A California Department of Education study found a direct correlation between students' levels of physical fitness and their academic achievement (see figure 7.5). Both physical and neurological benefits are cited for physical activity. As one would expect, basic motor skills improve, but so do reading and mathematics scores. The functioning and nourishment of the brain improve, and there are social-emotional benefits in self-esteem, energy, concentration, and overall behavior (Scheuer and Mitchell 2003).

The adult brain, although only about 2 percent of the body's weight, receives 16 percent of the blood supply, and per unit of mass, brain tissue receives ten times as much blood as muscle tissue. By the age of three

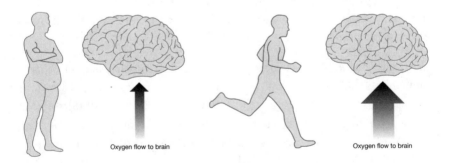

Oxygen flow to brain   Oxygen flow to brain

7.5 The more efficient the system, the more agile it becomes. Oxygen uptake to the brain is improved by structured physical activity.

the brain is 80 percent of its adult size and by the age of five reaches 90 percent of adult size. In adults the brain uses about 25 percent of the oxygen in the system, and in young children the figure is nearer 50 percent. Professor Susan Greenfield (1999) of Oxford University, one of the world's leading authorities on the brain, says, "The brain is very sensitive to what is happening to the body, and the more you are interacting and stimulating the circuits of the brain, the more agile are your brain cells." Case proven.

You've Got to Laugh about It

In 1982 I was working as a museum guide in the Lake District of northern England. My job involved telling groups of tourists about the literary associations of the area. I worked for a museum and would lead as many as twelve tours a day, each lasting forty minutes. I had recently graduated, I was not well off, and so I worked long hours seven days a week. One morning, midway through a sentence about Wordsworth's poetic method, I got a fit of the giggles. Nothing too extraordinary had happened. I had noticed the gardener, who doubled as the chief museum guide, wander by the window. As he did so, he looked in and pulled a face. I doubled over laughing and could not stop. As fourteen bemused Japanese tourists looked on, I laughed and laughed. Eventually, I had to give up the tour and go home for the day. My involuntary and uncontrollable laughing fit was my mechanism for relieving the physical stress of work.

There is a lot of research into laughter. In collaboration with the British Association for the Advancement of Science, Dr. Richard Wiseman at the University of Hertfordshire embarked on a quest to find the funniest joke. Wiseman created a website called "LaughLab" (http://www.laughlab.co.uk) to which visitors could submit and rate jokes. At its peak, with more than ten thousand jokes submitted from more than seventy countries, Laughlab was described as the world's most extensive psychology experiment ever. More than 100,000 people rated the jokes and, in doing so, revealed a lot about the differences between men and women, and among nations, in what is humorous. Males tended to favor more aggressive jokes, jokes with sexual innuendo, and jokes at the expense of women. Women preferred jokes containing word play. The joke ranked funniest of all was this one (announced in December 2001):

> The famous detective Sherlock Holmes and his partner,
> Dr. Watson, go camping, and pitch their tent under the
> stars. During the night Holmes wakes his companion and
> says, "Watson, look up at the stars and tell me what you
> deduce." Watson says, "I see millions of stars and, even if
> only a few of those have planets, it's quite likely that there
> are some planets like Earth and, if there are a few planets
> like Earth out there, there might also be life." Holmes
> replies, "Watson, you idiot. Somebody stole our tent."

Research also exists into laughter and learning. Laughter in a classroom can be a very positive way to reduce stress and aid learning. Laughter, when it precedes certain types of problem solving, can improve general performance. People are better able to deal with cognitive challenge when they approach the challenge through shared laughter with others.

Laughter also changes our physical state. It contributes to enhancing the immune system and increasing natural disease-fighting cells. It lowers levels of immunosuppressive hormones while boosting white blood cells. It lowers blood pressure and has a beneficial effect on conditions such as cancer and rheumatoid arthritis. It can reduce the symptoms of depression. Laughter is known to relieve stress, improve sleep, and produce a general sense of well-being.

The Association for Applied and Therapeutic Humor (http://aath.org)—where the therapy is known as "hee, hee healing"—has commissioned more than one hundred studies of the beneficial effects of humor. In one study by Dr. Jason Goodson (2001) of Utah State University, undergraduate students with signs of depression were given tapes of comedians to listen to for thirty minutes a day for four weeks. Prior to intervention the patients had an average depression score of 19. (Anything above 13 is considered mild to moderate depression). Post-intervention, the group mean score had dropped to 11, representing a significant, 42 percent reduction in symptoms. At Christmastime in 2001 the UK retailer Asda replaced the usual piped music in its stores with jokes in an attempt to relieve customers' stress and keep them shopping longer. With eleven million visitors to UK stores in the week before Christmas, Asda was playing for big stakes. This is one of the jokes the customers heard: "Who is never hungry at Christmas? The turkey—he's always stuffed!" Roll on Easter!

Researchers struggle to explain what is happening in the brain when we laugh. Laughter is understood to be an instinctive response programmed by our genes. Identical twins reared apart for forty years had identical laughs. Yet individuals who are autistic have great difficulty in understanding humor because they interpret things literally.

Laughter has a social function. Laughter provokes more laughter: You laugh with others and so it is good for relationships. If you tickle yourself, you do not laugh. Why not? Because of the social dimension of laughter; studies have shown that people are thirty times more likely to laugh in social settings than when alone. Even nitrous oxide ("laughing gas") loses much of its potency when taken in solitude. Extroverts (people who are outgoing) prefer sexual and straightforward jokes, while introverts (people who are shy) prefer nonsexual and more complicated jokes.

Each person has preferred types of humor—just like preferred ways of learning: Some people find visual jokes funny, others prefer auditory jokes, and others like physical (or kinesthetic) jokes. People laugh in similar but not identical fashion, often in variations of five notes. One will often hear

> Ha, ha, ha, ha, ha
> Ho, ho, ho, ho, ho
> He, he, he, he, he

But one will never hear

> Ha ho ha ho ha
> He ho he ho he

Research shows that males are better at getting laughs but females are better at laughing. Young children laugh on average three hundred times daily, but adults only twenty-five to thirty times.

Sing When You Are Winning

At football or baseball games it is not uncommon to hear fans sing in support of their team. Social commentators have assumed this is a form of tribalism that improves the performance of the players on the field. One popular favorite, "Sing When You Are Winning, You Only Sing When You Are Winning," is now known to have literal as well as metaphorical truth. Singing raises the level of antibodies in the body.

Research at the University of California at Irvine has shown physical and emotional benefits of singing.[4] Saliva swabs from thirty-two choristers who had just sung a Beethoven piece showed that immunoglobulin A levels had gone up dramatically. Immunoglobulin A (IgA) is used by the body's immune system to fight off disease. During rehearsals, levels of IgA increased by 150 percent and during performance by 240 percent. The authors—Professor Robert Beck and Dr. Tom Cesario—point out that "secretory immunoglobulin protein is associated with emotional arousal and mood, relaxation and sense of humor. If singing leads to higher levels of IgA, then it is beneficial to your health as we know that heightened levels of this protein are effective in the immune system."

Singing releases endorphins, it alters your breathing, it stimulates the nerves behind the stomach. Singing together is a good form of team building. Earlier I described how learning through music helps children remember related content. So, the class that sings together, wins together!

Chapter **8**

Engagement
How Do We Arouse and Direct the Brain?

This chapter contains the following sections:

Stress, learning, and the brain. A definition of stress. The physical changes that result from stress.

Dangerous dimensions of stress. The role of glucocorticoids. Good and bad ways to prepare for exams. How stress makes it difficult to create new memories.

Dealing with stressors. What to do to deal with stress. The stress responses that rats and humans share. Classroom tools for dealing with learner stress.

The four "F"s of classroom survival. Challenge versus stress: a vital difference to a learner. What happens to a classroom learner under stress? A summary of likely behavioral responses and what to do about each one.

Get yourself engaged. Emotions and their origin. How we all have different emotional palettes. Emotional adaptability and susceptibility.

A motivational model. A little more about motivation followed by a seven-stage motivational model.

It will answer the following questions:

- ▷ In what ways might stress get in the way of learning? How does challenge differ from stress?

- ▷ When I get stressed, what happens to my body?

- ▷ How do we know so much about stress?

- ▷ How can I recognize a learner under stress? What can I do when I recognize stress responses?

- ▷ What is the difference between engaged and disengaged emotions?

- ▷ Have you got something that will help me think my way out of a rut?

Introduction

In the last year, when have you been stressed? Did you experience stress that extended beyond the immediate moment? Did you feel out of control and unable to do anything about it? Did it affect your relationships? Appetite? General health? Energy levels? Enthusiasm for work?

If you answered yes to any or all of these questions, welcome to being an adult in the West in the twenty-first century. Adults in the West no longer die in great numbers from malaria, liver fluke, dysentery, leprosy, or tuberculosis. Instead, they die of stress-related illnesses such as diabetes, cancer, strokes, and ulcers. We have become accomplished at turning on the stress response. We are not so gifted at turning it off.

Professor Robert Sapolsky is a primatologist who specializes in glucocorticoids (a class of steroid hormones, also known as cortisol, secreted from the adrenal glands). He has spent years in the company of baboons. He gives wonderfully illustrated talks on stress in large primates. He compares the physical changes that baboons show under stress with those evidenced in humans. He starts his talks by pointing out how, in the West, we have slowly accumulated dysfunction over time, including the luxury of dying from stress-related illnesses (Sapolsky 2000).

Stress, Learning, and the Brain

A stressor is defined as anything from the outside world that puts us out of homeostatic balance. Thoughts can cause this imbalance, and if we think these thoughts chronically, we will get sick. A *stress response* is anything we do to restore the homeostatic balance. We can respond through thought, and if we do so well enough, we will recover. Professor Sapolsky affirms that we can turn on the stress response simply through thought but asks, Are we smart enough to turn it off again?

Your sympathetic nervous system mobilizes you to deal with threat, real or imagined. Your adrenal glands release adrenaline (also known as epinephrine) and other hormones that increase breathing, heart rate, and blood pressure. These chemicals quickly move more oxygen-rich blood to the brain and to the muscles needed for fighting or fleeing. Adrenaline causes a rapid release of glucose and fatty acids into your bloodstream to give you energy. Your senses become keener, your memory sharper, and your sensitivity to pain less.

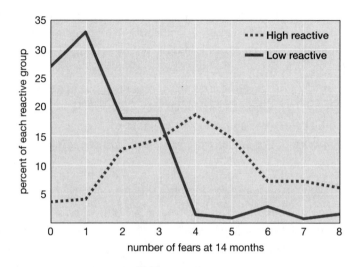

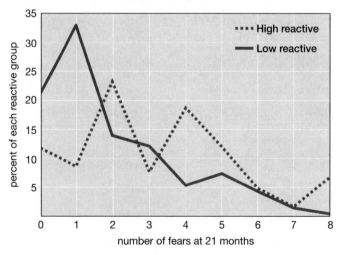

8.1 These charts show how young children cope differently with stress based on temperament and life experience. In each age range a set of physiological responses to an event that could be construed as fearful was measured. Some children showed little or no reaction. Others were disposed to demonstrate a stress response. Children who were deemed "highly reactive" at fourteen months were also found to be more susceptible to fearful events at twenty-one and forty-eight months.

Other functions shut down while all this is going on. While struggling for survival, you do not want to grow, have sex, or eat, and blood flow to the skin is reduced. That is why chronic stress leads to sexual dysfunction, increases your chances of getting sick, and may give you a rash. Under stress your body is in a temporary state of metabolic overdrive to prepare you to respond to a life-threatening situation. After you have responded and the danger has passed, your body tries to return to normal. It is incredibly easy to turn on the stress response, but it is incredibly difficult to turn it off. Scientists agree that the stress response is predetermined by genes and by childhood experience (see figure 8.1). It is voluntary only to a limited extent, and there is a subset of people who, for some unexplained reason, are better than the rest of us at coping with it.

In response to stress, the body may release any combination of eleven different chemicals. It will begin to do so within less than a second of a stressor being identified. The excitatory sympathetic nervous system jumps into action immediately, but it is very slow to turn off and allow the inhibitory, parasympathetic nervous system to take over and calm you down. Once the stress response has been activated, the system wisely keeps you in a state of readiness: The predator might come back. Remaining in a state of stress carries consequences for your health, as the following table shows:

Adaptive stress response	Stress-related disorder
Mobilize energy	Fatigue, diabetes
Raise blood pressure	Hypertension
Stop eating	Ulceration, colitis
Stop growing	Dwarfism
Stop having sex	Impotency, reduced libido
Suppress the immune system	Increased disease risk
Think faster	Eventual neural degeneration
Sharpen sensory systems	Death of neurons related to learning and memory

Some stress in learning is beneficial. Maze performance in rats goes up in the short term when they are injected with a stress hormone. It is at the point when a feeling of loss of control and helplessness kicks in that problems arise (see figure 8.2). This feeling is all too prevalent in everyday life in the West.

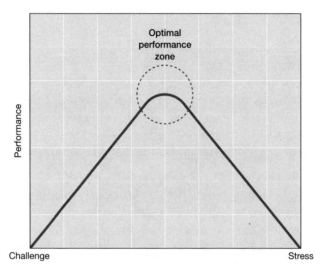

8.2 Challenge versus stress. In most learning, moderate or manageable stress in the form of challenge improves performance. At a point determined by the individual's capacity to accommodate stress, however, learning performance tips dramatically. High levels of anxiety characterize this phase. For teachers, balancing challenge with anxiety-related stress is part of their professional craft.

For the first hour or so, stress helps some types of learning. It helps route more oxygen to the brain in the short term. Neurons have more energy sources at their disposal. In this stage of engagement we learn better. Sadly, it does not last. After about six hours of unrelieved stress, short-term memory begins to go.

After about a week, we see neural networks begin to atrophy. The hippocampus is weakened and begins to show signs of aging faster. According to Professor Sapolsky, energy is diverted away from the hippocampus and cortex toward the cerebellum. Explicit memory is adversely affected and implicit memory is favored.

Dangerous Dimensions of Stress

Your lifestyle is also affected by stress. The most dangerous set of personality traits to hold onto are those of the "Type A" personality—particularly in men. If you know someone who habitually has a negative outlook on life, exhibits impatience, and is joyless, have a word with him or her. Remaining this way will affect the person's diet, immune system, growth, sleep, and ability to have children. The worst trait is the combination of hostility with impatience.

The bacteria contributing to stomach ulcers multiply faster when you are under stress. Your immune system is less effective, so you are more susceptible to disease. Testosterone levels in males go down, as does their capacity to reproduce. According to Sapolsky, choir boys in the Vatican have higher levels of testosterone than do young American marines going through boot camp. With excessive exercise and the stress it causes, female athletes stop ovulating. Children may not eat or grow normally. Stress-related dwarfism, although extremely rare, does occur. Remove the child from the stressor, and growth resumes.

To understand how stress affects learning and how some children fall victim to the stress response that will limit their learning before they ever get to a classroom, you must know about cortisol. Sustained stress can damage the hippocampus, the part of our limbic system central to learning, spatial recall, and memory. The presence of stress-induced cortisol for longer than it remains useful is the problem. During a perceived threat, the adrenal glands immediately release adrenaline. After a couple of minutes, if the threat is severe or still persists, the adrenals then release cortisol.

Once in the brain, cortisol remains much longer than adrenaline and continues to affect brain cells. Too much cortisol adversely affects brain function, especially memory. Human studies show a correlation between high cortisol levels and decreases in memory and cognitive functions like concentration and creativity. Learning and memory are all about long-term potentiation (LTP) in the hippocampus; that is, neurons being better able to communicate with each other. Hippocampal neurons are vulnerable. They age quickly. Months of stress will kill off hippocampal neurons outright. Post-traumatic stress disorder, sustained depression, and extended sexual abuse in childhood can have similar effects on the hippocampus.

Studying under high stress, such as the all-night cramming favored by adolescents, particularly boys, contributes to short-term memory loss. In a controlled experiment, researchers at the Washington University School of Medicine gave high doses of cortisol to a group of volunteers, while another group received a placebo. After four days the group that had taken the high dose of cortisol showed a significantly lower ability to memorize a written passage. The effect is reversible. After a week without cortisol, the volunteers found their memory quickly returned to normal.[1]

The timing of a stressful experience and its severity also correlate with the decrease in memory performance. Thirty minutes after rats were stressed by an unanticipated electrical shock, they were unable to remember their way around a maze. When the shock was given two minutes or four hours before the rats went through the maze, they had no difficulty. The memory loss lasts only a couple of hours, so the effect in this case is a temporary impairment of retrieval. The memory is not lost, it is just inaccessible or less accessible for a period of time. This time-dependent effect on memory performance correlates with the levels of cortisol circulating in the system, which are highest thirty minutes post-stress. The same thing happens when non-stressed rats are injected with cortisol. When cortisol production is chemically suppressed, there are no stress-induced effects on memory.

The presence of excess cortisol affects brain function in two ways (see figure 8.3). First, because stress hormones divert blood glucose to the large muscles, the amount of glucose—hence energy—that reaches the hippocampus is diminished. This creates an energy crisis in the hippocampus that makes it unable to create new memories. That fact explains why some people cannot remember a very traumatic event and why short-term memory is usually the first casualty of age-related memory loss. As we age, it becomes more difficult to turn off the stress response. We take longer to adjust, and the sensors in our blood vessels become less efficient at telling us when our blood pressure returns to normal. Second, as mentioned earlier, cortisol interferes with the function of neurotransmitters, the chemicals that brain cells use to communicate with each other. This leads to difficulty in thinking or accessing long-term

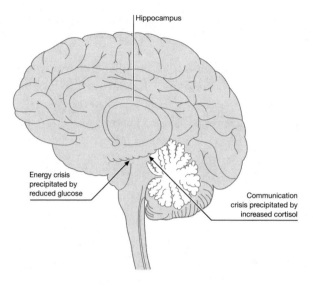

Hippocampus

Energy crisis
precipitated by
reduced glucose

Communication
crisis precipitated by
increased cortisol

8.3 Stress, cortisol, and learning. The hippocampus is highly affected by stress
chemicals. It becomes less efficient at memory creation. Connections
between neurons are also less efficient and long-term potentiation (LTP)
becomes more difficult.

memories. For this reason, many people become befuddled and confused
in a severe crisis—"the lines are down" and the mind goes blank.

Dealing with Stressors

So, what can we do to modify stress in ourselves, in our children, and in
our classrooms? First, we need to identify the causes of stress, acknowledge that the stress response varies by individual, and do what we can
to help stress-susceptible individuals manage the stressors in their lives.
This is where laboratory research helps. Professor Sapolsky (1998, 2000)
has conducted research on laboratory rats' susceptibility to stress-related
disorders such as ulcers. The stressors for rats are similar to the stressors
for humans:

▼ unpredictability

▼ sudden surprise

▼ lack of control over one's environment

▼ lack of stimulation in the environment

▼ no outlet for the stress response

▼ physical inactivity

▼ isolation

When isolated rats are given mild, unpredictable electric shocks, their susceptibility to ulcers increases considerably. When they are shocked in the presence of other rats, they are slightly less susceptible: They can take out their anger on another rat. When there is a warning signal ten seconds prior to a shock, stress is reduced. Being able to press a lever that the rat believes will control or decrease the shock reduces stress.

The speed with which the rat demonstrates a stress response is also shaped in part by the duration of weaning in its immature phase. Rats who were intensively groomed and licked showed more resistance to stressful situations and anxiety as adults. Removing juvenile rats from their mothers for a few hours a day increased the stress response. It is believed that the stress response is largely set during the prenatal and early childhood periods.

The implications for classroom learning are clear. When we look at the sorts of experiences that cause stress in classroom learning, we find many similarities between Sapolsky's rats and humans. The stressors for learners include

꘎ unpredictability

꘎ excessive risk

꘎ perceived threat

꘎ lack of feedback

꘎ poor progress measures

꘎ inability to connect to past, present, or future needs

꘎ lack of self-confidence

꘎ no outlet for stress response

꘎ lack of physical reprieve

꘎ no or little purposeful social interaction

According to Levine (1971) and Seligman and colleagues (Seligman 1975; Seligman, Rosellini, and Kozak 1975), the psychological modifiers of the stress response are as follows:

- outlets for frustration
- sense of predictability
- sense of control
- a perception of life improving
- social support

For a teacher this is a serious message. To create challenge without stress, build learning challenges on a familiar framework. Help learners perceive the benefits of learning and know where they are going and how they will get there. Ensure that they feel free from intimidation or put-downs and are encouraged to negotiate risk. Create a safe haven for managing challenge within your classroom. Create, and celebrate, a sense of collective achievement, and every now and again, enjoy a laugh together.

The Four F's of Classroom Survival

I suggested earlier that all meaningful learning involves risk. In circumstances where you feel safe, you will be willing to negotiate a higher level of risk. Some of us are risk tolerant, some of us are risk averse, and others fall at all points in between. If, in a learning situation, anxiety tips into stress, then what happens next is predictable. There are four categories of survival response available to students (see figure 8.4). Teachers and others who are involved in formally educating others are familiar with them. They are fight, flight, freeze, and flock. You show resistance to or fight the source of stress, you flee from it, you freeze in the face of it, or you hang out with others like you. If you have an accumulation of stressors that leaves you feeling out of control, then the four F's are what is left for you.

8.4 When high levels of anxiety are present in learning, the four Fs of survival prevail. Learners who feel intimidated, isolated by a sense of failure, put down, or out of control will use some combination of fight, flight, freeze, or flock. These are survival responses.

According to Robert Sapolsky, the reason a zebra does not get an ulcer is that while it is very good at mobilizing a stress response in the face of threat, it is also very good at turning off the stress response should it survive to be able do so. Humans, particularly adults in the West, are not as good at turning off the stress response. The survival options available to a zebra are similar to those available to a child in a classroom: It can flock—hang around with a bunch of other zebras and hope that the hungry lion picks on one of them. It can freeze—merge into the background, stay still, and hope the lion goes by. It can flee—get away fast and mobilize all of its running power to outrun the lion. Or, last option, it can fight—get power to the big limbs, raise the pain threshold, block out distractions, and become intensely focused on beating up that lion.

For a student in a classroom, flocking involves adopting the norms, values, and behaviors of the herd—in this case, the peer group. The peer group will police and, in some cases, collectively suppress learning performance in a classroom. In these circumstances, the flock, or peer group, shapes performance and it is difficult for individual students to be different.

Children will not volunteer ignorance, display enthusiasm, or show curiosity if they belong to a flock that promotes indifference.

Freezing is the default position when students get stuck or are suddenly asked a question to which they do not know the answer; it is like temporary paralysis. Teachers who pounce with their questions paralyze performance. Freezing happens when we cannot immediately access a high- or low-road response. It is as if the brain decides it needs more time to make a decision so suspends activity in the interim.

Flight is the use of every avoidance tactic known to schoolchildren the world over, in the hope the teacher engages with someone else. Many children develop skilled avoidance techniques from an early age: They keep their heads down, they do the minimum necessary to get by. In large classes where the teacher does not know individual children, avoidance techniques are more likely to be successful than in other settings.

Fight is any form of tantrum, rebelliousness, dissent, or mock outrage—and, in some schools, it can be physical as well. In fight mode—when the red mist descends—we resort to deep-seated, learned patterns of response. Learned responses come out when we are highly anxious. Tools for overcoming unhelpful learned responses are one of the gifts a teacher can bequeath to a child. In the anxiety of taking an exam, I have observed students default to answering English literature questions about novels they have never read! Their learned response was to write—and write as much as possible! The default mode in the stress of the exam is to get an answer down, get it down quickly, and inject as much content as possible. As I discussed earlier, learned responses can be altered at a number of levels. Mental rehearsals of positive patterns of behavior can displace less useful modes.

Get Yourself Engaged

Novelty engages curiosity. Curiosity engages attention. The effect of novelty and curiosity forms a U-shaped curve. There are only so many times an experience remains new. Novelty, curiosity, and attention are all served by a range of emotional systems. Separate emotional systems have their own developmental histories, their own trigger points for engagement and, within the brain, their own neural assemblies. No one center in the brain runs all emotional systems. Some emotions need to be present earlier in development than others do. It is useful for survival purposes to be fearful, so this emotion is present early. The startle response exists from the first few days. It is useful for survival purposes to attach oneself to an adult, so this also is present early. For other emotions, a more complex developmental history prevails. Anger may emerge from fear and attachment—maybe—but what survival value does sadness have? Each individual has a unique emotional palette.

The colors in the emotional palette come about partly as a result of genetic inheritance and partly through life experiences. The extent to which this palette can be applied successfully to give color and meaning to everyday experience varies by individual. Some people have a range of emotional colors in their palette and the palette ready to hand. Others have few colors in a palette that is awkward to use. Emotional adaptability, what I call an "engaged emotional response," is a measure of maturity. This response means being able to draw on and manage a range of appropriate emotional responses on a situation-specific basis. Emotional susceptibility, what I call a "disengaged emotional response," is a measure of immaturity. This person has few appropriate emotional responses to draw from in response to various situations. He or she is locked into patterns from which it is difficult to break free. Trying to do so may cause further upset, even trauma. I am not passing judgment on which colors and mix of colors form the best emotional palette. It is surely healthy to experience fear, sadness, anger, love, joy, loathing, disgust, surprise, and guilt. It is not so healthy to be locked into one of those emotions. When we are in an engaged emotional state, we have color and shape in our lives. When we are in a disengaged emotional state—in trauma or depressed or apathetic—we lack color, shape and, ultimately, choice. In such circumstances, what can be done?

A Motivational Model

Any individual who is clinically depressed or suffering from anxiety attacks, PTSD, or any other condition that is profoundly affecting his or her ability to make life choices needs professional help. If an individual needs to feel motivated again, to have a sense of purpose, to connect with a wider range of experiences—including emotional experiences—to break free from indifference, and to feel connected, then learning professionals can help.

Motivation is emotion in motion. A sufficiently motivated individual will experience physiological changes. The internal reward system is activated. Different circuitry—the amygdala, the nucleus accumbens, the basal ganglia, the brain stem, and the hippocampus—become involved. Research shows that with proper motivation, learning is quicker. More areas of the cortex become involved.

As teachers, we can create external reward systems, but engaging the internal reward system is more effective. How do we do this? By persuading the student of the benefits of whatever learning is being targeted. Because humans are complex creatures, this is not a simple selling job. Some of us are motivated toward success, others away from failure. For some, external material or peer reward is most effective (in the short term) while for others there is value and pleasure in the experience itself. What follows is a seven-stage motivational model. It is designed to be neutral on which benefits ought to accrue. It can be used individually or with groups. Use it if it is useful to you.

Stage 1. Conceptualize the outcome: What is it you want?

Stage 2. Test the outcome against experience and weigh its favorability: How is what you want better than what you currently have?

Stage 3. Mentally rehearse the outcome: If you get what you want, what will it look like? How will you know you have been successful? What will others say to you? How will you feel?

Stage 4: Become willing to move toward the outcome: When will you start to obtain your outcome?

Stage 5: Secure approval for movement: How will you remind yourself, or let others know, of your outcome?

Stage 6: Establish benchmarks of your movement toward the outcome: What will you do first? Next?

Stage 7: Remain optimistic throughout the process: What will you do to stay positive about your outcome?

To be able and willing to mentally rehearse positive personal outcomes, to conceptualize success—however framed—and to be self-aware throughout is a very useful set of lifelong learning tools to bring to any challenge. To be sufficiently emotionally resilient to accommodate adversity when things do not go right the first time is another. You need to be able to complete each stage in turn before graduating to the next. The seven-stage model is one way of facilitating emotional engagement. In the next chapter, I introduce a different form of brain engagement.

Chapter 9

Laterality
How Do We Develop Left and Right?

This chapter contains the following sections:

Purposeful asymmetry. The development of differences between the left and right hemispheres of the brain.

Does the left hand know what the right is doing? What makes someone left- or right-handed. The prevalence of handedness across different cultures.

Language and hemisphericity. How language is generated in the brain. Why some people do not understand jokes. Why others cannot stop telling lies.

Stay away from the medicine man. How asymmetry affects the emotions. Facts about depression and heart attacks. Classic voodoo death research and why it should be of interest to you.

The eyes have it. How what you believe is not what you see. The cross-lateral design of our optic systems. Japanese reading systems.

Listen to me when I'm talking. Dichotic listening. Why moving the telephone earpiece from one ear to the other changes the way you listen. The ear with which children hear best.

So what can we conclude about the left and right hemispheres? Conclusions about laterality and cerebral dominance.

What might these conclusions mean for formal learning? Too much of the same leads to boredom. Ten suggestions for holistic learning.

It will answer the following questions:

- How do differences between the left and right hemispheres of the brain develop?
- What determines handedness?
- What is so funny about a joke?
- How may a stroke affect the emotions?
- Why does a person with brain damage "see" the world differently?
- Do children have an ear preference?
- What should I know about differences between the left and right sides of my brain?
- How should I organize learning to accommodate hemispheric differences?

Introduction

A man has had a stroke affecting the left hemisphere of his brain. It has left him with some physical problems. Because the motor control areas in his left hemisphere were damaged, the right side of his body is affected. He has difficulty smiling. His smile is now lopsided. His speech is slurred, and he struggles to move his right hand freely. His wife tells him a joke.

> Patient: I've just swallowed a pillow.
> Doctor: How do you feel?
> Patient: A little down in the mouth.

He hears the joke and laughs. His face lights up, his eyes brighten, and both sides of his mouth lift in a natural smile. The unconsciously learned, spontaneous laughter response is primed by emotional centers in the brain, not by the motor cortex. Temporarily, the faulty circuitry in the left hemisphere is bypassed.

The difference in function between the left and the right hemispheres has caught more popular interest than any other area of brain research. So much so that the lines between fallacy, fad, and fact are badly blurred. Fueling this interest has been a strong desire on the part of the self-help movement, and some educators, for a one-line answer. In a well-intended desire to seek human integration at all levels, educators adopted the idea of left and right brain as a working metaphor for educating the whole person. Who can resist the idea that a realignment of education priorities might afford a more "brain compatible solution" to learning? To this end, a heavy industry of educators emerged who were willing to fulfill the brief of, for example, this professional development program for teachers advertised in September 2000: "Participants will learn how to teach the right-brained learner."

Meanwhile scientific research, which had long since forgotten to define the brain in such terms and no longer had an explicit focus on hemispheric difference, went on to ask increasingly sophisticated questions based on the fundamental organizing principle of asymmetry of function. Notions of right and left brain became considerations, not answers. It should be emphasized that there is no gene, no chemical, no neural assembly, no

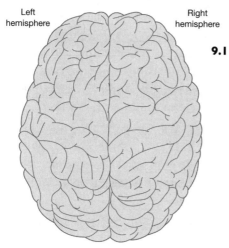

Left hemisphere

Right hemisphere

9.1 The hemispheres of the human brain are not identical, but both are involved in all complex tasks. There are hemispheric differences in how language is understood and produced and in the computation of spatial relationships. Chemicals related to emotional arousal and inhibition, selective attention, and managing impulsivity have unequal distributions in the hemispheres. The two hemispheres of male and female brains also differ.

lobe, no region, and no hemisphere in the human brain that is singly responsible for any behavior! Nor is any chemical or cell type or structure present in one hemisphere but not the other (see figure 9.1). When we understand this, we can leave behind forever the fad of the right- or left-brained learner!

Roger Sperry was awarded the Nobel Prize in Medicine in 1981 "for his discoveries concerning the functional specialization of the cerebral hemispheres." His work broke new ground in understanding how the human brain is lateralized. In his Nobel acceptance speech in Stockholm, he talked of the significance of some of his work for educators:

> The more we learn, the more we recognize the unique complexity of any one individual intellect, the stronger the conclusion becomes that the individuality inherent in our brain networks makes that of fingerprints or facial features gross and simple by comparison. (Nobelprize.org)

He went on to suggest a need for recognizing such individuality: "The need for educational tests and policy measures to identify, accommodate, and serve the differentially specialized forms of individual intellectual potential becomes increasingly evident." Sperry died in 1984. His work on hemispheric differences was colonized by the media, by the self-help movement, and eventually by some educators, and now has a residual metaphoric status. People describe themselves as "very right-brained," meaning they are creative, slightly disorganized, eccentric, and forgivably wacky. No one ever admits to being left-brained but, if they did, it would be code for dull, plodding, predictable, and ever so slightly and unforgivably anal. I did a quick search on Amazon.com to find out how many popular science books contain the words "right brain" or "left brain" somewhere in the title. The result? Forty-seven. There is obviously enormous interest and some scholarship in this field, so what do we know, and what does the current understanding of hemispheric differences in the brain tell us about human learning?

Purposeful Asymmetry

There is much virtue in having a body that is symmetrical. If a limb is torn off by a saber-toothed tiger, then you have another limb that looks and performs much the same to compensate. You can get on with being a hunter-gatherer or do a bit of compensatory foraging instead. Provided you survive the trauma, the loss can be accommodated.

Nature seemingly prefers symmetry. We look symmetrical. We have two of almost everything. Scientists call this *bilaterally symmetric evolution,* but the term is misleading. We are almost completely asymmetrical. We have a dominant, or preferred, ear, eye, hand, and so on. Attempt to walk in a straight line for as long as possible while blindfolded. You may discover one leg is longer than the other! The human brain appears to have identical left and right sides, but it, too, is asymmetrical. It has developed this way for a purpose. Understanding the asymmetry of the brain hemispheres leads us toward some of the most useful concepts relating to the human brain and learning.

From the very beginnings of life, the brain begins to develop a purposeful asymmetry in its circuitry. This leads to some specialization of function on each side of the brain. This *relative lateralization* influences how the mind represents and makes sense of everyday experience.

If you had bumped into a hunter-gatherer half a million years ago, could you have had a conversation? Would his, her, or its brain have been built the same way as yours? Corballis (1991) suggested that the humans who lived more than million years ago may have had speech specialization in the left hemisphere but that our modern flexible and rapid style of speech did not begin to develop until 150,000 to 200,000 years ago. Modern hemispheric asymmetry, he argues, derives from the period when tools began to be made and used as part of everyday life. The language necessary to share their production and use is largely generative, which is a function of the left hemisphere.

Asymmetry in the human brain is evident from birth, if not earlier. Within two days of being born, children given solutions of distilled water, sugar water, or citric acid showed approach or withdrawal signals occurring in different hemispheres. After tasting the sugar water, babies consistently showed an approach response with more activity in the left hemisphere. Approach responses are clearly marked from the earliest.

Growth spurts in the child's brain are also lateralized. Between the ages of four and six, the left frontal lobe grows more rapidly than the right. Between the ages of eight and ten, there is greater incremental growth in the right frontal lobe (Thatcher, Walker, and Guidice 1987). Growth also occurs within different areas of each hemisphere during this time. Children use the primitive communication tools of babbling and pointing, each of which is lateralized in a different hemisphere. At six months there is greater activation in the left hemisphere for speech and in the right for music. By twelve months, the difference has become more marked, with the left hemisphere clearly responding to names and the right to nonhuman sounds such as clicks.

Asymmetry for emotional responses is evident in the brain by the age of ten months. The frontal lobes are more active in perceiving and producing emotional responses than are the parietal lobes. The left frontal lobe is more active than the right in responding to positive emotions. Ten-month-olds sitting in their mothers' laps watched a video of an actress making facial expressions. The facial expressions evolved from happy to sad, happy to sad. The children were wired to electrodes that helped detect electrical changes in the brain. When they watched happy expressions, there was activity in the left frontal lobe. When they watched sad expressions, there was very little activity. In a follow-up experiment, infants were shown to use similarly differing areas of the brain when expressing happiness and sadness.

Does the Left Hand Know What the Right Is Doing?

The brain has a counterclockwise torque! It is twisted counterclockwise, with the right fontal lobe being larger than the left in front, and at the rear, the visual cortex being larger on the left than on the right (see figure 9.2). Your brain is more likely to be asymmetrical if you are right-handed than if you are left-handed.

There is a division of labor between your two hands, which you see in action when you write. Which hand writes? Which hand holds the page? Guiard (1987) proposed that the two hands work in what he called a kinematic chain, with the nondominant hand performing slow and labored movements having low temporal and spatial frequency, and the dominant hand performing quick and precise movements. The brain is also *contralateral,* with the left hemisphere controlling movement on the right side of the body and the right hemisphere controlling movement on the left side. In early childhood, a time when only gross movements are available to the brain, the movement areas are more fully developed

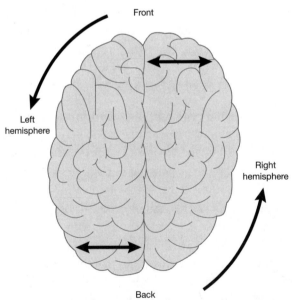

9.2 The brain develops a counterclockwise torque. In front, it is larger on the right, and in back it is larger on the right.

on the right side than the left. Is this why the right hemisphere becomes better at those slow, labored movements and thus becomes dominant for them?

Handedness is notoriously sensitive to changes in measures. Changing the measure changes the statistics regarding how many people are right- versus left-handed. Over time and across cultures it seems that humankind has a consistent pattern of right-handedness in around 94 or 95 percent of the population. Slightly more males than females are left-handed. Older people are more likely to write with the right hand and to throw with the left. Left-handers in the Western world seem more susceptible to certain types of illness: migraines, allergies, thyroid problems, and autoimmune diseases. Coren and Halpern (1991) suggested that they died younger, but it is difficult to establish what role handedness alone might play in this even if the statistics prove valid.

In Korea less than 1 percent of the population is left-handed, whereas in the United States, the figure is nearer to 13 percent. It is difficult to disentangle the effect of cultural norms on these statistics, but a pattern can nevertheless be inferred.

With left-handed writers, there is no neurological evidence that those who write inverted are wired differently from those who don't. Nor is there evidence that inverted writing arises because of some difference in motor control. The inverters who prefer the hooked position are about half of the left-handed population, though the figure goes down among the older generation and halves again among females. Research on inherited handedness is so contradictory it is not useful. There may be some basis for explaining handedness in the hormones your brain is awash with when you are in the womb.

After handedness, footedness is a good way of measuring hemispheric asymmetry. Which foot do you naturally kick a ball with? A warrior leads with the left foot, and so do armies when marching. More than 90 percent of right-handers show a preference for the right foot when kicking, but with left-handers the pattern is very different. As a group, they do not seem as left-footed as right-handers are right-footed: 82 percent of left-handers who prefer the left arm for throwing also prefer the left foot for kicking; 78 percent of left-handers who prefer the right arm for throwing prefer the right foot for kicking.

To collect information about handedness, questionnaires are often helpful. If a questionnaire has only one question, then it should be, With which hand do you write? In a more detailed questionnaire, one research team presented questions in the following categories:

- fine manual skill; for example, writing, drawing, holding a needle, using tweezers

- hand-wrist skill; for example, using a razor, combing hair, cutting bread

- hand-wrist-arm skill; for example, throwing a ball, holding a racquet, using a hammer

- strength; for example, which hand or arm is stronger

- activities that reflect preference but not necessarily skill; for example, picking up a small object or a book

Although we may have a preferred hand, foot, ear, and eye, lateral preference for the eyes and ears is less clearly expressed than hand preference. Watch people cross their arms: They will do so in a preferred way. Body laterality expresses itself in the smallest of gestures: Which eye do you wink with? Which hand claps and which is clapped? Oh, and by the way, experiments with cats suggest that you cannot breed for paw preference.

Does this mean that a teacher who constantly moves a child's pencil from the left to the right hand is working against the grain of that child's brain? Most probably.

A case has been made for identifying patterns of hemispheric dominance in a learner and linking those patterns to preferred learning styles (Hannaford 1997). The evidence for such a correlation is less than substantial. First, it is difficult to assess hemispheric dominance meaningfully. Second, it is difficult to get clean evidence of hemispheric dominance independent of cultural or lifestyle influences. Third, the quantification of learning style preference itself is not secure: It is neither a science nor is it objective. This is an area where more research is required. It may be fruitful to look at the prevalence of certain hormones in the brain. We do have evidence that bilateralism is associated with high mathematical ability (Benbow 1990; Benbow and Arjmand 1990; Benbow et al. 2000; Benbow and Minor 1990). A high percentage of precocious children are left-handed, have mixed hand dominance, or have a family history of left-handedness. Why? Perhaps the answer is related to levels of testosterone in the womb.

The left hemisphere is superior to the right for learning and using movements in sequence. This includes the sort of inhalation and blowing in sequence that is learned and used in playing a wind instrument. The right hemisphere is more useful in conveying a series of gestures, such as those used by a mime artist. These are not absolutes. Never allow yourself or anyone else in your hearing to say, "I could have played like Kenny G., but I'm too right-brained!"

Language and Hemisphericity

The left side of the brain is dominant for most language functions (see figure 9.3). These include talking aloud, making sense of what someone else says, and picking up on sound changes—including changes of inflection and tone of voice—and meanings of words. The right side is

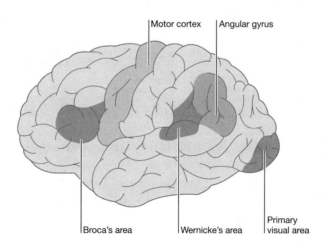

9.3 Different language functions reside in different parts of the brain, predominantly in the left hemisphere. In reading, the information is sent via the visual cortex and the angular gyrus to Wernicke's area. From there, it is transformed from sensory data to motor impulses in Broca's area. Sounds are then structured together into language. Impairment of any stage leads to reading difficulties.

used for context. Damage to the right side of the brain might result in difficulty comprehending jokes or innuendo, summarizing the gist of a passage of prose, recognizing satirical intent, or understanding metaphor. Right hemisphere damage also leads to problems in decoding cartoons that have no language component.

These facts are significant in a formal learning environment such as a classroom. Often the language of the classroom is coded, ambiguous, and negative, requiring complex decoding strategies: "Now, children, what do we not do when we go to assembly?" When people with aphasia (a language disorder resulting from brain damage) were given similar indirect requests—for example, "Can you play tennis?"—their ability to interpret them depended on where in the brain the damage had occurred. Ten subjects were asked to watch a film in which such questions were asked (Ornstein 1997). Those with damage in the left hemisphere—Broca's aphasics—could easily decode the indirect request and the appropriateness of the observed response. Those with damage in the right hemisphere could not. They understood the statements literally, but were not always able to interpret their meaning in context.

If an aphasic were told the first part of the joke I mentioned earlier

> Patient: I've just swallowed a pillow.
> Doctor: How do you feel?

then asked which of the following punch lines might be funniest,

> Patient: A little down in the mouth.
> Patient: Very full.
> Patient: Very sick. It's not easy to eat a pillow.

he or she would respond differently depending on where the brain damage was located. Those with damage to the right hemisphere are likely to choose option 3—"Very sick. It's not easy to eat a pillow"—because it is the most literal; whereas those with damage to the left hemisphere are more likely to choose option 1.

The following facts apply to the lateralization of language in the brain:

▼ Language tends to be located in the left hemisphere for most humans.

▼ In a significant population of humans, language is divided between the left and right hemispheres without any apparent loss of function.

▼ If an accident occurs and the left hemisphere is intact, speech production remains in the left hemisphere; speech comprehension migrates to the right even when the hemispheres are severely disconnected.

▼ The left hemisphere suppresses the right hemisphere's speech potential.

▼ When the left hemisphere has been removed or badly damaged, the right hemisphere takes over language functions.

We do not know if there is a sensitive period for learning a second language. Nor do we know if the brain areas used for acquiring a second language are the same for different people. When we know the answers to these questions, we will be able to create the optimal conditions for language learning. Studies in bilingualism suggest that phonemes and grammar need to be learned at an early age. Vocabulary and its meanings can be acquired throughout life. Is there such a thing as bilingualism? There is if you ask a citizen of the world. There is not if you ask a neuroscientist. Even in people who can switch flawlessly between languages, their languages do not have parity of status.

Scientists believe that one language is acquired in ways that make it the base, or mother, tongue. When we look at scans of an individual using his or her mother tongue, we see activity in the left hemisphere. When the individual shifts to another language, different processing centers are activated. For this reason it is possible, though not recommended, to destroy the ability of a person to learn a new language by removing an area of the brain the size of your thumb. Language areas of the brain differ in subtle ways by individual and reflect that individual's history of language exposure. Using fMRI, Dr. Joy Hirsch found that multilinguals used separate speech comprehension and speech production sites simultaneously. Wernicke's area (for comprehension) and Broca's area (for speech production) were activated separately. Yet when the speaker had learned both languages in infancy, activation in Broca's area was the same for both languages. The competition for neural real estate makes it hard to learn a second language after puberty—the areas of the brain needed for the new language may already have been used for something else.[1]

Individuals with damage to the frontal lobes often tell tall tales. They *confabulate*, telling stories that have no basis in truth without realizing they are doing so. There is no underlying psychopathology. No malice aforethought. It just happens.

Part of the explanation seems to lie, again, in the difference in function between left and right hemispheres. There is a higher incidence of confabulation among people who have had strokes. A stroke causes localized trauma, and the brain seeks to compensate by having other parts of the brain take over the lost functions. This takes time and practice. Ramachandran and Blakeslee (1998) explain confabulation as confused timing between left and right hemispheres. Generally, the left hemisphere establishes the sense of the memory, while the right hemisphere detects anomalies or discrepancies in the experience. The left organizes the disparate chunks of experience and the right acts as interpreter. If there is right-sided damage, as in some stroke cases, anomalies are no longer detected. The left hemisphere no longer has an interpreter to keep the experiences in check, and confabulation takes place.

Deliberately stimulating the right hemisphere by squirting ice-cold water into the left ear of a confabulating individual temporarily relieves the problem. Ramachandran and Blakeslee believe that stimulating the right hemisphere, or inducing rapid eye movement (REM), through the sensory shock of the cold water temporarily evokes the retrieval of lost memories. When the water warms, the confabulations return.

A favored view is that the left side is specialized for language and the right for spatial awareness. Another is that the left is better at focused attention tasks and the right at divergent, or diffuse, attention tasks. Yet another is that the left is analytic, whereas the right is holistic. Each of these dichotomies has a smattering of truth—but no more than a smattering. Accumulated research now suggests that we are unlikely to get a one-size-fits-all explanation of right and left brain differences. Both sides are involved in most activities.

The right hemisphere does not always assess the holistic aspects of an object more effectively than the left hemisphere does, nor does the left hemisphere always assess finer details more effectively than the right. It is believed that the left hemisphere is better at processing visual-spatial information of high frequency and the right at processing visual-spatial information of low frequency. The hemispheres differ in the way they process information, not in their structures. When we look at an object, some scientists believe that the left hemisphere makes more use of a categorization system that gives accurate information about the relative position of the object, while the right simultaneously uses a coordinate system giving information about distance and specific location (see figure 9.4). The hemispheres form a single, integrated information processing system, but they allocate their attention differently. Need dictates the processing system, and thus the hemisphere that gets used.

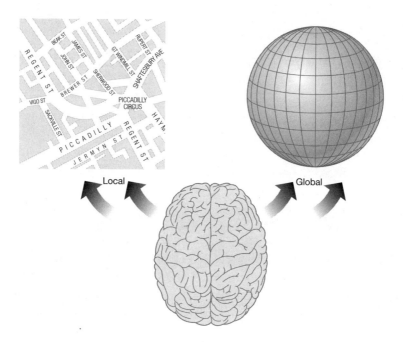

9.4 The left and right hemispheres differ in the way they process information, not in their structures.

Recall that the corpus callosum is the major fiber tract connecting the two hemispheres. It has at least two hundred million nerve fibers and acts like a conduit relaying some sorts of information between the left and right brain. There is considerable variation in the size of the corpus callosum by gender and by handedness. Left-handers have a larger corpus callosum, particularly those who are left-handed and male. Females in general, however, have a larger corpus callosum. There is little evidence that a larger corpus callosum improves hemispheric integration. Those who argue that women have better ability to multitask, to communicate under stress, and to be intuitive must look elsewhere for a biological explanation. The corpus callosum also functions as an inhibitory barrier. Activation in one hemisphere inhibits the level of excitation in the other. The corpus callosum plays a part in regulating the level of activation between the two hemispheres. It also contributes to reducing maladaptive cross-talk between the two halves of the brain.

Stay Away from the Medicine Man

Much of classroom success is based on the management of emotions. And much of emotion is, and has been, shaped by attention (see figure 9.5). Your brain cannot possibly process all the sensory information it receives, so it gives some stimuli attention and others it neglects. The technical terms are *attended* and *unattended* stimuli. The stimulus is there and you notice it, or it is there but your brain ignores it.

What is attended and unattended depends on goals and needs, which are in turn shaped by, among other things, experience and what you have done with it. When you decide you have had enough attending, you stop, a condition known as *extinction* or *habituation*. This is the "done that and got the T-shirt" of human attention systems. When your attention is engaged, this state is known as *vigilance*. Vigilance is the equivalent of the "watch out for the timeshare salesman" of human attention systems. Evidence suggests that the systems that run attention are asymmetrically organized in the brain.

People with damage to the right hemisphere have poorer levels of sustained attention than do people with similar left-hemisphere damage.

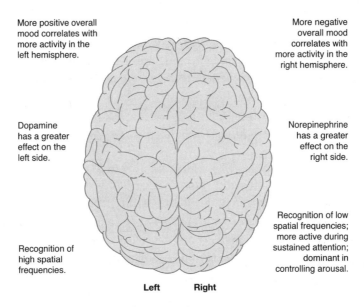

More positive overall mood correlates with more activity in the left hemisphere.

More negative overall mood correlates with more activity in the right hemisphere.

Dopamine has a greater effect on the left side.

Norepinephrine has a greater effect on the right side.

Recognition of low spatial frequencies; more active during sustained attention; dominant in controlling arousal.

Recognition of high spatial frequencies.

Left   Right

9.5 The systems for attention and emotion are asymmetrically organized in the brain.

It seems that the right hemisphere is more active than the left during a sustained attention task. The right hemisphere also plays a dominant role in controlling arousal and shows more sensitivity to pain than the left. Individuals with right-brain damage show higher pain endurance than those with left-brain damage.

Emotions such as sadness or joy are run by separate systems in the brain. Increased activity on the right side of the brain may be a signal of depression. Increased activity on the left can signal happiness, even euphoria. Research done at the University of Wisconsin shows how people with more chemical and electrical activity in the left hemisphere have a more positive overall mood, while people with more chemical and electrical activity in the right hemisphere are more negative overall (Ratey 2001). Some drugs have more effect on one side of the brain than the other: Drugs that depend on dopamine have more effect on the left hemisphere; drugs that depend on norepinephrine have more effect on the right hemisphere.

Researchers at Johns Hopkins University have identified an area of the brain that appears to be activated when we dwell on negative personal experiences. Subjects asked to describe family crises, financial worries, and situations causing personal stress on tape and then listen to the tapes while undergoing PET scans showed activity predominantly in the right frontal lobe. The right frontal lobe contributes to goal setting, planning, and evaluation of decisions. When the same subjects listened to tapes of themselves describing inconsequential, everyday events there was less activity in the right frontal lobe. The researchers inferred that some of the neural structures to do with worry lie in the right frontal lobe. All of which is very worrying.

Type A personalities are more prone to coronary disease. The type A personality, most often a man, exhibits hostility, anger, and impatience. The way the brain mediates emotions may play a part in exposing some of us to early death through heart attacks. Work with animals shows that inducing anger can cause myocardial ischemia. Depressives are also more susceptible to sudden cardiac arrest.

In 1942, a classic study of voodoo death showed that tribesmen died within hours of being cursed by a medicine man (Sapolsky 1998). Animal studies show that emotional stress can reduce the threshold for ventricular fibrillation; it can give you a heart attack. Brain mechanisms regulating emotion can play a significant part in inducing sudden death. A very good friend of mine had a family member who, after a lifetime of working in the local mill in a management position, was told that his services were no longer required. Due to a decline in business he and others were being laid off. He was told on a Friday morning. That afternoon he died at home of a heart attack. It is estimated that emotion plays a significant role in 20 percent of the 300,000 deaths due to cardiac arrest in the United States annually.

The brain-heart laterality hypothesis (BHL) suggests that the degree to which emotion is regulated by the left hemisphere rather than the right hemisphere (which is the norm), correlates to vulnerability to sudden death. The reason why emotion is generally lateralized to the right hemisphere of your brain may have to do in part with natural selection (Cacioppo, Tassinary, and Berntson 2001). Those who can maximize cardiac output in life-and-death situations are more likely to survive. At the same time, brain asymmetry confers greater cognitive abilities. What has changed more recently to reduce the survival value of this localization of function is the prevalence of diseases associated with unrelieved stress and the lengthening of life spans: Most sudden heart attack deaths occur in middle age. Thus, we have a brain that is lateralized for both emotional and intellectual demands. In cases where the lateralization is irregular, those individuals are correspondingly more vulnerable to unforeseen change.

The Eyes Have It

Work on seeing and hearing shows that we process visual and auditory information with different sides of the brain, depending on the source of information. When I stare at an object, the right side of my brain processes information in the right visual field, which is seen by the right sides of both retinas. The left side processes information in the left visual field, seen by the left sides of both retinas. A structure known as the optic chasm is the crossing point for this information (see figure 9.6). Individuals in whom the corpus callosum has been severed have difficulty perceiving whole objects that they are seeing without turning their heads. They can see the objects but have dif-

ficulty making them whole. Each hemisphere can only see half of what is in front of the person, and without the corpus callosum, the two hemispheres have no way to share and integrate the information. Turning the head so that each hemisphere can perceive the entire object is a compensatory strategy.

The visual system is based on simultaneous aggregation and disaggregation. As we look at everyday objects the visual information is broken down and sent simultaneously to separate

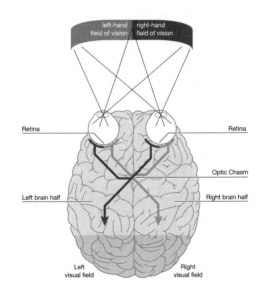

9.6 The optic pathways cross over at the optic chasm.

halves of the brain, where it is reassembled, albeit in different but entirely complementary ways. The notion of simultaneous aggregation and disaggregation is useful in thinking about the learning brain. In a learning challenge, the process of switching back and forth from the details to the big picture is constant. When big picture information is missing, switching becomes slower, messier, and more dislocated. For learning we need to be able to locate the detail in the wider context. The structure and organization of the brain point us to this basic learning premise: Seek and secure connections and constantly locate those connections in the wider context.

The Japanese language has a phonetic writing system known as Kana and a pictographic system known as Kanji (see figure 9.7). When normally functioning, literate Japanese were shown nonsense words in the right or left field of vision, hemispheric differences in how the two writing systems are processed were revealed. The sound system of Kana tends to be processed in the left hemisphere, while the visual system of Kanji is processed in the right (Sasanuma et al., cited in Springer and Deutsch 1998, 104). In his book *The Right Mind* (1997), Robert Ornstein points out that "Japanese people who suffer brain lesions in the left temporal hemisphere lose their ability to process phonetic Kana, both in reading

MEANING	KANA	KANJI
INK	イン キ (INKI)	墨 KANJI
UNIVERSITY	ダイガク (DAIGAKU)	大学 (GREAT LEARNING)
TOKYO	トウキヨウ (TOKYO)	東京 (EAST CAPITAL)

9.7 In Japan there are both syllabic and ideographic forms of writing: Kana is syllabic; Kanji is ideographic.

and writing, but can still process logographic Kanji; whereas those suffering lesions in the left parieto-occipital area suffer impaired processing of Kanji but not Kana."

The right hemisphere is more sensitive to low spatial frequencies and the left to high; thus, faces or letters may be processed more effectively by one or the other hemisphere depending on their spatial frequency characteristics. The consensus is however that this pattern becomes more dynamic with different types of processing. With early stages of perceptual processing, there is a right hemisphere advantage, but at later cognitive levels there is a left hemisphere advantage.

Listen to Me When I'm Talking

We are dichotic listeners; we listen differently by ear. In some telephone sales techniques, telemarketers are taught to switch the phone from ear to ear depending on the purpose of the call. When their goal is to close the sale and be matter-of-fact, attentive to detail, and focused on figures, they switch to the right ear. When they wish to be warm and empathetic, to engage with the emotional tone of the conversation, and they are in no hurry, then they switch to the left ear.

What you hear in your right ear is processed by the language centers in the left hemisphere. Information is passed simultaneously to both left and right hemispheres, but it is in the left hemisphere where language processing predominates. Dichotic listening tasks (DL) are used to assess laterality, particularly in language processing. When experiments are conducted with participants listening in one ear, information could still be processed in the other ear to a certain degree. There appears to be what is known as a right ear advantage (REA). In dichotic listening tasks, normally functioning participants report words more accurately when they are presented to the right ear rather than the left. Meaningless vowels and words played backwards also demonstrate left hemisphere/right ear advantage. Some nonverbal sounds such as birdsong, the melodic component of a musical piece, a dog barking, or a ship's siren show advantage in the right hemisphere.

Research completed in the 1960s and 1970s found that children showed better recall for one set of stimulus sounds when presented to the right compared with the left ear. Morton, Kershner, and Siegel (1990) found that normally achieving children performed differently than children with reading difficulties on a DL task when tested in the morning but not when tested in the afternoon. The normally achieving children were more strongly lateralized when instructed to listen selectively to the right ear input, as opposed to the sounds presented in either ear or to the sounds in the left ear. This difference may indicate that children with reading difficulties may have a lack of attention resources in the morning.

What do these findings mean for the telephone sales force? There is probably more value in the belief that switching makes a difference than in any subtle advantage offered by dichotic listening. Like many of the myths around left and right brain, this one has a tiny grain of truth.

So What Can We Conclude about the Left and Right Hemispheres?

The differences in function are relative rather than absolute. The left brain is not involved only in motor control and higher-order functioning, but also seems to be important in the autoimmune system. The right brain is more involved in the control of vital functions involving survival and coping with stress and external challenges. The right hemisphere contains more chemicals associated with emotional arousal and inhibition.

Science has until very recently relied on postmortem study of dysfunction—including of people with split brains—or on invasive techniques to find out about the workings of the brain. Nowadays blood and oxygen changes can be measured, overlaid with MRI, and mapped, and we can see the tremendous individual variance between left and right. Cerebral dominance is still a widely used term by specialists in this field. Yet researchers are more concerned with the degrees of, rather than absolute, difference between left and right. They are more likely to consider differences between the top and the bottom, or the front and the back, of each hemisphere than between the two hemispheres.

Facts about the Left and Right Hemispheres of the Brain

They are not identical in their capability or their organization.

They are both involved in all complex tasks.

They differ significantly with regard to the understanding and pro-duction of language.

They process complex spatial relationships differently.

The neurotransmitters that regulate attention, motor behavior, ap-proach-withdrawal, and self-regulation differ in their distribution across hemispheres.

Male and female brains differ in their asymmetry, largely as a result of hormonal levels within the womb.

There is little evidence to suggest that either hemisphere turns on to perform a specific task all by itself. Many areas of the brain are involved in the simplest of tasks.

What Might These Conclusions Mean for Formal Learning?

Much learning is curiosity driven but you do not "do" curiosity. It is not scheduled for a block period on Friday afternoon, nor is it on page 43 of the workbook. Damage to the hippocampus leads to lack of curiosity. Curiosity directs attention. Attention is at the core of cognitive engagement.

The idea of "whole-brain" learning has more metaphoric than scientific value. Too restricted a diet stunts growth. Too much of the same leads to boredom. If you want to grow plants to a particular shape, confine their space. There is no such thing as a right- or left-brained learner, but there are such things as stultifying learning environments, a slavish attachment to monotony, and restricted thinking about what is and is not good learning.

There is nothing in the research on hemispheric difference that says "teach like this or else." If you look closely at what the research tells us, it tells us to respect individuality and to engage the attention systems. To this end, I think the following commonsense learning approaches are consistent with some of the research findings about asymmetry. The list is not prescriptive. Nor is it surprising that it reads like what the best classroom teachers have been instinctively doing for years.

Multiple-Level Engagement
Assume multiple entry and exit points in the design of lessons. This cannot be done if all learners are expected to do the same thing, for the same duration, with the same success measures.

Global and Local Emphasis
When designing learning activities or inputs of new information, be aware of the need to provide a global context within which local data can sit.

Aggregate and Disaggregate
Secure opportunities for learners to build up and break down information. Make this a regular part of their learning. If, for example, you are teaching a Shakespearean sonnet, it makes sense to look at what Shakespeare wanted to evoke in the reader as well as the techniques he used to achieve that response. Alternatively, start with the smallest unit, the sound, and build up.

Sort by Similarity and Retrieve by Difference
Teaching classification skills, practicing identifying and specifying similarity and difference, generating comparative data, and using organizational models are all ways of developing sort-and-retrieve capability.

Seek Connections
At all levels and at all times, meaningful learning involves seeking and securing connections. An accomplished learner is practiced in surveying material for connections. An accomplished educator builds connections into everyday classroom interactions.

Cross-lateral Learning
Impose an occasional regime where a deliberate mix of visual and auditory learning coexists. For example, a learner self-consciously describes aloud what he is thinking as he constructs a graph or diagram.

Imitation and Gesture

Using open and closed movements—excitatory and inhibitory—learners practice through gesture. If you are able to mimic chemical transmission at the synapse and do so successfully, then learning has begun.

Learning Materials

Design learning materials to allow easy switching from high to low visual frequency and vice versa. At the simplest level, this principle could mean presenting summary information in larger and more open fonts in poster form alongside body text. Position these summary visuals in the left field.

Bilateral Classrooms

Check for lateralization using some of the measures described previously. Allow learners to find the hand they are comfortable writing with. Have left-handed equipment—for example, scissors—available in every classroom.

Sight and Hearing Lines

Where do you position yourself when giving information or asking questions? Do you position yourself where you can be easily seen and heard? Move to an established place in the classroom when giving vital summary information. Observe how children cock their heads to hear. Which ear predominates? Rotate their physical position from time to time.

In the next chapter we consider another possible dimension of difference: male and female brains.

Chapter **10**

Gender
How Do We Respect Difference?

This chapter contains the following sections:

Starting early. Differences in male and female brains exist but are not absolute. The degrees of male or femaleness evident in a brain. Sites within the brain that are more male or female. When differences emerge.

Let's not jump to conclusions! There is little basis in science for teaching boys and girls in different ways. The dangers of misinterpretation.

Do boys and girls learn differently? Practical case studies that explore possible differences.

What are the differences? What difference in learning behaviors of men and women are supported by research.

Can't we just talk about it? Differences in language functions between men and women.

Mathematical reasoning. Boys and girls approach mathematics in different ways. Why?

Your motor movement's gross! Significant differences in the way men and women maneuver themselves or an object through space. The gestures right- and left-handers make.

It will answer the following questions:

- At what point does a brain begin to be recognizably male or female?
- Should we teach boys and girls separately or differently?
- Do boys and girls learn differently?
- What are the major differences in the learning behaviors of men and women?
- Are women better designed for language?
- What sorts of things should I do when teaching math to make it boy/girl friendly?
- Who is more likely to be better at multitasking: men or women?

Introduction

One evening a woman found her partner standing over their baby's crib. Silently, she watched him. As he stared down at the sleeping infant, she saw a look of awe and wonder on his face. She sensed an engagement and curiosity she had never noticed in him before. His face was a mixture of emotions: tenderness, doubt and delight, amazement and mystification. She slipped her arm around him. "A penny for your thoughts," she said. "It's amazing!" he replied. "I just don't see how anyone can make a crib like that for $49.95."

Males and females behave differently. They look different. Their bodies are different. Do they learn differently? Some popular writers claim there are differences between male and female brains. If so, what are they? How significant are they? How do differences in the architecture of male and female brains map onto differences in how we think, remember, and learn? In what ways might such differences be a reflection of evolutionary history or of differing roles in society or of the way society and science tend to look for and position such differences? Might such differences play any part in learning preference?

Starting Early

Males show greater lateralization of function than females. There are differences in the asymmetry of male and female brains. Hormonal levels within the womb contribute significantly to the extent of the difference.

By the age of six months, research shows that a girl's left hemisphere is developing faster than her right, while the opposite is true for boys (Shucard and Shucard 1990). These gender differences have been linked to hormonal differences. Testosterone improves spatial memory and increases hippocampal size in male and female birds. At different times of the year—when navigation is important for finding and storing food, for example—the hippocampus grows. The hippocampus is essential in visual and spatial recall. In an investigation of spatial abilities in women throughout their monthly hormonal cycles, women's spatial ability was inversely related to their levels of estrogen (cited in Blakemore and Frith 2000). This has implications for taking tests. If the test involves an academic subject that requires insight into the organization of shapes, spatial relationships, or objects rotated in space or unfolded, then a young woman may do less well when her estrogen levels are high.

Testosterone is largely responsible for gender differences in brain asymmetry. Every organism requires multiple levels of control over maleness and femaleness. It is fascinating to recognize the number of areas of the brain in which gender differences exist, each with its own development timetable, mode of responding to hormonal levels, and mechanisms for interacting with other parts of the brain. It is as if some parts of the brain are more male or female than others—You have a very female emotional circuitry but are very male in your perceptual systems; I have a very female memory system but my musculature is very male.

In the central nervous system alone, the differentiation of sexual behaviors involves sexual dimorphism of the hypothalamus, preoptic area, amygdala, pituitary, spinal cord nuclei associated with pelvic musculature, perhaps the cortex, perhaps the hippocampus, and perhaps the pineal body; gender differences in exploratory behavior may involve the cerebral cortex, striatum, and hippocampus; gender differences in paternal and maternal behavior involve the hypothalamus, pituitary, and probably additional brain regions as well; gender differences in perception involve differential organization of a variety of sensory processing pathways and associative connections (Lewis and Diamond Cleeves 1998).

Let's Not Jump to Conclusions!

‘ Knowledge about individual and group differences in how people think, learn, and remember is essential for understanding human cognition and developing educational programs and theories that can identify cognitive weakness and capitalize on cognitive strengths. The real enemy is the potential for misuse of knowledge, not the knowledge itself. (Springer and Deutsch 1998) ’

Before we look at what science has got to tell us about the learning of men and women, boys and girls, let's start with a few caveats (Halpern 1996):

▼ Variability within the sexes is as significant as variability between the sexes. There is a great deal of overlap in the distribution of ability across men and women.

▼ Despite research demonstrating differences in male and female brains, the results are too often equivocal and subject to different interpretation. It is difficult to get "clean" outcomes.

▼ Gender differences in higher mental functions are typically on the order of one-fourth of a standard deviation.

▼ Premature articulation of findings occurs. Because some rats happened to navigate successfully through a maze and they happened to be male does not mean women cannot read maps!

▼ Gender remains no better a determinant for shaping educational policy than handedness, limb length, or shoe size.

The real danger is in the possible misuse of emerging findings about male and female brains. What we do not want is whimsy trickling into educational policy. While there may be practical or religious reasons for strategies such as single-sex schooling or separating boys and girls in science or sitting students in boy-girl pairings, there is nothing in brain science that supports doing so from an educational perspective.

Science has demonstrated some clear physical differences between male and female brains. Male brains, although larger and heavier, are—surprisingly to some people—less dense. A team from McMaster University in Ontario, Canada, led by Sandra Witelson found that the frontal lobes of women's brains are more tightly packed with cells ("Mapping the Mysteries"). This area controls so-called higher mental processes such as judgment, personality, planning, and working memory. Women were found to have up to 15 percent more brain cell density. As they age, however, women appear to shed cells more rapidly from this area than men do. By middle age, the density is similar for both sexes.

Here we have in cameo the problem for researchers. What conclusions should we draw from these findings? Could we infer that women naturally have better judgment, more personality, more astute planning, or a better memory for where they put things? I will leave that to you. Greater density of cells does not mean that women can outperform men. It could be one way by which nature compensates for women's smaller brain size.

Male brains are larger in the anterior temporal lobes, the area just in front of the ears. This area includes the amygdala, an area associated with emotional arousal, and the anterior hippocampus, which is associated with long-term memory. A major study also found that the anterior cingulate cortex, another area involved in emotional sensitivity, is larger in women (Good et al. 2000). In face-processing tasks, female participants showed bilateral brain activity, whereas gifted males showed significantly inhibited left hemisphere activity. The suggestion is that this specialization allowed less interference for the right hemisphere to check for affective context.

Independent of handedness, the corpus callosum is larger in women and there is a tendency toward larger absolute callosal areas in women. Some writers have seized on this as evidence that women are better at communicating under stress, multitasking, and deriving intuitive insights. They argue that because the corpus callosum provides a relay system for whole-brain integration, because it is involved in "whole-brain functioning," therefore women ought to be better at holistic behaviors. The science behind this conclusion is weak. In general, the neuroscience of gender is fascinating and sometimes conflicting. It points to a correlation between hemispheric organization and gender differences, but relating these differences to specific behavioral patterns is difficult.

The consequences of brain injury differ for male and females. In some studies damage to the left hemisphere in men resulted in greater impairment to verbal IQ than nonverbal IQ, with damage to the right hemisphere showing the opposite pattern. In contrast, women showed no site-of-lesion patterns. Language and spatial abilities appear more bilaterally controlled in females than in males.

Nature and nurture explanations can be given for these findings. Ontogeny reflects phylogeny. The organization of your brain reflects its interactions with its environment. If you constantly interact with the world around you in patterned ways, and all of your forebears who have provided you with your genetic structure have done the same, then who can say if your brain has shaped, or is shaped by, those interactions? Are the differences innate or learned?

Despite accumulated evidence from cognitive psychologists that men and women perform in very different ways on specific tasks, it is a bold leap to say that they are so different we should teach them in different ways. Perhaps science will eventually provide some answers.

Do Boys and Girls Learn Differently?

In a BBC television program called "Women on Top," we began to test some of the learning differences between boys and girls. I collaborated with a London school and Professor John Williams, a mathematician who works for MENSA (an organization for people of high intelligence), to devise tests on behalf of the BBC. To start, we set out to examine some physical differences.

Are there swerving differences? Males and females demonstrate propensities to turn either left or right. This is affected by dopamine. Females turn to the left more. In a test we used simply as a means of identifying locomotor differences we asked six-year-olds to run through a set of cones positioned in a play area about three feet apart. This swerve test involved four boys and four girls. We asked them to run the course again and again. What we noticed was, at this age, the boys tended to be better at moving independently off either foot, they used their arms more, and they were more competitive. The boys have physical advantages that make this task easier. They seemed to be better at manipulating themselves in two dimensions. Might they also be better at manipulating objects in two or three dimensions?

To look for play differences, we then observed boys and girls between the ages of five and ten in the play area at morning recess and at lunch. We recorded some of what happened on film. While many individual differences were obvious, some patterns of children's play emerged. The boys seemed to command more of the physical space of the play area. They ran around more and engaged in more exploration of the perimeter.

They interacted in smaller social groupings. They appeared to be more competitive but less focused in their play. Games were more fluid, beginning and ending haphazardly and with changing participation. We tried to identify isolates. Boys seemed to remain on their own for longer. As a general rule, girls played with girls and boys with boys. This pattern broke down in one-on-one interactions between an individual boy and girl from time to time, but the tendency was for separate play.

The girls seemed less robust in their physical play. They ran around less and confined their physical play to more limited areas of the playground. An interesting cameo was observed during morning recess. A group of five girls brought out some toys such as wobble boards, hoops, and jump ropes. They began to use these toys to play individually. Very quickly a group of boys commandeered the wobble boards, hoops, and jump ropes and took them off for their own use. Shortly thereafter, the girls got them back again when the boys abandoned them for some new activity!

We observed a higher proportion of girls on the periphery of the main play area. Many sat against, by, or on top of a wall in social groups. Mostly they clustered in small units of three or four, but in one case a large group of girls sat side by side on the wall conversing and observing the proceedings. The girls who played in groups out in the play area were focused around an activity or a prop. We observed skipping to what appeared to be rules. We also observed turn-taking with hoops.

Are there differences in throwing? We replicated a test conducted by Kimura and Lunn that involved throwing a ball covered in Velcro hook-and-loop fastener underhand toward a target. We repeated the test overhand. The original test investigated the targeting abilities of boys and girls between the ages of three and five; we did our test with five-year-olds. Boys were significantly better in underhand throwing and dramatically better in overhand.

Might different phases of physical development and experiences of targeting activities in sports account for the difference? Undoubtedly, but as boys and girls get older, the differences may well remain. Men would appear to be better at throwing and catching accurately than women are. One of the most widely recognized differences between men and women is in throwing objects at a target. Factors such as muscle tone and bulk, bone density and length, endurance, strength, and speed may also contribute to the differences.

Men may also gain satisfaction from engaging in an activity in which they are more likely to succeed than their female peers. They may thus be more likely to practice and reinforce their success. There may also be real differences that persist over and above temporary variables.

In research involving men and women throwing darts, the men were more consistently accurate than the women by at least a full standard deviation. In a similar experiment conducted in the same lab, men were better at an interception task (Kimura 1999). What is interesting about this research is that there was no correlation between performance in tasks that might be thought to demand similar abilities, such as mental rehearsal of spatial information. This suggests that targeting is a relatively separate ability (32–33).

In the tests we ran, we attempted first to establish certain obvious differences in the physical dispositions of the boys and girls. Having done this, we then ran tests to look at cognitive differences. These test were conducted with students in first grade at Horsenden Primary School in Ealing, London. Tania Borsig, the class teacher, expressed the opinion that the boys and girls in her class "behave differently and learn differently, but don't achieve differently." We set out to research some of her observations of patterns of behavior.

Are there differences in simple construction tasks? We wondered, if offered the choice of playing Scrabble or Lego, would the boys choose Lego and the girls, Scrabble? As in all great research traditions, we started with a setback. There was not a strong pattern of preference based on gender across the class. Secretly, I was pleased. We then moved to an activity that had more "science" behind it—a test of reaction to concrete apparatus. Specifically we observed what strategies boys and girls used when asked to sort multicolored, multishaped blocks.

In single-sex friendship pairs and separately, with minimal prompting, the boys and girls were asked to play with the plastic blocks. What happened again and again was that the boys sorted by function and the girls by some classificatory system. The girls built low, flat, and extended connected structures. The boys went high and independent. The boys' structures threatened to topple. The girls' structures threatened to fall off the edge of the table. When asked what they had produced, the boys cited phenomena from the outside world: Pokémon characters, a castle, a car. The girls used words like "shapes," "pictures," or "tessellations." The boys experimented a little more and seemed willing to take apart what they'd done and start again. The girls settled into a pattern of performance. The girls occasionally found each other a suitable color or shape; there was less observed collaboration among the boys. Throughout all the experiments, the BBC television cameras rolled.

And therein is the key to this. The experiments were designed for their visual quality. They were also designed to lend something to a television program whose thesis was, If the brains of boys and girls are so different, ought we to be teaching them in different ways? We set up one final experiment to test this thesis.

To find out about differences in switching from a routine, we organized boys and girls in three teams of three: nine boys, nine girls. The children were randomly selected ten-year-olds. The test they were to do was a variation on the Luchins water jug test. The original test involved problems of the kind, "You have a four-pint jug, a five-pint jug, and a seven-pint jug. Using as few pourings as possible, how do you measure out two pints of water?"

Traditionally, the subjects are shown how to solve the problem using all three jugs, do a few problems requiring three jugs, then encounter a problem admitting the use of either three or two jugs, then encounter one requiring the use of two jugs (see figure 10.1). They tend not to notice the opportunity to use two jugs in the penultimate problem or

10.1 With water jugs of different capacity, can you pour the water between the jugs so as to be left with two pints? How long will it take? What will be your method?

to recognize how to do so when required in the final problem. Even if these two test problems are introduced earlier in the series, the subjects still resist switching to the simpler solution. Previous research suggests that girls develop a habitual approach to problem solving earlier in the series than boys do and are less likely to switch.

What happened in practice was the reverse! Perhaps our sample was not large enough. Perhaps we had not been sufficiently rigorous in setting up the conditions. Maybe we did not run the experiment enough times. Or perhaps we just got a reminder that life and learning are a lot messier than theorists would sometimes like. The girls were no less adept at switching than the boys were. Both sets of three followed similar paths of hypothesizing, performing mini-trials, debating, and speculating, then agreeing to get on with it. We had expected the girls to become accomplished very quickly, to fall into a pattern, and to be resistant to breaking out of that pattern. We had also expected that they would be able to accommodate other simultaneous challenges, provided they did not have to break out of the pattern. We had thought they might be quicker to habituate. As it happened there was considerable ingenuity and flexibility among both boys and girls. One outcome that did conform to our expectations was that under pressure, the boys' performance improved disproportionately to the girls'. Against the challenge of getting a result in a limited time, they did much better.

Against the context of these limited but useful experiments we can examine what cognitive scientists say about the differences between men and women.

What Are the Differences?

The following lists are compiled from a variety of published sources on behavioral differences. They do not have their immediate origin in brain research, so we cannot with any authority surmise that they are a result of architectural differences in male and female brains. Such a conclusion would be a "bridge too far." They do, however, pose questions that, at some time in the future, neuroscientists may like to try to answer:

Why Is It That Women Do Better At . . . ?

- tasks that involve perceptual speed, such as the ability to rapidly identify matching items
- most language functions
- tasks of ideational fluency (for example, listing objects of the same color) and of verbal fluency (for example, name words that begin with the same letter)
- tasks that involve arithmetic calculation
- remembering whether an object or a series of objects has been displaced
- controlling distal musculature (the muscles farther from the trunk)
- tasks requiring precise manual control, such as replicating fingertip-touching patterns
- coordinating several movements
- rapid access and retrieval of information from memory
- landmark-based as opposed to geometrical navigation
- remembering faces and associating them with feelings
- studying by separating things out, practicing one component until it is mastered, then moving on to the next

Why Is It That Men Do Better At . . . ?

- tasks that are spatial in nature, such as navigating in two and three dimensions and through a maze
- mechanical skills, including assembling pictures, manipulating blocks, and mentally rotating objects
- guiding or intercepting projectiles using gross motor movements
- simple, repetitive movements, such as hitting a single key
- tasks that involve mathematical calculation
- seeing and thinking in concepts and patterns; finding abstract relationships and forming links based on them

- concentrating on an abstract idea or theorem and dissociating it from other "distracting" information
- unembedding shapes from their surroundings
- covert counting (that is, in their heads)
- persisting longer in covert retrieval (answering from memory)
- geometrical as opposed to landmark-based navigation
- Breaking down a task and therefore persisting with it (mature males)

Can't We Just Talk about It?

There appears to be a gender difference in the areas of the brain contributing to speech and language, although the findings are intriguing rather than definitive. In the processing of speech sounds, activity is triggered in the left inferior frontal gyrus for males, whereas the pattern in females is activation of more diffuse neural systems involving both hemispheres.

An area crucial for language comprehension in the left temporal lobe, the planum temporale, is more highly active during language tasks in men than in women. A listening study of twenty men and twenty women found that men use the left side of the brain—traditionally associated with understanding language—to pick up conversations. women used both hemispheres. Participants listened to excerpts from John Grisham's novel *The Partner* while researchers from the Indiana University School of Medicine monitored brain activity using fMRI.[1] Scientists have believed for some time that male brains are more lateralized than female brains. One view is that language centers are more compactly located in male brains and more widely dispersed in female brains.

Consider this task: In your head, go through the alphabet and count the number of letters that end in the long e sound, including the letter e. How many are there? Now go through the alphabet again, and this time, in your head, count how many capital letters have curves. How many are there?

Your score may reflect your gender: Females, on average, tend to do better on the sound task; males, on average, tend to do better on the shape task (Springer and Deutsch 1998). Females, on average, perform better than males on tasks that require the use of language. These include verbal fluency, speed of articulation, and grammar. In word tasks gifted subjects activated the frontal regions of the brain to a greater extent than control subjects, who tended to activate the temporal regions. In the western world, girls tend to speak earlier than boys. Their vocabulary is larger early on. Statistics cited lightheartedly by memory researchers Marilee Springer and George Deutsch (1998) suggest that women in the West use an average of about seven thousand words daily, and men about two thousand. The question then becomes, What do you do when you are with a man and he reaches his quota?

Parents in the West contribute to these language differences by talking differently to their sons and daughters and by having different expectations for behavior, social interaction, and play. If you are a parent, monitor the way you talk to your sons and daughters for a day. Look at the distribution of praise and discipline. Who gets it and for what? By implication, this balance of praise and correction, the noticing that goes with it, reinforces certain patterns of behavior. You get more of what you reinforce. When was the last time you praised your daughter for risk taking and physical prowess, for persistence, for scoring high on a computer game, for "being like Daddy"? When was the last time you praised your son for tidiness, neatness, accuracy in schoolwork, reading a story to its end, playing quietly, sharing toys, saying something correctly, or "helping mommy"?

Mathematical Reasoning

The international Organisation for Economic Co-operation and Development (OECD) published a report in December 2001 citing a worldwide disparity between the reading literacy of boys and girls (OECD 2001). At present, boys are poorer readers than girls the world over. OECD also reported that worldwide there was no such disparity in math, and that in many countries boys were slightly ahead. When interviewed in the journal *Educational Leadership*, Brian Butterworth explained that women were far more likely to self-denigrate their abilities in math and to undervalue their performance (D'Arcangelo 2001). According to MENSA, boys are more likely than girls to be highly talented in mathematics (John Williams, personal communication, August 2001). Girls are better on calculations, and males on mathematical reasoning.

Carr and Jessup observed that boys and girls engage in different processes to complete everyday calculations. [2] Girls use procedural, overt counting such as touching their fingers to find their answers better and more often than boys do. Boys are more successful with counting in their heads. Boys persist longer in trying to retrieve information from memory, though they are worse at it than are girls, who use other backup strategies. Girls are more likely to see each area of study as an entity and to need to feel confident about it before moving on to the next. The boys are more likely to be "atomizers." They can dissociate the task at hand more readily. They get better at persisting as they get older, particularly if they have atomized a task. Testosterone may play a part in resisting fatigue to allow this to occur.

Here are some ideas to help both boys and girls develop all-around mathematical ability:

▼ Use lots of physical objects that students can manipulate, feel, unfold, and relate to the two-dimensional problems in their workbooks.

▼ In class use number cards, whiteboards, and paired discussion to allow processing time before asking students to volunteer answers to math problems. Thoughtful answers are always better than quick answers.

▼ Provide opportunities for individuals to talk through their thinking as they problem solve.

▼ Use the descriptive, reflective, speculative process: (1) This is what I notice. . . . (2) I think it happens because. . . . (3) The next time I do it I will. . . .

▼ Break down tasks into the smallest possible units; review for understanding and consolidation before moving on.

▼ Reward persistence and risk taking, not just neatness and accuracy.

Connect to practical uses. Avoid rote homework; instead give shorter assignments with real-life applications, and discuss them extensively in class rather than formally grading them.

Your Motor Movement's Gross!

The right side of your brain seems better adapted than the left for navigating you, or an object you are controlling, through three dimensions. The right is used for defining depth, dimension, shape, and movement. It is more involved than the left side when mentally rehearsing the look of an object unfolded in three dimensions.

Many boys seem to be better at tasks that involve mentally rotating an object or imagining objects unfolded in three dimensions. They may be good at imagining their way around a large object like a ship or a power station or a medieval castle. They certainly enjoy construction in three dimensions. I can personally attest to having cut out a dozen or so African animals from the back of cereal boxes by the age of ten—sometimes before the cereal was eaten. They hung on my "trophy wall" at the foot of my bed. The types of books that show cutaways or cross-sections through various objects are likely to be highly popular with boys.

Boys are generally better at target-directed gross motor skills and interception, such as catching and throwing. This is not an absolute. I can remember secretly admiring girls who were adept at hopscotch and who were also good at throwing and catching tennis balls against a wall in sequence with both hands, sometimes three at a time. The balls moved in a blur, the exercise was accompanied by a song, and at the end of each verse another girl would jump in and take over the throwing and catching.

Girls generally do better on precision manual tasks such as peg boarding. Fine movement of the fingers is not fully coordinated in young children until about the age of five, and often later than that in boys. In the great wars of the twentieth century, women were recruited into munitions work and were particularly good at the speedy and accurate manipulation required for the assembly of bullets. I worked for a short period in a woolen mill. I worked in the dye house: all heavy lifting, heat, steam, and men. In the carding and spinning area all was delicate fibers, noise, tying broken threads, and women. The Purdue Pegboard, which looks like a cribbage board, was designed as a dexterity test in the recruitment of factory workers for intricate assembly-line work during World War II. It involves the speedy manipulation of light metal pegs and washers into the holes on the board. Women always outperform men on the pegboard test.

Doreen Kimura (1999), a Canadian-based researcher, and others argue that women are better at controlling the distal musculature—that is, the muscles farther from the trunk. She and others also claim that women are not only better at precise control such as replicating fingertip-touching patterns, but also at coordinating several movements simultaneously.

This may come as no surprise to many women who are familiar with the notion of multitasking, but may disappoint men who think that, by right, they are better at driving a car, manipulating a CD into the CD player, and holding a conversation on a cell phone that is trapped between neck and chin, all while looking for the right exit off the freeway.

Without any trace of irony, Kimura goes on to write, "Men, however, tend to be better at performing a single movement, such as tapping one key repeatedly with the same finger" (37). The next time you try to wean your son away from his PlayStation 2, be aware you are fighting destiny!

Some argue that the left hemisphere is more active with open-loop movements and the right with closed-loop movements. An open-loop movement is one that requires no correction or fine adjustment based on sensory feedback; for example, sawing, cranking an engine, stirring soup. Closed-loop movements are slower, modified regularly, and adjusted based on feedback; examples are shooting pool, typing, playing an instrument, or throwing a ball. Kimura showed that an important function of the left side of the brain is to control the sequencing of articulatory movements of the mouth and tongue and of changes in limb posture. Damage to the left side of the brain can result in individuals recognizing sequences of movement but being unable to do them. When you smile you do so unevenly! For verbal and nonverbal movements, the right side of your mouth opens wider and faster. For emotions, the left side of your face—which is controlled by the right hemisphere—is most expressive.

In conversation, right- and left-handers make different types of gestures. Both are equally likely to make self-touching gestures with both hands. Right-handers make more open gestures—movements with the hands or arms away from the body—with their right hand than do left-handers. Why? Doreen Kimura and others believe this has to do with the fact that the centers for speech specialization and for sequencing articulatory movements are located in the left hemisphere.

Chapter 11

Memory
How Do We Remember?

This chapter contains the following sections:

Thinking allowed. Priming, context, and cues in thought and recall. The difference between priming and cuing. Memory research using divers and using music.

You forget for a purpose. Forgetting is part of an effective memory. What would happen if your memory were perfect. False memory syndrome. Why each memory is an act of reconstitution.

The mechanics of memory. Memories are formed through a process of chemical and electrical changes known as long-term potentiation. A breakthrough discovery in memory.

Three parts of the brain used in memory. A model of memory. The role of the amygdala, hippocampus, and frontal cortex in memory formation and recall.

Short and long: the systems of memory. Different systems of memory. How information is transferred from short-term to long-term memory. How much information you can store.

Place, space 'n' face. Research with London taxi drivers. Why you are good at remembering faces. How schoolchildren used visual memory to make dramatic improvements in recall on tests.

Put on your memory SPECS. A technique for improving recall that is more than 2,000 years old. A simple memory tool for you or your students. The place of rote learning.

It will answer the following questions:

- Why does an answer to a question come to me when I am not expecting it?

- In self-help books I read, "You have a perfect memory—if you know how to use it." Is this true?

- What is a memory? Does it exist somewhere in the brain?

- Why do some people lose their memory? How can brain damage affect memory?

- I read a telephone number, I go to dial it, but I forget it before I can do so. Why?

- Does my brain grow with use?

- What is the best way to remember anything?

Introduction

My great-great-grandmother was, according to my mother, a Scots Highland "seer." She had a sixth sense and would occasionally rule on some issue of family destiny. This meant she got the best chair in the house and no one dared challenge her word. She would sit brooding in the corner by the fireplace with a furrowed brow and a slightly pungent aroma. From time to time she would utter some cryptic and necessarily gloomy judgment, "Yon bairn will ne'er hae a frosty pow." This was said in reference to my mother's newborn cousin who later, as a merchant seaman in the last war, lost his life when his ship was bombed: He never reached old age and never had grey hair ("ne'er hae a frosty pow").

Mind and memory must surely be more than the sum of the parts of electrical and chemical connections between neurons. Consciousness research, because of its controversial and beguiling nature, attracts disparate disciplines, all offering radically different perspectives. So too does memory research. Memory research has benefited a great deal in recent years from multiple perspectives. What is and what is not memory? How do memories form and fail to form? What role does forgetting play in memory and is it essential for a good memory? Memory involves not only what we consciously recall and reconstitute, it is what is inhibited rather than erased. Memory "loss" may also be an important part of creativity: Remembering too much detail prevents you from seeing the pattern. Memory, like my great-great-grandmother's intuitive insights, may operate on the edges of conscious awareness, suddenly coming together as a result of an accumulation of previously unnoticed cues available to some of us but only some of the time. Our starting point in looking at the brain and memory is to look at the role of intuitive learning and the value of forgetting.

Do you need to be conscious of an experience in order to learn from it? Can learning occur without conscious awareness? If there is such a thing as unconscious learning, how would we know that it had occurred? Would there be an ideal developmental stage for it? What circumstances would need to be in place for it to occur?

Thinking Allowed

I borrowed my partner's car to go shopping, a rare event on a number of counts. I found myself afterwards in the parking lot of a very large shopping mall looking for my car. I could not find it. The shopping cart wheels were ground almost to nothing by the time I gave up. I decided to sit down and take a breather, at which point a car drove by with two shopping bags on its roof. The shopping bags sitting there upright and on their own seemed absurd. I was unable to help. The car drove off. It was at that point, having been diverted from my preoccupation, that I realized I had been looking for my own car, but I had come in my partner's car. I found it straight away (see figure 11.1).

I believe that my narrowing preoccupation with limited data—my car and what it looks like—had inhibited me from thinking more broadly and remembering the important cues. A diversion had readjusted the focus for me.

11.1   Narrow thinking leaves me carless. It takes a paradigm shift involving bags of shopping to solve the problem.

Priming is also part of the process of recall. Priming can be loose or tight, direct or indirect. When it is direct, someone defines the category for us; when it is indirect—the shopping bags on the car roof—some inadvertent situation triggers the memory.

There is danger in priming too tight a set of categories from which to draw information in recall. Learning is about seeking and securing connections. Prime too narrowly and you do not get the connections. What does the word *green* evoke for you? I recall the face of a boy with whom I went to school. You may think of the park near your house. To a professional pool player, green may mean the felt on the pool table. To a professional golfer, hit it on the first shot or go home with no prize money! Creativity and breadth of thought can be stifled by priming that is too narrow. Offering lots of categories for recall seems better than giving only a few. You have to watch the categories, however: More categories require harder thinking. Or do they?

The theory of flow suggests that the best thing to do in order to engage creatively is to stop thinking about it. Thereby, other items from other categories are more likely to be evoked. With regard to links between brain cells, inhibitory effects decline more quickly than excitatory ones. Flow involves willingly suspending disbelief. Edison is credited with the quotation, "If you want to have a good idea, have lots of good ideas." For Professor Nick Rawlins of the University of Oxford, "We can learn implicitly through cues from phenomena at the periphery of our senses. As we have discussed earlier, complex rules can be learned via exposure to sequences that adhere to the rules, without having explicitly learned them" (Berns, Cohen, and Mintun 1997).

Surprisingly, some findings from brain research run counter to what intuitively feels like good teaching practice. Memories can be retrieved at a phenomenally fast rate. Professor Steven Rose, of the Brain and Behaviour Research Group at the UK Open University, describes the activation sequence in the brain as a particular memory is retrieved. Activation of the visual cortex occurs within 100 milliseconds, then within 300 milliseconds the frontal cortex is activated, followed by Broca's area at 600 milliseconds, then, as a choice is made, by 900 milliseconds the right parietal cortex is activated. The speed of this activation suggests that decisions can, and do, get made outside of conscious attention. There is, for example, a great deal of learning that goes on outside of conscious attention. The brain processes information that is neither attended to nor noticed, and this process is pervasive and ongoing. Children can, in some situations, learn without the involvement of the teacher. What is the significance of this for learning? You may well have to stop yourself mid-sentence when you start to say, "You'll never learn unless you pay attention."

For some types of learning we can speed the process by cuing. Memories are often context dependent. Restore the context and you reconstitute the memory (see figure 11.2). Vivid contexts are good for learning because they are rich in cues, but changing the context can be enough to ensure recall. Alan Baddeley (1982), of the University of Bristol, taught two

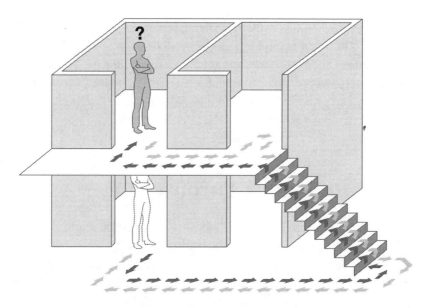

11.2   Context cues can precipitate connections and facilitate recall. Cues can be conscious or unconscious and can be accessed mentally or physically. Going from one room to another takes ten seconds. On arrival, you discover you have forgotten what you came for. What do you instinctively do?

groups of volunteers long lists of words. The first group learned the words in a classroom while the others learned them at the bottom of a swimming pool wearing full scuba gear. Recall was then tested for both groups. Baddeley found that those who learned in the classroom remembered better in the classroom while those who learned underwater remembered better underwater. What does this prove? Context is useful in shaping recall. Restore or approximate the original context and recall improves.

Music can provide an important contextual cue for improving recall. Participants in a context experiment viewed a list of words, one at a time. Two days later, they were given a test in which they simply had to recall as many of the learned words as possible. Like Baddeley's divers, for these individuals, learning and recall took place in the same or in different contexts, but in this case the contexts were musical. There were three different learning conditions: one group heard a Mozart piano concerto (K491 in C), another a jazz piece ("People Make the World Go Around," by Milt Jackson), and the third no background music. During the recall test, groups were subdivided so that they received either the same music (or quiet) that was present during learning or different music (or quiet).

Recall was best when the music was the same during learning and recall. Quiet during both events did not aid memory. The worst recall occurred when the musical context was changed and was found to be due to a memory process, rather than to possible distraction. Music, used as part of learning, can enter into memory and aid recall, even when it is not consciously attended to.

You Forget for a Purpose

A television commercial in the 1980s showed a black youth running aggressively toward an elderly white man in a public street. There was fear on the old man's face. The youth ran straight at him and pushed him violently to the ground. Both fell together, the youth on top of the old man. Then, almost simultaneously, a section of a wall crashed down where the old man had been standing seconds before. A voiceover said, "Don't take things at face value." At least that is how I remember the commercial. But I may be wrong. As they say, "Of all the liars, memory is the smoothest."

Forgetting is part of an effective memory. At the molecular and cellular levels of the brain, memory is highly dynamic rather than fixed. If your memory were "perfect," how miserable your life would be! Solomon Shereshevski, the world's most celebrated memory man, could memorize strings of numbers just by glancing at a chalkboard. He performed memory feats for a living, recalling strings of numbers backwards or forwards months and years after learning them. Assessed for thirty years by Russian psychologist Alexander Luria, Shereshevski complained that he could remember things only by picturing them and that this hindered his mental capacity. His cognitive abilities never developed beyond those of an adolescent because he could not think in the abstract. His mind was entombed in clutter. He could remember the numbers 2345, 3456, 4567, 5678 but could not, no matter how hard he tried, see any sort of pattern in the series (see figure 11.3).

1	8	3	6
2	**9**	**4**	**7**
3	10	5	8

11.3 Solomon Shereshevski had a near-perfect memory for particular types of information. His memory was pictorial and synesthetic. He was poor at discerning contexts and patterns. He was also deeply unhappy.

Shereshevski could remember anything with amazing detail because he did so through the confused sensory system he was born with. He had synesthesia, which meant that he subjectively experienced sensations from senses that were not being stimulated: He "heard" colors, "saw" tastes, "felt" sounds, and "smelled" shapes! He could also detail the perceptions surrounding his memory feats: "The color feels rough and unpleasant, and it has an ugly taste. . . . You could hurt your hand on this." What sounds very confusing is actually a clue to an excellent way of encoding memory. By deliberately conflating the physical qualities of an experience, we make it more memorable. Shereshevski would also deploy a pegging technique to help him retrieve memories. He would imagine a series of facts in relation to a town that he had created for this purpose in his head. The town had features that were highly familiar to him: streets, houses, private homes, public buildings and facilities, meeting places, and so on. When he was given a new fact, he would associate it with a feature of the town and do so in a highly synesthetic way: "I smell the date that is on the flag of the town hall by the brightly colored square," thus combining two memory techniques—pegging and synesthesia.

One in four people is susceptible to false memory syndrome. With prompting and coaxing, one in four of us can be led to believe that something has occurred in our past that, in fact, never did. Each year in the United States 77,000 people are charged with crimes based solely on eyewitness evidence and, according to U.S. National Institute of Justice figures for 1999, five have been sentenced to death on eyewitness testimony alone. After the major 1992 Amsterdam plane crash, a study showed that an impossible 66 percent of Dutch people interviewed claimed to have seen the event. Eyewitness testimony is vulnerable to suggestibility and in particular differs in reliability based on age, race, presence of a weapon, and duration of exposure to the experience. Older people are more likely to pick someone from lineup. The phenomenon of own race bias means that one is more accurate at identifying someone of one's own race than someone of another race. In the presence of a weapon an eyewitness focuses in a tunneled way on the weapon, not on the person at the other end of it (Memon 2002). Successful bank robberies using carrots and eggplants prove this!

It can be seen that memory is a more malleable phenomenon than everyday experience would lead us to believe. This makes the "truth" itself more uncertain, particularly when a fallible individual is drawing upon it. In order to survive and lead balanced and healthy lives, people have become accomplished practitioners of false memory syndrome. Thankfully, this is a very necessary part of everyday existence: a survival imperative. What would your life be like if you could remember everything?

In truth, each memory is an act of reconstitution. The process of recall is influenced by many variables, including emotional state, physiological condition, context, and how the memory may connect with others. An event can never be remembered exactly as it was. Every recall is a reconstitution that slightly distorts the original. In some cases we cannot remember something because the event was not encoded as worthy of recall in the first place. We failed to give it serious significance so it never hit our radar. Some scientists believe that many memories are simply put out of everyday reach through a process known as inhibition. Inhibition is useful because it prevents a confusing clutter of memories. People like Shereshevski are believed to have poor inhibitory mechanisms. Not being able to forget can affect your health. Quite aside from the constant reliving of a traumatic experience, the bane that is PTSD, being unable to inhibit memories can lead to depression. People who tend to mull over events excessively experience longer periods of depression than those who do not. Inhibition uses up mental resources. Low IQ scores often correlate with the presence of PTSD and extended depression. Perhaps less working memory is available for dampening down unwanted recollections.

With regard to memory it is important to distinguish between measures of recognition (the awareness that something is familiar) and measures of recall (accessing specific information). Multiple-choice and true-false tests prompt recognition whereas essay tests demand recall. It is also important to understand that memory is complex, messy, changing, multilayered, and imperfect. It is designed to be. Do not be seduced by those who promise that "your memory is perfect—if only you know how to use it." It is designed to be imperfect! If it were otherwise, life would be a never-ending nightmare of data tumbling out and at us.

The Mechanics of Memory

At the smallest level in the brain, memories are formed through a process of chemical and electrical changes known as long-term potentiation (LTP). LTP is the mechanism, neurologists believe, through which memories are encoded and so become capable of recovery (see figure 11.4).

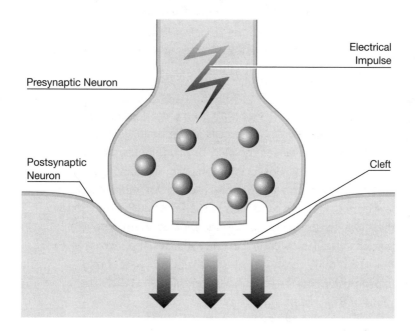

11.4   Mind the gap. Long-term potentiation is a long-lasting increase in the efficacy of a synapse. Proteins produced in the first neuron must find their way to specific receptors on the receiving neuron and bind to them. This changes the structure of the synapse and permanently increases its sensitivity to an incoming signal.

At the cellular level in the brain, each new experience causes some neurons to form new connections and other connections to deteriorate. Little chemical and electrical messengers are sent on their way from one neuron to another. The more certain neural connections are reinforced, the more alternative connections are neglected. A single neuron produces almost a tenth of a volt and the total electrical activity in the brain is easily measurable with an EEG.

The connections take the form of small electrical charges. The patterns of connections become the raw material of memory. If and when the pattern of connections is reactivated, a process known as potentiation begins to occur. This makes subsequent connections easier and more likely. The process of memories becoming more permanent is known as LTP. From what we know of LTP, we could argue a strong case that learning is like exercise for the brain. Regular "intellectual stretching" of the brain will produce more capillaries to help carry oxygen and glucose, more supportive glial cells, more all-around capacity to meet the metabolic and nutritional demands of the neurons. What would happen in a period of extended lethargy? If neurons in the pattern are allowed to weaken, then the memory weakens. If we do not use it, then we live with the possibility of losing it. John Ratey (2001, 194) describes the process like this:

> An initial stimulation triggers a communication across the synapse between two nerve cells in the brain. Further stimulation then causes the cells to produce key proteins that bind to the synapse, cementing the memory in place. If LTP—and hence a memory—is to last for more than a few hours, proteins produced in the first neuron must find their way to specific synapses and bind to them, an event that changes the structure of the synapses and increases their sensitivity to an incoming signal. This process may explain the need for rehearsal in learning as well as the value of REM sleep.

LTP is the most compelling explanation for the workings of memory. To use a horticultural analogy, creating a memory is akin to hacking clear a path and then walking that pathway. Neglect the pathway and it becomes overgrown. Use the pathway and it remains a viable communication route and is easier to walk on every subsequent journey.

Antonio Damasio (2000) describes the process of memory in terms of "convergence zones." Convergence zones are points that are physically near the sensory neurons that first registered the event. Think of ripples in a pond moving outward and from time to time running into other ripples from a different source (see figure 11.5). Damasio proposes a hierarchy of convergence zones. Lower convergence zones link the cues that allow us to understand the general concept of dog, while higher convergence zones allow us to recognize specific dogs. There may be convergence zones linking the two that recognize different elements of a dog—tail, head, coat—and specific types of dogs.

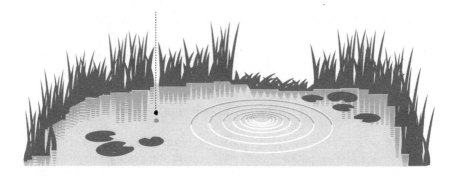

11.5   Neurons send out signals to others clustered nearby and they, in turn, respond by sending on or returning the signal. The effect is like ripples in a pond.

Does a sea slug have a good memory? What about a fruit fly? Both are being used in breakthrough research into the mechanics of memory. Given that it does not have a very long life span, a fruit fly has a surprisingly useful memory. Recent research with fruit flies suggests that short-term memory utilizes proteins that are present at the synapses (Cahill 1996). Long-term memory requires a different process. To shift a memory from short-term into long-term memory requires other proteins that recon-figure synapses. This synthesis is controlled by a protein known as CREB. CREB acts like a switch to trigger or turn off the production of new proteins. CREB has two opposing functions—to activate and to suppress. The activator promotes long-term memory formation; the repressor impairs the memory.

Scientists found that they could either speed up the formation of memories or block them in fruit flies by altering the levels of repressor and activator proteins. Normally, following ten training sessions with a short rest between each one, fruit flies learned that an odor signaled an impending electric shock. Flies with extra activator protein remembered more effectively. One lesson was enough for them. Flies that overproduced the repressor, however, could not form a specific long-term memory, even after many training sessions.

Researchers found that alterations in activator and repressor levels also affected the memory of mice for complex tasks. In one test, mice had to rely on lasting memories to find a hidden dock in a pool of water. Those with lots of activator protein swam to the dock and stood on it easily. Those with high repressor levels swam and swam without finding the dock. In another experiment, they had to choose a meal that matched the smell of a fellow mouse's breath. The mice with low levels of CREB activator could not remember the smell and so did not eat as well. The researchers pinpointed the hippocampus as one of the brain areas where CREB exerts its power. Mature rats that had their CREB activity disrupted only in the hippocampus showed a deficiency in long-term memory function.

Working with mice, Cold Spring Harbor Laboratory researcher Dr. Alcino Silva discovered the importance of "wait time" in learning. Mice improved their learning performance when given short periods of rest during training sessions. The speculation is that the brain uses this time to recycle CREB.[1] One of the outcomes of the CREB research is that scientists are testing on rodents a large number of existing drugs that may be able to enhance memory by affecting CREB levels.

Three Parts of the Brain Used in Memory

The brain has multiple memory systems for storing information, a fact that has been known for many years (see figure 11.6). Patient H., who suffered from epileptic seizures and had to have drastic surgery to separate the two halves of his brain, has been locked into the moment of surgery ever since. His recall of his life prior to his operation is intact.

He believes he is still in the 1950s of his youth. If, however, you were to visit him, he would not be able to remember your name or who you were by the end of a twenty-minute conversation. Oliver Sacks, a clinical neurologist, describes in detail how patients whom he treated suffered unusual aberrations in memory as a result of illness (Sacks 1985; see also <http://www.oliversacks.com>).

One man who came to him was a music teacher who, during the first office visit, turned his ears, not his eyes, toward Sacks. His gaze seemed "unnatural, darting and fixating" on the doctor's features one at a time. He had come with his wife, who sat next to him throughout the interview. When it ended the man appeared to grasp his wife's head and try to lift

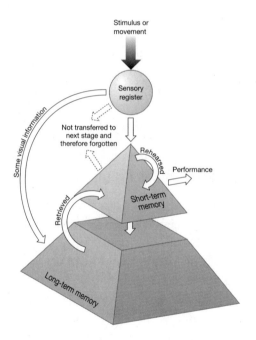

11.6   A model of memory. A physical experience registers in the sensory register, where it is held for a short period. Its fading is like the decline of an echo. The information needs to be transferred out of the sensory register in order to be retained. Some visual information goes directly to long-term memory. Some goes to short-term memory if we have attended to it and decided, at some level, that we need to use it. Once information is in short-term memory, rehearsal or application is needed to transfer it to long-term memory. Recall involves transferring back held data from long-term memory to short-term memory. Every act of retrieval is, in fact, a reconstitution so we never get back a verbatim transcript of the remembered experience.

it off and put it on his own head. He had, as Sacks says, mistaken his wife for a hat! The wife, in turn, gave no hint that anything out of the ordinary had occurred!

A second interview took place at the man's home. He was unable to recognize the rose in Sacks's lapel, describing it as a convoluted red form with a linear green attachment. Encouraged to speculate on what it might be, he guessed it could be a flower. When he smelled it, he came to life and recognized it. His wife explained that her husband made sense of everyday things through his senses. He functioned by making up little songs about what he was doing—dressing, washing, eating, and so on—and if the song was interrupted, he had to stop. Then he waited until he found a sensory clue on how to proceed. There is a site within the brain that contributes to facial recognition. Damage to it results in aberrant behaviors, and the individual has to resort to other methods to perform simple recognition tasks.

Memory for everyday experiences (episodic memory) uses different brain structures from memory for facts and information (semantic memory). Some individuals with profound amnesia cannot remember who you are a minute after you have introduced yourself but can talk to you with relative ease. We use different areas for encoding memory and retrieving memory. It does not come out in the way it went in!

John Ratey, associate professor of psychiatry at Harvard Medical School, describes memory as "the centripetal force which pulls together learning, understanding and consciousness" (2001, 185). In talking about the brain and memory he goes on to say that "the brain is more like an active ecosystem than a static, pre-programmed computer. There is no single center for vision, language, emotion, social behavior, consciousness or . . . memory." This is a point worth reinforcing. There are no single centers in the brain where specific memories are located. An act of remembering is like a unique coming together. A family gathering for a wedding anniversary would be a better metaphor for understanding memory than a computer or a library or an archive. Memory is not static. The act of remembering is part of the memory itself.

We cannot separate the act of retrieval from the memory itself. The memory in its quiescent state does not exist. It is as though, in our imaginary wedding anniversary, invitations are sent out to family members and friends and maybe a few acquaintances. The family members expect the invitation and are primed for a quick response; the friends, surprised by the invitation, have to be prompted; you have to work much harder to contact that acquaintance of your father's whom he has not seen for thirty years. The memory is as much in the uniqueness of their coming as it is in the event itself. This is like what happens in your brain when it remembers.

Three parts of the brain have a controlling function in memory. They are the amygdala, the hippocampus, and the frontal cortex (see figure 11.7). Their roles are like those necessary to organize your parents' wedding anniversary celebrations. The amygdala decides on the emotional value of the event. This is like deciding on how extravagant a celebration to hold. The amygdala is asking, Does this mean something to me? How significant is this to me? It then gives the occurrence an emotional tag based on its significance. The tag is like a value. If the amygdala is malfunctioning as a result of some sort of trauma or dysfunction, this will affect the emotional valuation given to the experience. If your general emotional state is depressed or is artificially high, that also alters the emotional value that is tagged to the memory. Brother and sister share the same parents but their experience of being parented differs. They may tag the event of the wedding anniversary differently.

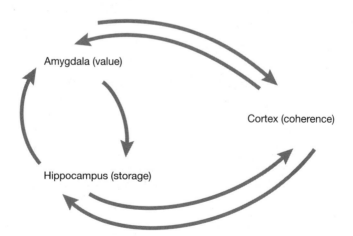

11.7   In retrieving memory the amygdala, hippocampus and frontal cortex are all involved. The amygdala assigns an experience an emotional 'value.' The hippocampus decides on where and how the information is stored. The cerebral cortex helps package the memory into a coherent whole.

The amygdala strongly tags negative emotional events, particularly those arousing fear or sadness, and they are better remembered than events with neutral emotional content. Adults observed while watching horror films showed a surprising link between activity in the amygdala and the number of frightening events. What is fascinating about this study is that it showed arousal of emotion in the brain even when the subjects claimed not to be affected by the films in any way.

It seems another area of the brain—the hippocampus—is more involved in remembering events that are emotionally fairly neutral. Information is routed simultaneously to the hippocampus and the cortex. The hippocampus is located in both hemispheres, and it has a central role in remembering. Memory may indeed be about dismembering and then remembering, with the hippocampus being central to both stages. In our extended metaphor of memory and anniversary party, the hippocampus seems to act like the family members who decide who should and who should not come. Not everyone is invited, not everyone is told of the event. Similarly, the hippocampus decides what information goes where. A proposal comes in, it is considered, evaluated, acted upon, and the relevant contacts made. This is what the hippocampus is doing with the tagged information it receives from the amygdala.

The third area of simultaneous involvement is the frontal cortex. It acts like an overall planning executive that oversees the decisions being made about whom to invite to the celebration. The frontal cortex is involved in planning, evaluating consequences, and determining goals. This part of the brain develops late and, when damaged, can lead to impulsive and reckless behavior. In the brain, it is the frontal cortex that neatly organizes the pieces of memory into a chronological, logical, and meaningful story.

You go from one room in the house to another to get something. You travel ten feet, it takes four seconds, and when you get there you have forgotten what you went in for. An explanation of this short-term memory phenomenon will follow somewhere toward the end of this sentence, but in order to understand it, you need to remember the beginning until you arrive here, at the end. Make sense? What is sometimes referred to as *working memory* enables us to remember on a moment-by-moment basis. Working memory is part of the executive function of the prefrontal cortex in the brain (see figure 11.8). Its essential feature is minute-by-minute

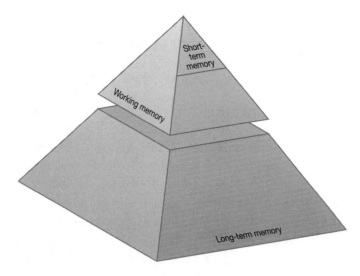

11.8 Working memory is a general term for all memory that is not long-term memory. Working memory allows us to exist on a moment-by-moment basis. It is part of the executive function of the prefrontal cortex and includes the sensory register. Selection, deletion, and distortion of memories occurs in working memory. Short-term memory, a temporary storage space for new information, is a subset of working memory. Short-term memory can be limited by duration or by digit span.

decision making on the basis of past experience. Working memory lends coherence to experience. Without it, we would be enslaved to the trivia of each moment.

Working memory acts as a gatekeeper at the front gate of consciousness, allowing only certain valued experiences to be encoded. If it did not do so, we would become habitual archivists, paralyzed into inactivity by the constant bombardment of disconnected sensory data.

Work done by Elizabeth Loftus and colleagues at the University of Washington in Seattle on planting false memories suggests about one in four of us believes them to be real (Carry et al. 1996; Loftus and Ketcham 1994). As the original memory is "recalled," the experience begins to feel real. Later it will be this feeling of reality that will authenticate the memory. We recall a vague feeling of authenticity alongside the memory. We are then seduced into believing in its truth. According to Dr. Daniel Wright, a psychologist working with the UK Eyewitness Research Unit, in 20 percent of lineups, crime victims identify a person whom police know to be innocent (Memon and Wright 2000; Wright and Davies. 1999; see also Gary Wells's homepage on the Iowa State University website). Wright is among many who believe that false memory, and thus wrongful conviction, is more prevalent than generally believed.

Wright conducted an experiment in which forty students individually looked at a picture book that showed a crime being committed at a pool hall. The book contained photographs of two men and a woman. The woman stole a wallet from one of the men. Unbeknownst to the students, half of them saw a picture book showing the woman loitering with an accomplice and the other half saw pictures of her on her own. When questioned afterwards individually as to whether the woman had an accomplice thirty-nine out of forty gave an accurate response. Then the groups were put into mixed pairs, where one member of each pair had seen the picture containing the accomplice and the other had seen no accomplice. They were then asked what happened. None of the pairs ought to have reached agreement. Yet only four failed to reach an agreement. The rest compromised. Sixteen pairs persuaded themselves one way or another, with nine reporting no accomplice and seven reporting an accomplice. When we are given information, we use it to fill gaps. Having someone describe an event is a powerful way of altering a memory.

So working memory involves a certain amount of selection, deletion, and distortion. False memory syndrome is a distortion of a natural process that shows memories can be planted. If you give people a selection of childhood memories, three of which are real and one of which is false, many respondents will come to believe with absolute certainty that all are real. Memory involves selection. Selection occurs at a number of levels, both conscious and unconscious. We store by similarity; we retrieve by difference.

Short and Long: The Systems of Memory

Short-term memory, a subset of working memory, is analogous to RAM: It is there while we need it, but as soon as the computer is switched off we lose it. Short-term memory is largely defined by its susceptibility.

When subjects were asked to remember new information while counting backwards from one hundred, recall of the new information consistently declined to zero after about ten seconds.

If you were asked to take a random sequence of numbers and repeat them back to me, how many would you be able to remember before you made an error? Try this using the following list. Read out the first set of numbers in sequence, then close your eyes and pause before repeating the sequence. Try each set in turn. At what point do you make an error?

```
7324
4718
32901
51899
064528
348371
8137649
5633407
21440753
93057312
219843781
520791642
4852066738
65782179342
91524837623
```

This is a very crude measure of digit span. Interestingly, it is influenced by the sounds contained in the spoken number. The more sounds, the more information the brain is asked to carry, and the less efficient our memory may be. In languages where the names of numbers are short and varied, performance goes up. Most people in the West can manage about seven digits, some nine or ten, and some only five or six. Recall is also influenced by method of rehearsal. Saying them aloud aids recall. So does saying them in a rhythm. Looking for patterns, chunking the numbers, and visualizing them also provide slight improvements in performance.

Short-term memory needs some sort of meaningful activation in order for the temporary storage to become more permanent. Long-term memory is like storing the information on the computer hard drive so we can use it again and again. How does the conversion from short-term memory to long-term memory occur? What is the sequence of events in the brain?

11.9 When asked a question, we need time to hear the question, assimilate it, compare it to others we have been asked before, formulate a response from a possible range, and express the response in language. All of this takes time—processing time.

Conversion does not occur until the prefrontal cortex sends the information to the hippocampus, and research suggests this takes time. The time required is the length of time it takes for the neurons to synthesize the necessary proteins for LTP. For learning, "wait," or processing, time is vital. For this reason educators ought to be good at pausing after asking a question. The learner needs to hear the question, assimilate it, formulate a response, and then express the response in some way (see figure 11.9). Asking for a response too quickly interferes with processing time.

Good teachers use tools to encourage a wide range of categories in a learner's thinking. This is a form of giving processing time. They ask questions like, What alternatives should we also consider? How might someone else approach this problem? Let us think about this one upside down or back to front or inside out! One teacher I know approaches difficult problems by physically pretending to take off her own head and put on someone else's: How would the principal approach this? What about the board of directors? What about a parent?

Sleep is also a form of processing time—if it's the right sort of sleep. Research done in Israel with laboratory rats revealed that the type of sleep affects recall. Interrupting REM sleep repeatedly led to complete blockage of recall. Repeated interruption of non-REM sleep did not.

Long-term memory is classified in a number of ways. The main types are declarative versus procedural memory (see figure 11.10). Declarative memory encompasses episodic and semantic memory. Procedural memory includes motor memory and conditioned responses. Declarative memory is the "what"; procedural is the "how." Formal education focuses excessively on the what. As humans, we are naturally better at doing the how.

Declarative memory includes both episodic and semantic types of recall. Episodic memory is a time-tagged memory of the moment. With episodic memory, you remember the experience and its circumstances. The structures that are activated in recall are distributed throughout the brain, but different types of memory have high dependency on certain areas.

Semantic memory is the memory for meanings and related information, facts, figures, faces, places, and things. These data are directly accessible to our conscious awareness but are not necessarily connected to a time or a place. The fact that Paris is the capital of France is not necessarily linked to the first time you discovered this. Semantic memory is rapidly retrievable when effectively rehearsed, unreliable when poorly rehearsed. It involves both the cortex and the hippocampus.

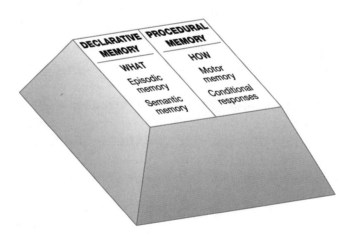

11.10 The main types of long-term memory are declarative and procedural, declarative being the "what" and procedural the "how." Declarative memory encompasses episodic and semantic memory, procedural memory includes motor memory and conditioned responses.

Procedural memory involves the recall of a sequence of steps. Examples are habits and skills that, once rehearsed thoroughly, become implicit; that is, they do not have to be consciously accessed: walking, throwing, catching, riding a bicycle. They are slowly retrieved, inflexible, and thoroughly reliable. Procedural memory relies on the basal ganglia and the cerebellum, both involved in the control of movement. A component of effective learning is the ready ability to turn declarative learning—specifically explicit memory—into procedural learning and, specifically, implicit memory. As a skill progresses from explicit to implicit, its location in the brain changes.

Research into Parkinson's disease, which affects the basal ganglia, shows that declarative memory can remain intact while some procedural memory is lost. People with Parkinson's disease can understand who they are, remember their past, know facts and figures, and recognize faces but struggle to perform a series of habituated movements such as walking or talking. In contrast, some people with Alzheimer's disease lose their declarative memory for names, places, faces, facts, and their own identity but retain procedural skills such as knitting. Amnesiacs often acquire motor skills at a rapid rate, often more quickly than do people with an unimpaired memory. They retain such procedural memories even when memory for everyday facts is lost.

The development of semantic memory is similar in some ways to the development of motor memory. Both benefit from distributed rehearsal. New information and skills become stored in long-term procedural memory through rehearsal. The best sort of rehearsal is distributed. In other words, practice a little and often. According to Dr. Larry Cahill, of the University of California at Irvine, this is true throughout the "learner kingdom": "From fruit flies to humans, distributed learning works better than amassed learning, and so adding more content comes at a price" (Cahill 1996; see also Cahill Profile).

Place, Space 'n' Face

Visual long-term memory has been described as a special case in humans. We are really good at remembering places, spaces, and faces. Studies with children show that they have photographic-like recall for visual memory until about the age of six, by which time most have been to school for about a year. Anthropologists studying peoples without written language talk of their photographic-like ability to recall objects and places. How old is the act of reading? Written language evolved among humans some 10,000 years ago, 90,000 years after the human brain had evolved to its present form. The phenomenal capacity we have for visual recall reflects our evolutionary history. We are naturally good at remembering the look of things and their spatial relationships.

Dominic O'Brien is the current and eight-time winner of the World Memory Championships. He can recall forty decks of cards and has done so against the clock with only one mistake; he has learned one hundred names and faces in half an hour, a five hundred-word poem in fifteen minutes, and a deck of cards in thirty-six seconds. He is not a freak! He decided only fourteen years ago to train his memory and now makes his living from it. How does he do it? One of the methods he uses involves physical locations. He has in his head, should he need them, eighty pre-learned possible journeys with fifty-two stops each (O'Brien 2002). He has little difficulty navigating the rehearsed sequence of stops, and at each he quickly makes exaggerated associations with the new information. He assigns the unfamiliar to the familiar and organizes it via a visual and spatial sequence.

People use visual memory to navigate, to recall the physical location and shape of objects, and to maneuver themselves or objects in space. Visual-spatial memory is imperative for survival and always has been. At its most sophisticated, it is James Bond recognizing his enemy's position by tracking the slow movement of his shadow. A homing pigeon uses the same sophistication to find its three-foot-square coop from four hundred miles away. The same sophistication allows you to recognize that the lines of color on a Picasso canvas in front of you represent the consequences for a nation of a bombing raid that occurred more than sixty years ago.

People with Alzheimer's disease can suffer from two forms of visual-spatial memory impairment, depending on the location of their brain lesions. Lesions in the right hemisphere inhibit their ability to understand the big picture. At the circus, they would see the clown's large shoes, the star on the elephant's head, and the chalk on the trapeze artist's hands but not be able to make sense of them all. Lesions in the left hemisphere inhibit their ability to understand the particulars. They would see the brightly colored tent and the audience, experience the excitement and laughter, but not appreciate what was happening and why.

A growing field of research suggests that specific genes are responsible for place memory. Some of us may be better disposed to spatial recall than others. Dr. Tsusumu Tonegawa at MIT discovered a gene responsible for long-term episodic memory. His work, along with that of Eric Kandel at Columbia University, showed that this gene in the hippocampus is responsible specifically for place memory. When this gene is enhanced, rats show an amazing photographic memory, resulting in one-time learning. Without it, they require twenty or more trials to achieve the same result.[2]

As part of an accelerated learning initiative at a London school, children were encouraged to look at learning posters containing key information that were placed around the classroom. The posters contained limited amounts of chunked information and were easy to see and read. Children were encouraged to test their recall of the look of each content poster, to draw them in their notebooks, to teach them to others, and to try to draw them from memory. At the end of the year the children's performance improvement on their standardized tests was among the highest in the country. They could remember the look of key information and its spatial relationship with what surrounded it. In a wonderful moment of serendipity, neuroscience explained why the following year.

In September 2000 I was traveling in a taxi to Paddington railway station from the Institute of Cognitive Neuroscience in London. I had been to a seminar on neuroscience and learning, and I had sneaked out early. This does not always happen in London, but I got to talking amicably to the driver. He asked me what I had been doing in London. I told him. He told me that he could remember customers by associating them with places. For example, he had dropped off a student at the institute two years before, one of only two occasions he had been there. She was a tea drinker and a sociology student. He told me he remembered this because he had picked her up again about a year later and had asked her if she was still drinking tea. As she had only just got into the cab and had not said anything, she was taken aback and later said as much. How could he have remembered her all that time later? His story was interesting, and I told him about the University College research on London taxi drivers' brains published earlier that year.

Tests conducted with fifteen London taxi drivers, some of whom had more than forty years' experience, revealed that their brains had adapted to help them hold a map of the city in their heads. The research team, led by Dr. Eleanor Maguire, used MRI techniques to compare the brains of taxi drivers with those of fifty other people in a control group (Maguire, Gadian, and Johnsrude 2000). They found that each taxi driver had a larger hippocampus compared to the control group, and that part of the hippocampus grew larger as the driver spent more time on the job (see figure 11.11).

11.11 Evidence that structural changes can occur in healthy human brains was provided by research into London taxi drivers. Part of the hippocampus grew larger as the taxi drivers spent more time on the job.

The only area of the taxi drivers' brains that was significantly different from the fifty other control subjects was the left and right hippocampus. The posterior hippocampus was bigger, and the anterior hippocampus smaller, in the taxi drivers compared to the control group. As Dr. Maguire explained, the structure of the hippocampus apparently changed to accommodate the drivers' huge amount of navigating experience. The findings are very interesting because they show there can be structural changes in a healthy human brain.

The development of the posterior hippocampus also reflected the amount of time individuals had been taxi drivers. There seems to be a definite relationship between the navigating they do as taxi drivers and the changes in their brains. The evidence that the brain is able to change physically according to the way it is used could have important implications for people with brain damage or diseases such as Parkinson's disease. For a long time scientists have believed that the adult brain had only a limited amount of plasticity. Perhaps rehabilitation programs in the future could utilize this kind of knowledge.

The taxi driver who picked me up from the institute told me it takes, on average, about four years to "learn" London and the suburbs. He memorized 'the knowledge' in seventeen months. I asked him what he had done to learn the information so quickly. He was a Cockney, he had a moped, and he had been ill—all of which was relevant to his success. He used lots of rhyming slang in everyday speech and was good at manipulating language sounds. He remembered by rehearsing the sounds of street names in his head. He used acronyms: Chelsea, Albert, and Battersea bridges became CAB. Then he became ill, and as a result was confined to bed, at first in hospital and then at home, for several weeks. During this time he pored over the maps of London and mentally rehearsed the routes in his head, again and again. If you visit London, you will see lots of very large men on very small mopeds in the most obscure streets. Attached to their handlebars is a plastic map holder. They are physically rehearsing their knowledge of London geography by getting out and driving it.

How long would it take you to gain perfect recall of all of central London and the suburbs, including streets, landmarks, places of interest, galleries, museums, theaters, hotels, and restaurants? Taxi drivers have to demonstrate this knowledge before they are licensed to drive a cab in London. If you had taken a leaf out of my taxi driver's book and learned by hearing, seeing, and doing, then I would suggest, you could master the information a lot more quickly than if you had used simple rote rehearsal.

Memory for faces uses different parts of the brain. Working memory can transfer information to long-term memory within sixty seconds of encoding and, as we age, we rely more and more on the left prefrontal cortex and less on the right visual cortex. As soon as we meet a person, rather than remember the visual image of the face, we use the associations, thoughts, and impressions associated with it. The implication of this finding is that even as we attempt to describe information held in working memory, we use different structures of the brain to do so. Thus, every memory is an act of reconstitution. We make it up as we go along!

When you see an attractive face, sites that are associated with reward become active. A team in the Institute of Cognitive Neuroscience at University College, London, asked sixteen volunteers to rate the attractiveness of forty different unfamiliar faces on a scale of one to ten (Knut et al. 2001; Maguire, Frith, and Cipolotti 2001). The volunteers were asked to look for qualities such as radiance, empathy, cheerfulness, and even motherliness, in addition to conventional beauty. Faces deemed attractive by the subject, irrespective of gender, activated the ventral striatum, the brain's reward center. This activation occurred only when the viewer could make eye contact with the face in the photograph, not when the photograph showed an averted gaze. Studies with monkeys and rats have shown that this part of the brain lights up in anticipation of a reward such as food or water. It is also implicated in addiction. The research also shows that an attractive face is recognized by the brain in a matter of seconds, suggesting the process is automatic, perhaps even hardwired into the brain.

Our ability to recognize faces is remarkable. People's faces are very similar. Yet we can instantly tell whether a face we see before us is a friend, a relative, or a complete stranger. The apparently simple task of recognizing a face actually takes a huge amount of processing power. The task is so brain intensive, in fact, that our facial recognition system only works with faces that are the right way up. In figure 11.12, notice how much more quickly you recognize the face that is the right way up than the faces that are upside down.

11.12 Three faces. One the right way up, another upside down, and another upside down apart from the eyes and mouth. Notice how much more quickly you recognize the first.

Ralph Haber collected thousands of slides of faces and places and spent a morning session showing them to his psychology students at the rate of one per second (Haber 1998; see also Haber 1981, 1982, 1985). The slides contained images of people and of locations in and around the area where Haber lived. The students would not have recognized them. A couple of days later he showed the same slides, but each was now shown alongside a new slide randomly positioned to the left or right. Asked to say which was the slide they had seen before from a collection of now more than two thousand, students identified them with 90 percent accuracy. Without any practice or rehearsal, they had somehow secured the visual information in long-term memory. We are really good at doing this sort of thing, and yet many learning environments and textbooks are bereft of visual cues.

Put on Your Memory SPECS

Techniques for improving memory are surprisingly enduring. The methods taught nowadays in expensive management seminars are no different from methods used in Greek or Roman times. The basic message is I, F, and R: Intent, File, and Rehearse. Decide that some information is important to recall (by doing so you give it significance), then store it through some mechanism (for example, using mnemonics or association), then rehearse it (go over it until you are comfortable you will be able to access it in a variety of situations). The methods taught in management courses focus on the second stage—File—and are variations on ways of giving information significance.

To make something memorable, put on your memory SPECS! Focus on what you wish to remember, then See it, Personalize it, Exaggerate it, Connect it, and Share it—SPECS (see figure 11.13).Throughout, remember that experiences that have emotional resonance are remembered best—so really go for it!

What follows is a basic memory improvement package in a paragraph. It is a description of a process. Pay attention at the back! Motivation is important in recall. Here goes.

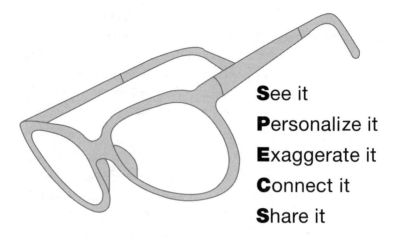

See it
Personalize it
Exaggerate it
Connect it
Share it

11.13 The SPECS memory filing technique. To enhance recall, use the SPECS method: See the information, Personalize it, Exaggerate it, Connect it, and Share it.

Tag the experience as significant by deciding what it is you want to remember. **Prime** your memory by identifying what sort of information it is and how it connects to what you already know. **Sell** yourself on the benefits of knowing this information. (As a result of doing this, I will be better off because. . . .) You have now given significant attention to the activity of remembering and are ready to **encode** the memory. To encode—or file—it use the SPECS method: See the information, Personalize it, Exaggerate it, Connect it, and Share it. Be consistent—if you rehearse in a particular place or in a particular way, continue to do it that way. To conclude, **rehearse,** or go over, the information frequently and **test** yourself.

Finally, is there a place for rote learning? There is certainly value in distributed rehearsal and in spaced testing. Distributed rehearsal, or "a little and often," is fundamental to the maintenance of any skill. Recall scores go up with spaced testing. Rote learning is a subset of distributed rehearsal but with an emphasis on verbal familiarity. Separate fMRI studies looked at brain responses to rote repetition of vocabulary items. The areas of the brain used for speech production were also used for rote repetition.

The significance of this finding is that with material learned by rote, recall is prompted by verbal cues coded within speech networks (Blakemore and Frith 2000). Some believe that learners with poor neuronal capability for learning information by heart can nevertheless learn through other means; brain imaging will, in time, reveal whether this is the case. It is certain, however, that the capacity for learning information by rote is highly individualized.

For many young learners, there is security in being able to demonstrate immediate knowledge. Your child may feel good about being able to recite the seven times table at the drop of a hat, but is such memorization a good use of neural real estate and limited class time? Rote learning does not invite students to understand connections. It does not open up alternative categories of knowledge. It does not deepen their sensitivity to a poem's message. Nor does it give insight to the application of math facts. It does provide many learners with a set of tools that may have use over and above their immediate application.

As a child attending Sunday school in Scotland, I had to learn the books of the Old and New Testament in order from the King James Bible. What use has this been to me? Very little in everyday life, but maybe it has had some deeper value in reminding me that I can do it. Perhaps it has played a part in developing verbal fluency and a better understanding of patterns of sound and, most significantly, it has helped activate the neural circuitry for similar needs should they arise. Rote learning will always be controversial. It has its place. If I am on an international flight, I want the pilot to know by heart the safety drill in the event of engine failure. How he or she remembers it is a different issue.

3

PART THREE

The Brain's Finally behind It

Chapter **12**

The Findings

1 The outcomes of research into the workings of the human brain, particularly in the field of learning dysfunction, offer a great deal to educators. A lot of teaching that has been based on intuition and common sense could benefit from many of the informed insights neuroscience offers.

2 More effort is needed to convey research findings to educators accurately and intelligibly. At present there is no consistent mechanism for such communication. Without authoritative and informed insights, the education community remains susceptible to glib truths such as the 10 percent myth.

3 Monitoring of health is crucial in pregnancy and in early childhood. More effective conduits to get information to parents, especially about lifestyle choices and links to learning, are desirable.

4 The idea of the sensitive period is useful for the education community to know about and understand. More work on the extent and duration of such windows—for example, whether they exist for different areas of human endeavor—is needed. The concept of brain development being both dependent and expectant is also useful in reminding us of a balance between nature and nurture in learning.

5 The brain has natural and separate circuits for language and for number. Development of these circuits starts early. Children acquire and store language earlier than commonly believed, provided they have repeated exposure to it. Exploration of the world of number starts in infancy and needs subsequent structured intervention.

6 There is a need to invest in primary education but with a more informed, and perhaps more appropriate, pedagogy. For far too many children, hothousing can be antagonistic to positive lifelong learning dispositions.

7 A second—or any additional—language or languages need to be taught early. Language acquisition favorably alters the structure of the brain. Is it worth the struggle to institutionalize language learning in high school, at a chronological phase when it has already become more difficult for the learner?

8 It is vital to retain the motion and emotion components of learning through movement and music.

9 Core skills and some factual information need to be taught. Teaching should align with and make use of what is known about brain development and structure. For example, teaching should provide structured challenge, multilevel engagement, imitation, aggregation and disaggregation, connections, real contexts, and regular and reflective rehearsal.

10 Respecting difference is less about badges of distinction—race, gender, disability—than it is about accommodating different entry and exit points.

Chapter 13

Recommendations

For Parents, Educators, and Policymakers

For Parents

1 Choose a lifestyle of learning. With the brain, what you don't use, you lose. The brain circuitry developed in childhood provides the basis for all subsequent learning.

2 Monitor your lifestyle in pregnancy and when trying to conceive. The mother's poor diet; excessive stress; or use of alcohol, nicotine, and drugs may all affect the developing baby's brain.

3 The best care is "kangaroo care." In the early months of life particularly, skin-to-skin contact helps develop emotional bonds between parent and child. This is a time when the child's stress response is being set for life.

4 Monitor your child's health, particularly hearing, eyesight, and physical abilities.

5 Play with your child and exploit imitation skills. This is the first learning style.

6 Harsh words may alter a child's brain for life. Be constantly positive in the things you do and say with your child.

▶▶7 Be there to share. One of your child's greatest needs is to talk about things that happen with a consistent adult.

▶▶8 Speak to, with, and around your child from the earliest days. Never underestimate an infant's capacity to store words.

▶▶9 Be aware that the brain develops in spurts and plateaus, and also that there are ideal times for certain learning experiences to occur.

▶▶10 Avoid beginning formal learning too early. There is no real evidence that starting formal learning early advantages your child.

For Educators

▶▶1 Respect your own professionalism. Stay up-to-date with new research, particularly in fields such as learning disability. Our understanding is evolving.

▶▶2 Plan for multiple levels of engagement and global and local emphasis. Assume multiple entry and exit points in the design of your classroom learning activities. Always set chunked information in a wider global context.

▶▶3 Scaffold challenge. Be aware that there is an emotional curriculum that lies below the surface and that those emotions direct attention. When a learner tips out of anxiety and into stress, the behavioral response is predictable and bad for learning.

▶▶4 An understanding of both physical and physiological variables assists your teaching. Use variables such as the room setup, time on task, and movement to help your learning outcomes. Be aware of the physiological state of the learners in front of you.

▶▶❺ Model by proximity. Demonstrate desired behaviors through what you do and say. Be aware that learners need to approximate to a role model before they can adopt his or her practices. If the model is too remote, modeling does not work.

▶▶❻ Seek connections. At all levels and at all times, meaningful learning involves seeking and securing connections. An educator builds connections into everyday classroom interactions.

▶▶❼ Optimize structured language exchange within each learning activity.

▶▶❽ Teach and model mnemonic skills.

▶▶❾ Allow processing time and build in reflective rehearsal.

▶▶❿ Challenge naïve assumptions and easy truths about what the human brain is and is not. To do this you need to stay informed.

For Policymakers

▶▶❶ Argue the case for more professional understanding of developmental stages of the human brain as part of teacher preparation programs. Train more colleagues in dealing with learning disorders and in the early use of diagnostic tests.

▶▶❷ Create a research community of educators and neuroscientists to share findings and "cross the bridge" between scientific understanding and educational practice. Encourage educators to ask more specific questions of the science community with regard to learning.

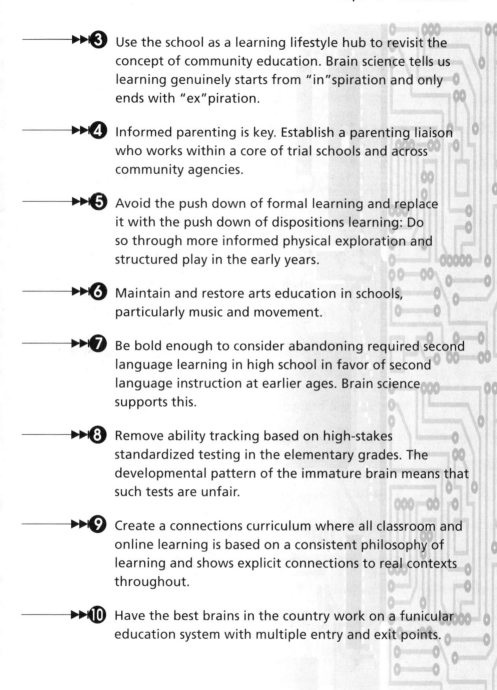

3 Use the school as a learning lifestyle hub to revisit the concept of community education. Brain science tells us learning genuinely starts from "in"spiration and only ends with "ex"piration.

4 Informed parenting is key. Establish a parenting liaison who works within a core of trial schools and across community agencies.

5 Avoid the push down of formal learning and replace it with the push down of dispositions learning: Do so through more informed physical exploration and structured play in the early years.

6 Maintain and restore arts education in schools, particularly music and movement.

7 Be bold enough to consider abandoning required second language learning in high school in favor of second language instruction at earlier ages. Brain science supports this.

8 Remove ability tracking based on high-stakes standardized testing in the elementary grades. The developmental pattern of the immature brain means that such tests are unfair.

9 Create a connections curriculum where all classroom and online learning is based on a consistent philosophy of learning and shows explicit connections to real contexts throughout.

10 Have the best brains in the country work on a funicular education system with multiple entry and exit points.

Chapter 14

Questions

and Where to Find the Answers

Recommended Websites

The Author

Alite (Contact me via my website!)
www.alite.co.uk

Aging

Alliance for Aging Research
www.agingresearch.org

Alzheimer's Association
www.alz.org

Child Development and Prenatal Care

Alliance for Childhood
www.allianceforchildhood.net

Child Development Institute
www.cdipage.com

Sheila Kitzinger, midwifery specialists' homepage
www.sheilakitzinger.com

National Institutes of Health, U.S. National Library of Medicine Medline
http://www.nlm.nih.gov/medlineplus/prenatalcare.html

Gender Differences in Learning

American Psychological Association: Women & Men
http://www.apa.org/topics/topicwomenmen.html

Science.ca Scientist Profiles: Doreen Kimura
(contains information on gender-based differences in brain organization)
www.science.ca/scientists/scientistprofile.php?pID=10

Giftedness

Council for Exceptional Children
www.cec.sped.org

EdWeb: Theory of Multiple Intelligences
www.edwebproject.org/edref.mi.intro.html

National Association for Gifted Children
www.nagc.org

National Research Center on the Gifted and Talented (NRCG/T)
www.gifted.uconn.edu/nrcgt.html

Institutes and Professional Organizations

American Academy of Child and Adolescent Psychiatry
www.aacap.org

American Academy of Neurology
www.aan.com

American Psychological Association
www.apa.org

British Psychological Society
www.bps.org.uk

Institute for Brain and Immune Disorders
www.winternet.com/~briminst

King's College London Institute of Psychiatry
www.iop.kcl.ac.uk/IoP/index.stm

Medical Research Council (UK)
www.mrc.ac.uk

Medical Research Council Cognition and Brain Sciences Unit
www.mrc-cbu.cam.ac.uk

National Institute of Neurological Disorders and Stroke
www.ninds.nih.gov

University College London, Institute of Neurology
www.ion.ucl.ac.uk

Learning Difficulties

Attention Deficit Disorder in the UK (links on ADD)
www.pavilion.co.uk/add/english.html

Brain Injury Association of America
www.biausa.org

British Dyslexia Association
http://www.bda-dyslexia.org.uk/main/home/index.asp

Dyspraxia Foundation (for information on apraxia)
www.dyspraxiafoundation.org.uk

International Dyslexia Association
www.interdys.org

LD Online (good overview site)
www.ldonline.org

LD Resources: Resources for the Learning Disability Community
www.ldresources.com

Optometrists' Network: Attention Deficit Disorder FAQs
www.add-adhd.org

The Stroke Association
www.stroke.org.uk

Libraries and Databases

Washington Open MRI
www.washingtonopenmri.com

Proceedings of the National Academy of Sciences (PNAS)
www.pnas.org

Seeing, Hearing and Smelling the World
(a Howard Hughes Medical Institute report)
www.hhmi.org/senses

Washington University School of Medicine Neuroscience Tutorial
http://thalamus.wustl.edu/course

The Whole Brain Atlas
www.med.harvard.edu/AANLIB/

Virtual Hospital, Dissections of the Real Brain
www.vh.org/Providers/Textbooks/BrainAnatomy/BrainAnatomy.html

Music and Learning

CODA Music Trust
www.mri.ac.uk/index.html

MIND Institute Research (contains research on the Mozart effect)
www.mindinst.org

The Mozart Center (Tomatis Method)
www.mozartcenter.com/index.html

MuSICA Music & Science Information Computer Archive
www.musica.uci.edu

Society for Education, Music, and Psychology Research (SEMPRE)
http://www.sempre.org.uk

Physiology and Learning

British Sleep Society
www.british-sleep-society.org.uk

Brain Gym® International
www.braingym.org

International Association for the Study of Dreams
www.asdreams.org

International Bottled Water Association
www.bottledwater.org.

Loughborough Sleep Research Centre
www.lboro.ac.uk/departments/hu/groups/sleep

Publications

Archives of General Psychiatry
http://archpsyc.ama-assn.org

Beemnet: Brain ExchangeElectronic Mentorship Network
www.beemnet.com/dana/

Brain, A Journal of Neurology
http://brain.oupjournals.org

Nature Neuroscience
www.nature.com/neuro

Science magazine
www.sciencemag.org/

New Scientist magazine
www.newscientist.com

Neurobiology of Learning and Memory
http://www.elsevier.com/wps/find/journaldescription.cws_home/622924/
description#description

Publishers and Bookstores

Caine Learning (a brain-based learning site with good links)
www.cainelearning.com

Crown House Publishing
www.CHPUS.com

New Horizons for Learning (materials to do with brain-based learning)
www.newhorizons.org

Research Laboratories

Birkbeck University of London, Centre for Brain and Cognitive Development
www.psyc.bbk.ac.uk/cbcd/cbcd.html

Boston Neurosurgical Foundation
www.boston-neurosurg.org

Center for the Study of Emotion and Attention (CSEA)
http://www.phhp.ufl.edu/csea/center_main.html

Inserm's Cognitive Neuroimaging Unit (Stanislaus Dehaene)
http://www.unicog.org/main

Project Zero at the Harvard Graduate School of Education
http://pzweb.harvard.edu

University College London, Institute of Neurology
www.ion.ucl.ac.uk

University of California at Irvine, Neurobiology and Behavior research
http://neurobiology.uci.edu/frames/ri_frameset.html

Training and Development Organizations

Brain Connection
www.brainconnection.com

Collaborative for Academic, Social, and Emotional Learning
www.casel.org

21st Century Learning Initiative
www.21learn.org

de Bono Thinking Systems
www.aptt.com

Learning Disability Resource Community (a good learning-to-learn site)
www.snow.utoronto.ca/Learn2/sitemap.html

Glossary

ACTH
A hormone that produces the body's long-term reaction to an environmental stressor.

adrenaline (epinephrine)
A hormone that stimulates glucose release as a way of dealing with short-term stress.

agnosia
Literally "not knowing," agnosia is the condition of not recognizing sensory stimuli. For example, someone with visual agnosia would have no trouble seeing an object but would lack the ability to understand the image.

Alzheimer's disease
A degenerative, age-related form of dementia.

amnesia
A cognitive disorder involving memory loss, typically as a result of a traumatic injury or degenerative brain condition.

amygdala
A part of the basal ganglia named for its almond shape. The amygdala is thought to be involved with emotion and memory formation.

androgens
The male hormones produced in the testes, one of which is testosterone.

angular gyrus
A section of the left temporal lobe involved in language processing; it connects the occipital cortex with Wernicke's area.

anterior
Front

anterior cingulate gyrus
A component of the limbic system associated with motor control, pain perception, cognitive function, and emotional arousal.

aphasia
Partial or total loss of the ability to express or comprehend spoken or written language, resulting from damage to the brain caused by injury or disease.

apraxia	An impairment in the planning and execution of complex, coordinated movements in the absence of sensory or motor impairment; it may also affect general learning abilities.
attention	The selection of stimuli to which we direct conscious thought.
attention-deficit/ hyperactivity disorder (ADHD)	A syndrome characterized by short attention span and poor impulse control.
auditory feedback	The process by which humans learn to speak using hearing and vocalization. In auditory feedback sounds heard are repeatedly imitated and fine-tuned until they can be perfectly reproduced.
autonomic nervous system	Also called the visceral nervous system. Located outside the brain and spinal cord, this system obtains sensory information from internal organs and provides feedback to them.
axon	An extension of a neural cell that transports information away from the cell body, usually via an electrical impulse.
basal ganglia	A series of subcortical structures in the center of the brain that are principally responsible for motor tasks.
blind spot	A spot in the visual field of each eye where the eye cannot see. The blind spot corresponds to the point in the retina where the optic nerve exits the eye and which is devoid of photoreceptors.
brain stem	The major route by which the forebrain communicates with the spinal cord and peripheral nerves. The brain stem controls, among other things, respiration and regulation of heart rhythms.

Broca's area	The central region for the production of speech. Located in the frontal lobe, typically in the left hemisphere.
central executive	A component of working memory models associated with coordinating cognitive functions.
central nervous system (CNS)	The "central station" to which the peripheral and visceral (autonomic) systems send their sensory information. The CNS takes that sensory information and responds by sending motor instructions back to the peripheral and visceral systems. The two main structures of the CNS are the brain and the spinal cord.
cerebellum	A large structure located high inside the hindbrain and connected to the pons, medulla, spinal cord, and thalamus. It helps control movement and some aspects of motor learning.
cerebral cortex	The outer, highly convoluted layer of the cerebral hemispheres responsible for perception, emotion, thought, and planning.
cerebral hemispheres	The halves of the brain, each of which has its own specific functions. The left hemisphere is typically associated with speech, writing, language, and calculation; the right hemisphere is typically associated with spatial perception, visual recognition, and aspects of music perception and production.
cerebral palsy	A developmental disorder characterized by motor control difficulties that results from perinatal damage to brain tissue.
chromosome	A threadlike structure of the cell nucleus that contains genetic information. Chromosomes occur in characteristic matched pairs for each species; humans have twenty-three pairs.

cingulate gyrus

A cortical structure, part of the limbic system, that is directly over the corpus callosum along the medial side of each hemisphere. It is involved with regulating emotion and attention and in tagging.

circadian rhythms

The basic daily rest-activity cycle of the body. It is regulated by a structure in the brain known as the suprachiasmatic nucleus (SCN), which determines levels of wakefulness over a twenty-four-hour period.

cognition

The mental processes by which knowledge or awareness is applied to comprehension and problem solving.

cognitive interference

The theory that certain cognitive processes in the brain may conflict with other cognitive processes.

cognitive map theory

One theory concerning how the brain represents physical spaces.

consciousness

One's immediate awareness. Consciousness is arguably what makes us human. A highly controversial field of study, consciousness is also an area where no one theory prevails. Being able to understand, self-regulate, and share one's own thoughts are at the core of consciousness.

contralateral

Related to the opposite side of the body, as when functions on the right side of the body are controlled by the left side of the brain.

corpus callosum

A large bundle of nerve fibers that connects the left and right cerebral hemispheres.

cortical plasticity

The ability for connections between neurons to be modified within the cortex.

corticospinal tract

The direct pathway from the cortex to the spine, involved in voluntary motor control.

cortisol

A long-term stress hormone that maintains high blood pressure and produces glucose for energy at times of stress.

decussation

A crossing over of nerve fiber tracts from one side of the body to the other. Typically, it results in the right hemisphere of the brain controlling the left side of the body, and the left hemisphere controlling the right side of the body.

dendrite

A branching extension from the neuron cell body that receives information from other neurons.

deoxyribonucleic acid (DNA)

A long, threadlike molecule contained in the nucleus of cells that encodes the genetic information of an organism. DNA is a remarkable molecule because it can self-replicate. Half of a child's DNA contains genetic information from the mother and half from the father.

dopamine

A neuromodulator acting principally through structures of the basal ganglia. Dopamine is associated with reward pathways, and low levels of dopamine are characteristic of Parkinson's disease.

dorsal

Relating to the back of the body.

dorsolateral prefrontal cortex

An area on the lateral aspect of the brain near the front that is associated with executive functions, decision making, and working memory.

dyscalculia

A disability of mathematical calculation.

dyslexia

A disability of reading and writing.

epilepsy

A neurological disorder caused by uncontrolled electrical activity that spreads throughout the brain, causing seizures that can last from seconds to several minutes.

episodic memory	A type of long-term memory that references events and time.
estrogen	A hormone that helps define femaleness and is involved in creating female body shape.
executive processes	Cognitive tasks related to decision making, associated with the frontal lobe of the brain.
frontal cortex	An area of the brain associated with higher cognitive functions, including planning and motor control.
frontal lobe	One of the four divisions of each hemisphere of the cerebral cortex. (The others are the parietal, temporal, and occipital). The frontal lobe is the site of emotions, personality, and cognitive and motor functions.
functional magnetic resonance imaging (fMRI)	A technique for imaging brain activity using a magnetic field. It differs from MRI in that the latter produces static images.
gene	The smallest unit of hereditary information; a section of DNA that encodes a protein.
glial cells	A range of cell types that act to support the neural network by providing structure and nourishment. In some cases, glia may be involved in modulating neural signals.
glucocorticoids	Any of a group of steroid hormones that affect glucose metabolism.
hemisphere	Half of the brain, the right or left.
hippocampus	A cortical structure near the center of the brain that plays an important role in memory. The hippocampus is named for its seahorse-like shape in cross-section.

hypothalamus | The master control structure for the autonomic nervous system and the secretion of hormones.

inferior colliculus | A cluster of cells responsive to sound that are found in the brain stem below the superior colliculus.

inhibitory | Describes anything that has a dampening effect; used specifically in reference to a synaptic connection that decreases the electrical excitability of the postsynaptic neuron.

ipsilateral | Related to the same side of the body; used, for example, to describe the right hemisphere controlling movement on the right side of the body.

kinesthesia | The sense by which muscular motion, weight, position in space, and the like are perceived.

lateral | Refers to a structure that is close to the side or surface of another structure (the opposite of medial). For example, the lateral part of an egg is the egg white, and the medial part is the yolk.

limbic system | A group of brain structures that work to regulate emotions, memory, and certain aspects of movement. It includes the amygdala, hippocampus, cingulate gyrus, septum, and basal ganglia.

longitudinal fissure | A deep sulcus (groove) that runs down the middle of the cortex and provides a prominent landmark for separating the brain into the left and right hemispheres.

long-term potentiation (LTP) | A long-lasting increase in the efficacy of a synapse.

magnetic resonance imaging (MRI)	A technique for imaging soft tissues, especially the brain, using a magnetic field. While MRI provides a static image of the brain, a related technique called fMRI (functional magnetic resonance imaging) can image changing activity within the brain.
medial	Refers to a structure that is towards the midline of another structure, such as the body (opposite of lateral). For example, the medial part of an egg is the yolk, while the lateral part is the egg white.
medulla oblongata (myelencephalon)	An area located within the brain stem, or hind brain, that is responsible for controlling respiration, circulation, and other bodily functions.
melatonin	A sleep-inducing hormone secreted by the pineal gland during the hours of darkness.
memory space theory	A theory of hippocampal function suggesting that the hippocampus acts to encode environmental episodes rather than spaces in particular. (Opposed to the cognitive map theory.)
modality	A mode of sensation; for example, hearing, touch, smell, taste, or vision.
myelin	A glassy, white sheath surrounding the axons of some neurons. Myelin acts as an insulator, helping neural signals travel more quickly and over greater distances than they could in an uninsulated axon. Myelin is composed of Schwann cells that wrap themselves concentrically around the neural axon.
neglect	The slow demise of a system.

neocortex	Literally meaning new cortex, the most recently developing part of the brain. Located in the anterior, or front, part of the brain, the neocortex is especially large in higher primates and is responsible for sensory and motor processing, as well as abstract reasoning and association.
neonate	Newly born.
neuron	The cellular unit of the central and peripheral nervous systems.
neurotransmitter	A chemical released by neurons to relay information to other cells.
noradrenaline	A short-term stress hormone that works in conjunction with adrenaline and gives a short-lived feeling of alertness. It impairs short-term memory, and scientists now believe it can promote the growth of bacteria.
nucleus accumbens	The principal pleasure center of the brain, containing one of the largest stores of dopamine. Highly involved in motivation and reward systems, the nucleus accumbens is studied extensively in addiction research.
occipital lobe	A rounded projection at the back of the brain devoted mostly to vision. It contains the primary visual cortex.
olfactory	Of or relating to the sense of smell.
orbitofrontal cortex (also known as Brodmann's area 47)	A region of the frontal cortex that is involved in motor function and communicates with the basal ganglia as well as other limbic structures. This structure may be involved in mood-related disorders as well as motor dysfunction.

parietal lobe	An area separated from the frontal lobe by the central sulcus and from the occipital lobe by the parieto-occipital sulcus. The parietal lobe contains somatosensory and sensory integration areas.
pathway	A route of information flow in the nervous system.
perinatal	Occurring shortly before, during, or just after birth.
peripheral nervous system	The nerves located outside the brain and spinal cord that obtain sensory information from the external world and provide motor output to the voluntary muscles to allow us to move.
phoneme	The smallest unit of speech that carries meaning. (*Cat* and *bat* have different meanings because *c* and *b* are phonemes.) Phonemes are combined into syllables and words.
pituitary gland	A small gland at the base of the brain that secretes hormones regulating most of the other glands in the body. It is often referred to as the master gland.
planum temporale	A cluster of neurons believed to be important for language processing; in most people, it is larger in the left hemisphere than in the right.
pons	A structure at the top of the brain stem containing a number of nuclei and many fiber tracts connecting the cerebellum and medulla to the higher brain areas.
positron emission tomography (PET)	A technique for imaging brain activity using radioactive dyes injected into the bloodstream.
posterior	Rear

posterior parietal cortex	The rear portion of the parietal cortex, which is involved in transforming visual information to motor commands.
postsynaptic	On the receiving side of the synapse. A post-synaptic cell receives neurotransmitters from a presynaptic neuron.
prefrontal cortex	An area of the brain associated with higher cognitive functions, including planning and working memory.
premotor cortex	A region in the frontal lobe involved in the sensory guidance of movement and in activating proximal and trunk muscles.
prenatal	Relating to the time before birth.
primary motor cortex	Cortical area in the frontal lobe that is directly involved in producing muscle contractions.
primary visual cortex	An area of the occipital lobe that receives the earliest information from the eyes by way of the thalamus.
procedural memory	A type of unconscious memory for motor skills that does not require the hippocampus for formation.
prosopagnosia	An inability to recognize faces following brain injury.
psychometric	Relating to the measurement of mental processes.
rapid eye movement (REM) sleep	A phase of sleep in which some consolidation of memory, and therefore learning, is thought to occur.
saccadic eye movements	High-velocity, jerky eye movements from one point to another point that occur when panning one's gaze over a scene.

serotonin

The oldest neurotransmitter in the brain; important for emotional processing and sleep.

slow-wave sleep

A phase of sleep that is particularly deep.

somatic nervous system (also voluntary nervous system)

A component of the peripheral nervous system that controls voluntary actions by carrying signals to skeletal muscles to make them contract.

somatosensory

Relating to tactile, temperature, pressure, and position information perceived through sensory organs in the skin and muscles.

stress

A state of high physical, emotional, or mental activity in preparation to deal with a potential danger. In the context of this book, anything from the outside world that tips a person out of homeostatic balance.

stroke (cerebral vascular accident, or CVA)

A blockage or bursting of a blood vessel (or vessels) in the brain that disrupts blood flow. Symptoms include difficulty with voluntary movement, impairment of sensation, and confusion or loss of consciousness.

Stroop task

A test that measures cognitive interference, the role that one stimulus characteristic plays in the perception of another characteristic. The Stroop effect is an increase in reaction time evident when an individual has to identify one stimulus property that conflicts with a more salient stimulus property. For example, if the word *blue* is written in red ink, a person has more difficulty identifying the ink color than when the ink is blue.

subcortical

Located beneath the cortex; used in reference to brain structures that are not a part of the cerebral cortex.

supplementary motor area (SMA)	Region in the frontal lobe involved in the planning of complex movements and in two-handed movements.
synapse	The gap over which electrochemical transmission between two neurons passes.
temporal lobe	One of the four major projections of the brain; it is primarily responsible for hearing and memory or learning. It is separated from the frontal lobe by the lateral sulcus.
testosterone	The hormone that defines maleness. It has been linked—controversially—with male aggressiveness, male libido, and impatience. Males who are victims of violence suffer a significant drop in testosterone levels. Stress also lowers testosterone levels.
thalamus	A structure in the brain that receives sensory information (vision, hearing, and touch) coming into the brain and routes that information to appropriate areas of the cerebral cortex.
visual cortex	Areas of the cerebral cortex principally associated with vision.
voluntary nervous system (somatic nervous system)	A component of the peripheral nervous system that controls voluntary actions by carrying signals to skeletal muscles to make them contract.
Wernicke's area	An area of the left temporal lobe that is crucial for language comprehension.
working memory	A type of memory where information is readily available for a very short period of time.

Notes

Chapter 1

1. Thinking about the educational implications of genetics research will be a hugely important task for the future. The jump from gene to behavior is much greater than the jump from brain to behavior. The work to be done in terms of bringing neuroscience into contact with education will facilitate the work that will eventually have to be done to bring insights from genetics to bear on teaching and learning.

2. *Brain in the News* 4(11): 4, 13. (New York: Dana Press).

Chapter 2

1. From a presentation by Alison Gopnik at Brain Expo, San Diego, January 4, 2001.

2. Dr. Jusczyk's research is described on his faculty web page: <http://www.psy.jhu.edu/faculty/jusczyk.html>

3. From my notes taken at the Royal Institution Seminar, "What Can Brain Science Tell Us about Learning?" led by Sir Christopher Ball, September 21, 2000.

4. From my notes taken at a talk by Susan Greenfield, professor of pharmacology at Oxford University, given to the Technology Colleges Trust at the Royal Society, May 2000.

Chapter 3

1. Debra Yurgelen Todd, interview with the author, McLean Medical School, Boston, August 1999.

2. See Liz Lipton, "Morphometrics Opens Door to More Precise Brain Studies," *Psychiatric News* (May 2000); Diana Phillips Mahoney, "Insight" feature. *Computer Graphics World* (January 2000); John Lauerman, "Brain Atlases Reveal Individual Terrain, *Brainwork*, The Dana Foundation Magazine (January 2000); all available at <http://www.loni.ucla.edu/~thompson/MEDIA/media.html>

Chapter 5

1. These findings were published in *Brain Research*, October 2000.

Chapter 6

1   From my notes taken at the Brain Research and Learning conference held at the Royal Institution, London, spring 2000.

2. From my notes taken at the Early Learning and the Brain conference held at the Royal Institution London, July 12, 2000.

3. Retrieved from <http://www.researchmatters.harvard.edu/section_list.php?section=mind>.

Chapter 7

1. See "Sleep and Dreaming," special issue of *Behavioral and Brain Sciences* (Cambridge University Press, 2001).

2. From my notes of "How Circadian Rhythms and Light Impact the Human Brain," presentation at Brain Expo, San Diego, January 19, 2000.

3. Ibid.

4. UCI Newsroom March 2001.

Chapter 8

1. See <http://research.medicine.wustl.edu/ocfr/research.nsf>.

Chapter 9

1. *Brain in the News*, August 15, 1997, 5.

Chapter 10

1. From my notes of a talk given at the Radiological Society of North America Annual Meeting in 2001 on the research of Joseph T. Lurito. See also, "Temporal Lobe Activation Demonstrates Sex-Based Differences during Passive Listening," *Radiology* 220 (2001): 202–7. Available from <http://radiology.rsnajnls.org/cgi/content/abstract/220/1/202>.

2. *BrainWork*, July 15 1997, 6.

Chapter 11

1. *BrainWork*, January–February 1997, 9.

2. *Brain in the News*, 15 January 1997, 2.

Selected Bibliography

1. Pre-wiring:
What Happens to the Brain in the Womb

Diamond, M. 1988. *Enriching heredity: The impact of environment on the anatomy of the brain.* New York: Free Press.

Eliot, L. 1999. *What's going on in there? How the brain and mind develop in the first five years of life.* New York: Bantam Books.

2. Wired to Fire:
Brain Development in the First Five Years

Blakemore, S-J. 2000. Early years learning. Paper prepared for the Parliamentary Office of Science and Technology (POST). Available online at <www.parliament.uk/post/pn140.pdf>.

Gopnik, A., A. Meltzoff, and P. Kuhl, P. 1999. *How babies think.* London: Weidenfeld and Nicolson.

Siegel, D. J. 1999. *The developing mind: Toward a neurobiology of interpersonal experience.* New York: Guilford Press.

3. Wired for Desire:
The Brain and the Onset of Puberty

Dawkins, R. 1989. *The selfish gene.* Oxford: Oxford University Press.

Harris, J. R. 1998. *The nurture assumption: Why children turn out the way they do.* London: Bloomsbury.

Howard, P. J. 1994. *The owner's manual for the brain—Everyday applications from mind-brain research.* Austin, TX: Bard Press.

Kotulak, R. 1996. *Inside the brain.* Kansas City, MO: Andrews and McMeel.

McCrone, J. 1996. *Going inside.* London: Faber and Faber.

Ratey, J. 2001. *A user's guide to the brain: Perception, attention, and the four theaters of the brain.* New York: Pantheon Books.

Restak, R. 1980. *The brain: The last frontier.* New York: Warner.

Scientific American book of the brain: With an introduction by Antonio Damasio. 1999. New York: Scientific American.

4. Wired to Inspire:
The Completion of Brain Development

Butterworth, B. 2000. *The mathematical brain.* London: Papermac.

Calvin, N. 1996. *How brains think: Evolving intelligence then and now.* London: Weidenfeld and Nicolson.

Carter, R. 1998. *Mapping the mind.* London: Weidenfeld and Nicolson.

Dehaene, S. 1997. *How the mind creates mathematics.* London: Penguin.

Greenfield, S. 1997. *The human brain: A guided tour.* New York: Basic Books.

———. 2000. *Brain story.* London: BBC Publications.

Hogarth, R. 2001. *Educating intuition.* Chicago: University of Chicago Press.

Perkins, D. 1992. *Smart schools.* New York: Free Press.

Sacks, O. 1985. *The man who mistook his wife for a hat and other clinical tales.* New York: Simon & Schuster.

Sternberg, R. J., ed. 1997. *The nature of creativity.* Cambridge: Cambridge University Press.

Zohar, D., and I. Marshall. 2000. *Spiritual intelligence: The ultimate intelligence.* London: Bloomsbury.

5. Wired to Misfire:
Learning from Dysfunction

Barkley, R. A. 1995. *Taking charge of ADHD: The complete authoritative guide for parents.* New York: Guilford Press.

Niehoff, D. 1999. *The biology of violence: How understanding the brain, behavior, and environment can break the vicious circle of aggression.* New York: Free Press.

Volavka, J. 1995. *Neurobiology of violence.* Washington, DC: American Psychiatric Press.

Walker, H., and R. Sylwester. 1991. Where is school along the path to prison? *Educational Leadership* 49 (September): 14–17.

Weiss, G., and H. L. Trokenberg. 1993. *Hyperactive children grown up.* New York: Guilford Press.

6. Wired to Retire:
Aging and the Brain

Heston, L., and J. A. White. 1991. *The vanishing mind.* New York: W. H. Freeman and Co.

Khalsa, D. S. 1997. *Brain longevity.* London: Century.

Vernon, M. 1992. *Reversing memory loss,* Boston: Houghton Mifflin.

7. Physiology:
How Do We Maintain the Brain?

Carlson, N. R. 1991. *Physiology of behavior.* Boston: Allyn and Bacon.

Druckman, D., and R. A. Bjork. 1991. *In the mind's eye: Enhancing human performance.* Washington, DC: National Academy Press.

Logue, A. W. 1991. *The psychology of eating and drinking.* New York: W. H. Freeman and Co.

Portwood, M. 1999. *Developmental dyspraxia: identification and intervention.* 2nd ed. London: David Fulton Publishing.

Shapiro, F. 1995. *Eye movement desensitization and reprocessing,* New York: Guilford Press.

8. Engagement:
How Do We Arouse and Direct the Brain?

Csikszentmihalyi, M. 1990. *Flow: The psychology of optimal experience.* New York: HarperCollins.

Damasio, A. 2000. *The feeling of what happens: Body and emotion in the making of consciousness.* London: Vintage.

Goleman, D. 1995. *Emotional intelligence.* New York: Bantam Books.

Kalin, N. H. 1993. The neurobiology of fear. *Scientific American* (May): 195–205.

Lewis, M., and J. M. Haviland-Jones. 2000. *The Handbook of emotions,* New York: Guilford Press.

LeDoux, Joseph. 1998. *The emotional brain.* New York: Simon and Schuster.

Parasraman, R. 1999. *The attentive brain.* Boston: MIT Press.

Pert, C. 1997. *Molecules of emotion.* New York: Scribner's.

Ramachandran, V. S, S. Blakeslee, and O. Sacks. 1999. *Phantoms in the brain: Probing the mysteries of the human mind.* London: Fourth Estate.

Sapolsky, R. 1998. *Why zebras don't get ulcers: An updated guide to stress, stress-related diseases, and coping.* New York: W. H. Freeman and Co.

Van der Kolk, B. A. 1996. *Traumatic stress: The effects of overwhelming experience on mind, body and society.* New York: Guilford Press.

9. Laterality:
How Do We Develop Left and Right?

Davidson, R. J., and K. Hugdahl. 1996. *Brain asymmetry.* Boston: MIT Press.

Hellige, J. B. 1993. *Hemispheric asymmetry: What's right and what's left.* Cambridge, MA: Harvard University Press.

Ornstein, R. 1997. *The right mind: Making sense of the hemispheres.* New York: Harcourt Brace.

Springer, S. P., and G. Deutsch. 1998. *Left brain, right brain: Perspectives from cognitive neuroscience.* New York: W. H. Freeman and Co.

10. Gender:
How Do We Respect Difference?

Kimura, D. 1999. *Sex and cognition.* Boston: MIT Press.

Moir, A., and D. Jessell. 1991. *Brain sex: The real difference between men and women.* New York: Carol Publishing Group.

Rogers, L. 1999. *Sexing the brain.* London: Weidenfeld and Nicolson.

11. Memory:
How Do We Remember?

Baddeley, A. D. 1986. *Working memory.* Oxford: Oxford University Press.

Gordon, B. 1995. *Memory: Remembering and forgetting in everyday life.* New York: Mastermedia.

Hobson, J. 1988. *The dreaming brain.* New York: Basic Books.

Luria, A. 1986. *The mind of a mnemonist: A little book about a vast memory.* Cambridge, MA: Harvard University Press.

Mirsky, N. 1994. *The unforgettable memory book.* London: BBC Publications.

Rubin, D. C., ed. 1996. *remembering our past: Studies in autobiographical memory.* Cambridge: Cambridge University Press.

Rupp, R. 1998. *Committed to memory: How we remember and why we forget.* London: Aurum Press.

Schachter, D. 1996. *Searching for memory: The brain, the mind, and the past.* New York: Basic Books.

———. 2001. *The seven sins of memory.* Boston: Houghton, Mifflin.

Further Reading

Blackmore, S. 1999. *The meme machine.* Oxford: Oxford University Press.

Blakemore, S. J., and U. Frith. 2000. *The implications of recent developments in neuroscience for research on teaching and learning.* London: Institute of Cognitive Neuroscience.

Bloom, F. E., and A. Lazerson. 1988. *Brain, mind and behavior.* New York: W. H. Freeman and Co.

Brandt, R. 2000. On teaching brains to think: A conversation with Robert Sylwester. *Educational Leadership* 57(April): 7.

Brothers, L. 1997. *Friday's footprint: How society shapes the human mind.* New York: Oxford University Press.

De Bono, E. 1986.*CORT thinking program,* Oxford: Pergamon Press.

de Fockert, J. W., G. Rees, C. D. Frith, and N. Lavie. 2001. The role of working memory in visual selective attention. *Science* 291: 1803–6.

Elbert, T., and C. Pantev. 1995. Increased cortical representation of the fingers of the left hand in string players. *Science* 270 (5234): 305–7.

Feuerstein, R., Y. Rand, M. Hoffman, and R. Miller. 1980. *Instrumental enrichment.* Baltimore: University Park Press.

Gardner, H. 1991. *The unschooled mind: How children think and how schools should teach.* New York: Basic Books.

———. 1993. *Frames of mind: The theory of multiple intelligences.* New York: Basic Books.

Gazzaniga, M. 1992. *Nature's mind.* New York: Penguin Books.

———. 1998. *The mind's past.* Berkeley: University of California Press.

Kandel, E. R., J. H. Schwartz, T. M. Jessell, eds. 1995. *Essentials of neural science and behavior.* New York: Appleton and Lange.

Maguire, E. A., R. N. Henson, C. J. Mummery, and C. D. Frith. 2001. Activity in prefrontal cortex, not hippocampus, varies parametrically with the increasing remoteness of memories. *Neuroreport* 12 (3): 441–44.

Perkins, D. 1995. *Outsmarting IQ: The emerging science of learnable intelligence.* New York: Free Press.

Pickup, G. J., and C. D. Frith. 2001. Theory of mind impairments in schizophrenia: symptomatology, severity and specificity. *Psychology and Medicine* 31 (2): 207–20.

Posner, M. I., and M. E. Raichle. 1997. Images of mind. New York: Scientific American Library.

Sternberg, R. J. 1988. *The triarchic mind: A new theory of human intelligence.* New York: Viking.

——. 1996. *Successful intelligence: How practical and creative intelligence determine success in life.* New York: Plume.

Sylwester, R. 1995. *A celebration of neurons: An educator's guide to the human brain.* Reston, VA: ASCD.

——. 2005. *How to explain a brain: An educator's handbook of brain terms and cognitive processes.* Thousand Oaks, CA: Corwin Press.

Wolfe, P. 2001. *Brain Matters: Translating research into classroom practice.* Alexandria, VA: ASCD.

Wolfe, P., and P. Nevills. 2004. *Building the reading brain, Pre K-3.* Thousand Oaks, CA: Corwin Press.

References

Anderson, S. W., A. Bechara, H. Damasio, D. Tranel, and A. R. Damasio. 1999. Impairment of social and moral behavior related to early damage in human prefrontal cortex. *Nature Neuroscience* 2: 1032–37.

Ash, R., and M. Nelson. 1998. Iron status and cognitive function in UK adolescent girls. *Proceedings of the Nutrition Society* 57: 81A.

Baddeley, A. 1982. *Your memory: A users' guide.* New York: Macmillan.

Barkley, R. A. (1997). *ADHD and the nature of self-control.* New York: Guilford Press.

———. 1998a. Attention-deficit hyperactivity disorder. *Scientific American* 279(3):66–71.

———. 1998b. *Attention-deficit/hyperactivity disorder: A handbook for diagnosis and treatment.* New York: Guilford Press.

Bechara, A., H. Damasio, A. R. Damasio, and G. P. Lee. 1999. Different contributions of the human amygdala and ventromedial prefrontal cortex to decision-making. *Journal of Neuroscience* 19 (13): 5473–81.

Bechara, A., D. Tranel, H. Damasio, and A. R. Damasio. 1996. Failure to respond autonomically to anticipated future outcomes following damage to the prefrontal cortex. *Cerebral Cortex* 6: 215–25.

Bekoff, M. 2001. Social play behavior: Cooperation, fairness, trust, and the evolution of morality. *Journal of Consciousness Studies* 8: 81.

Benbow, C. P. 1990. Sex differences in mathematical reasoning ability: Further thoughts. *Behavior and Brain Sciences* 13: 196.

Benbow, C. P., and O. Arjmand. 1990. Predictors of high academic achievement in mathematics and science by mathematically talented students. *Journal of Educational Psychology* 82: 430–41.

Benbow, C. P., D. Lubinski, D. L. Shea, and H. Eftekhari-Sanjani. 2000. Sex differences in mathematical reasoning ability: Their status 20 years later. *Psychological Science* 11: 474–80.

Benbow, C. P., and L. L. Minor. 1990. Cognitive profiles of verbally and mathematically precocious students: Implications for identification of the gifted. *Gifted Child Quarterly* 34: 21–26.

Benton, D. 1997. Psychological effects of snacks and altered meal frequency: A comment. *British Journal of Nutrition* 77: S118–20.

Benton, D., and P. Y. Parker. 1998. Breakfast, blood glucose and cognition. *American Journal of Clinical Nutrition* 67: 772S–78S.

Benton, D., O. Slater, and R. T. Donohue, R. T. In press. The influence of breakfast and a snack on memory and mood. *Physiology and Behavior.*

Berk, L. E. 1994. Why children talk to themselves. *Scientific American* 271(5):78–83.

Berns, G. S., J. D. Cohen, and M. A. Mintun. 1997. Brain regions responsive to novelty in the absence of awareness. *Science* 276(5316):1272–75.

Blakemore, S. J. 2000. Early years learning. Paper prepared for the Parliamentary office of Science and Technology (POST). Available online at <http://www.parliament.uk/post/pn140.pdf>.

Blakemore, S. J., and U. Frith. 2000. *The implications of recent developments in neuroscience for research on teaching and learning.* London: Institute of Cognitive Neuroscience.

Brown, H. D., and S. M. Kosslyn. 2003. Hemispheric differences in visual object processing. In *The Asymmetrical brain,* ed. K. Hugdahl and R. J. Davidson, 93. Cambridge, MA: MIT Press.

Bruer, J. T. 1997. Education and the brain: A bridge too far. *Educational Researcher* (November): 4–16.

BUPA Health News Journal (September 3, 2001). Retrieved from <http://www.bupa.co.uk/health_news/030901pregnancy.html>.

Butterworth, B. 1999. *What counts: How every brain is hardwired for math.* New York: Free Press.

Cacioppo, J. T., L. G. Tassinary, and G. Berntson. 2001. *Handbook of psychophysiology.* 2nd ed. Cambridge: Cambridge University Press.

Cahill, L. 1996. The neurobiology of memory for emotional events: Converging evidence from infra-human and human studies. In *Function and Dysfunction in the Nervous System,* Symposium 61, vol. 61, 259–64. Cold Spring Harbor, NY: Cold Spring Harbor Laboratory Press.

Cahill Profile. <http://darwin.bio.uci.edu/neurobio/Faculty/Cahill/cahill.htm>

Cahill, L., and J. L. McGaugh. 1998. Mechanisms of emotional arousal and lasting declarative memory. *Trends in Neurosciences* 21: 294–99.

Carry, M., C. G. Manning, E. F. Loftus, and S. J. Sherman. 1996. Imagi-
nation inflation: Imagining a childhood event inflates confidence
that it occurred. *Psychonomic Bulletin and Review* 3(2): 208–14.

Carter, R. 1999. *Mapping the mind.* London: Weidenfeld and Nicolson.

Castellanos, F. X., J. N. Giedd, and P. C. Berquin et al. 2001. Quantitative brain magnetic resonance imaging in girls with attention-
deficit/hyperactivity disorder. *Archives of General Psychiatry* 58(3).

Castro-Caldas, A., K. M. Petersson, A. Reis, S. Stone-Elander, and
M. Ingvar. 1998. The illiterate brain: Learning to read and write
during childhood influences the functional organization of the adult
brain. *Brain* 121(6): 1053–63.

Chan, A. S., Y. C. Ho, and M. C. Cheung. 1998. Music training improves
verbal memory. *Nature* 396: 128.

Coffey, C. E., J. F. Lucke, J. A. Saxton, G. Ratcliff, L. J. Unitas, B. Billig,
and R. N. Bryan. 1998. Sex differences in brain aging: A quantitative
magnetic resonance imaging study. *Archives of Neurology* 55 (2):
69–79.

Conway, M. 2002. Memory, brain, self and culture. Memory Matters
Seminar presented at the Institute for Cultural Research, London
University, February 16–17, 2002

Corballis, M. C. 1991. *The lopsided ape: Evolution of the generative
mind.* Oxford: Oxford University Press.

Coren, S., and D. F. Halpern. 1991. Left-handedness: A marker for
decreased survival fitness. *Psychological Bulletin* 109: 99.

Cortisol levels during human ageing predict hippocampal atrophy and
memory deficits. 1998. *Nature Neuroscience*, May.

Cromie, W. J. 2001. Toddling toward the birth of knowledge: Psychologist Spelke focuses on how infants become acquainted
with the world. *Harvard Gazette,* Nov. 29. Retrieved from <http:
//www.news.harvard.edu/gazette/2001/11.29/03-spelke.html>.

Damasio, A. R. 1994. *Descartes' error: Emotion, reason and the human
brain.* New York: Putnam.

———. 2000. *The feeling of what happens: Body and emotion in the
making of consciousness.* London: Vintage.

D'Arcangelo, M. 2001. Wired for mathematics: A conversation with
Brian Butterworth. *Educational Leadership* 59(3): 14–19.

DeCasper, A. J., and W. P. Fifer. 1980. Of human bonding: Newborns
prefer their mother's voice. *Science* 208: 1174–76.

Dehaene, S. 1997. *The number sense: How the mind creates math-ematics.* London: Penguin Press. for Elizabeth Spelke see <http://www.news.harvard.edu/gazette/2001/11.29/03-spelke.html>.

Dehaene, S., G. Dehaene-Lambertz, and L. Cohen. 1998. Abstract representations of numbers in the animal and human brain. *Trends in Neuroscience* 21(8): 355–61.

Dehaene, S., E. Spelke, P. Pinel, R. Stanescu, and S. Tsivkin. 1999. Sources of mathematical thinking: Behavioral and brain-imaging evidence. *Science* 284 (5416): 970–74.

Devlin, B., M. Daniels, and K. Roeder. 1997. The heritability of IQ. *Nature* 388 (31 July): 468–71.

Elbert, T., and C. Pantev. 1995. Increased cortical representation of the fingers of the left hand in string players. *Science* 270 (5234): 305–7.

Eliot, L. 2000. *What's going on in there? How the brain and mind develop in the first five years of life.* New York: Bantam Books.

Elliott, R., K. J. Friston, and R. J. Dolan. 2000. Dissociable neural responses in human reward systems. *Journal of Neuroscience* 20(16): 6159–65.

Everhart, D. E., J. L. Shucard, T. Quatrin, and D. W. Shucard. 2001. Sex-related differences in event-related potentials, face recognition, and facial affect processing in prepubertal children. *Neuropsychology* 15(3).

Fast ForWord for Language. 1998. Oakland, CA: Scientific Learning Corporation. <http://www.scilearn.com>.

Field, T. M., D. Cohen, R. Garcia, and R. Greenberg. 1984. Mother-stranger face discrimination by the newborn. *Infant Behavior and Development* 7: 19–25.

Frith, U. 1985. Beneath the surface of developmental dyslexia. In *Surface dyslexia,* ed K. E. Patterson, J. C. Marshall, and M. Coltheart, 301–30. Hove: Lawrence Erlbaum Associates.

Furlow, B. 2001. Play's the Thing. *New Scientist* 2294 (June 9): 28–31.

Gage, Fred. 1997. Untitled article. *Brain in the News* 4(4): 1.

Gary Wells homepage. <http://www.psychology.iastate.edu/faculty/gwells/homepage.htm>.

Gazzaniga, M. S. 1998. *The mind's past.* Berkeley: University of California Press.

Gjone, H., and J. Stevenson. 1997. The association between internalizing and externalizing behavior in childhood and early adolescence: Genetic or environmental common influences? *Journal of Abnormal Child Psychology* 25(4):277–86.

Gleick, J. 1999. *Faster: The acceleration of just about everything.* New York: Random House.

Gold, P. E. 2003. Acetylcholine modulation of neural systems involved in learning and memory. *Neurobiology of Learning and Memory* 80(3):194–210.

Goleman, D. 1995. *Emotional intelligence.* New York: Bantam Books.

Good, C. D., I. Johnsrude, J. Ashburner, R. N. A. Henson, K. Friston, and R. S. J. Frackowiak. 2000. Voxel-based morphometry analysis of 465 normal adult human brains. *Neuroimage* 11(5): S607.

Goodson, J. 2001. An investigation into the effects of humor on depressive symptomatology. Paper presented to the First International Summer School and Colloquium on Humour and Laughter: Theory, Research, and Applications. Queen's University, Belfast, Northern Ireland, June 30. Abstract available online at <http://www.psychologie.unizh.ch/perspsy/humor/files/ISS01ColloquiumAbstracts.pdf >

Gopnik, A., A. Meltzoff, and P. Kuhl. 1999. *How babies think.* London: Weidenfeld and Nicolson.

Greenfield, S. 1999. *Brain power: Working out the human mind.* London: Element Books.

Guiard, Y. 1987. Asymmetric division of labor in human skilled bimanual action: The kinematic chain as a model. *Journal of Motor Behavior* 19(4):486–517.

Haber, R. N. 1981. The power of visual perceiving. *Journal of Mental Imagery* 5: 1–16.

Haber, R. N. 1982. It's silly to equate imagery with learning. *Journal of Mental Imagery* 6(1): 32–34.

——. 1985. One hundred years of visual perception: An ahistorical perspective. In *A century of psychology as science: Retrospectives and assessments,* ed. S. Koch and D. E. Leary, 250–81. New York: McGraw-Hill.

——. 1998. Retrieving lost memories: A review of Erdelyi's *Recovery of Unconscious Memories. Journal of Hypnosis* 32: 56–88.

Haber, R. N., and C. A. Levin. 1989. The lunacy of moon watching: Some preconditions to an explanation of the moon illusion. In *The moon illusion,* ed. M. Hershenson, 299–318. Hillsdale, NJ: Lawrence Erlbaum Associates.

Halpern, D. F. 1996. Changing data, changing minds: What the data on cognitive sex differences tell us and what we hear. *Learning and Individual Differences* 8: 73–82.

Hamann, S. B., L. Cahill, and L. R. Squire. 1997. Emotional perception and memory in amnesia. *Neuropsychology* 11: 1–10.

Hannaford, C. 1997. *The dominance factor: How knowing your dominant eye, ear, brain, hand & foot can improve your learning.* Arlington, VA: Great Ocean Publishers.

Harris, J. R. 1998. *The nurture assumption: Why children turn out the way they do.* London: Bloomsbury.

Harris, P. 1989. *Children and emotion.* Oxford: Blackwell.

Herbal remedies "boost brain power." *BBC News Online* April 14. Retrieved from <http://news.bbc.co.uk/hi/english/health/newsid_713000/713087.stm>.

Herzmann, C., Torrens J. K., de Escobar, G. M., et al. (1999). Maternal thyroid deficiency during pregnancy and subsequent neuropsychological development of the child. *New England Journal of Medicine* 341: 2015–17.

Hobson, J. A., and R. Stickgold. 1994. A neurocognitive approach to dreaming. *Consciousness and Cognition* 3 (1): 1–15.

Hurwitz, I., P. H. Wolff, B. D. Bortnick, and K. Kokas. 1975. Nonmusical effects of the Kodaly music curriculum in primary grade children. *Journal of Learning Disabilities* 8: 45–51.

Huttenlocher, P. R. 1979. Synaptic density in human frontal cortex: Development changes and effects of aging. *Brain Research* 163: 195–205.

——. 1987. The development of synapses in striate cortex of man. *Human Neurobiology* 6: 1–9.

——. 1993. Morphometric study of human cerebral cortex development. In *Brain development and cognition: A reader,* ed. M. H. Johnson. Cambridge, MA: Blackwell.

Iacoboni, M., R. P. Woods, M. Brass, H. Bekkering, J. C. Mazziotta, and G. Rizzolatti. 1999. Cortical mechanisms of human imitation. *Science* 286: 2526–28.

Institute of Cognitive Neuroscience. Retrieved from <http:// www.icn.ucl.ac.uk/members/Csibr25/>.

Iwaniuk, A. N., S. M. Nelson, and J. E. Pellis. 2001. Do big-brained animals play more? Comparative analyses of play and relative brain size in mammals. *Journal of Comparative Psychology*, 115(1): 29–42.

Jeannerod, M. 1994. The representing brain: Neural correlates of motor intention and imagery. *Behavioral and Brain Sciences* 17: 187–202.

Kastner, S., and P. De Weerd. 1998. Mechanisms of directed attention in the human extrastriate cortex as revealed by functional MRI. *Science* 282(5386): 108–11.

Kimura, D. 1999. *Sex and cognition.* Cambridge, MA: MIT Press.

Knut, K., W. Kampe, C. D Frith, R. J. Dolan, and U. Frith. 2001. Psychology: Reward value of attractiveness and gaze. *Nature* 413: 589

Kotulak, R. 1996. *Inside the brain: Revolutionary discoveries of how the mind works.* Kansas City, MO: Andrews and McMeel.

Lamb, S. J., and A. H. Gregory. 1993. The relationship between music and reading in beginning readers. *Educational Psychology* 13: 19–26.

LeDoux, Joseph. 1998. *The emotional brain.* New York: Simon and Schuster.

Levine, S. 1971. Stress and behavior. *Scientific American* 224 (1): 26–31.

Lewis, D. W., and M. Diamond Cleeves. 1998. The influence of gonadal steroids on the asymmetry of the cerebral cortex. In *The Asymmetrical brain,* ed. K. Hugdahl and R. J. Davidson, 42. Cambridge, MA: MIT Press.

Liu Y, J-H. Gao, H-L. Liu, and P. T. Fox. 2000. The temporal response of the brain after eating revealed by functional MRI. *Nature* 405: 1058–62.

Loftus, E. F., and K. Ketcham. 1994. *The myth of repressed memory.* New York: St. Martin's Press.

MacLean, P. D. 1990. *The triune brain in evolution: Role in paleocerebral functions.* New York: Plenum.

Maguire, E. A., C. D. Frith, and L. Cipolotti. 2001. Distinct neural systems for the encoding and recognition of topography and faces. *Neuroimage* 13(4): 743–50.

Maguire, E. A., D. G. Gadian, and I. S. Johnsrude. 2000. Navigation-related structural change in the hippocampi of taxi drivers. *Proceedings of the National Academy of Sciences* 97(8): 4398–4403.

Maquet, P., J. Peters, J. Aerts, G. Delfiore, C. Degueldre, A. Luxen, and G. Franck. 1996. Functional neuroanatomy of human rapid-eye-movement sleep and dreaming. *Nature* 383(6596): 163–66.

"Mapping the Mysteries of the Mind." McMaster University website. Retrieved from <http://www.mcmaster.ca/ua/opr/times/fall98/witelson.htm>.

Maslow, A. H. 1982. *Toward a psychology of being.* 2nd ed. New York: Van Nostrand Reinhold.

Mason, J. W., L. H. Hartley, T. A. Kotchen, E. H. Mougey, P. T. Ricketts, and L. G. Jones. 1973. Plasma cortisol and norepinephrine responses in anticipation of muscular exercise. *Journal of Psychosomatic Medicine* 35: 406–14.

Maszuda, M., Y. Liu, S. Mahankali, Y. Pu, R. A. DeFronzo, P. T. Fox, and J-H. Gao. 1999. FMRI study of the altered hypothalamic response to oral glucose intake in obese humans. *Diabetes* 48: 1801–6.

Meltzoff, A. N. 1999. Persons and representation: Why infant imitation is important for theories of human development. In *Imitation in infancy,* ed. J. Nadel and G. Butterworth, 9–35. Cambridge: Cambridge University Press.

Memon, A. 2002. Eyewitness testimony. Presentation given at Memory Matters seminar, Institute for Cultural Research, London University, February 16–17.

Memon, A., and D. B. Wright. 2000. Factors influencing witness evidence. In *Behaviour, crime and legal processes: A guide for forensic practitioners,* ed. J. McGuire, T. Mason, and A. O'Kane. Chichester and New York: John Wiley & Sons

Meyer, G., B. P. Hauffa, M. Schedlowski, C. Pawlak, M. A. Stadler, and M. S. Exton. 2000. Casino gambling increases heart rate and salivary cortisol in regular gamblers. *Biological Psychiatry* 48(9): 948–53.

Morton, L. L., J. R. Kershner, and L. S. Siegel. 1990. The potential for therapeutic applications of music on problems related to memory and attention. *Journal of Music Therapy* 4(17): 195–208.

Müller, M. M., C. S. Herrmann, A. D. Friederici, G. Csibra, and M. H. Johnson. 2001. Object processing in the infant brain. *Science* 292: 163.

Nagarajan, S., H. Mahncke, T. Salz, P. Tallal, T. Roberts, and M. M. Merzenich. 1999. Cortical auditory signal processing in poor-reading adults. *Proceedings of the National Academy of Sciences* 96: 6483–88.

National Health and Nutrition Examination Survey (NHANES). 2000. Atlanta: Centers for Disease Control and Prevention, National Center for Health Statistics. Retrieved from <http://www.cdc.gov/nchs/nhanes.htm>.

Nelson, M., F. Bakaliou, and A. Trivedi. 1994. Iron deficiency anaemia and physical and academic performance in adolescent girls from different ethnic backgrounds. *British Journal of Nutrition* 72: 427–33

Nichelli, P., J. Grafman, P. Pietrini, D. Alway, J. C. Carton, and R. Miletich. 1994. Brain activity during chess playing. *Nature*, 369: 191.

Nobelprize.org. Roger W. Sperry—Nobel Lecture (December 8, 1981). Retrieved from <www.nobel.se/medicine/laureates/1981/sperry-lecture.html, Nobel Lecture>.

"Obesity and smoking cut brain power." 1998. *BBC News Online*, November 9. Retrieved from <http://news.bbc.co.uk/hi/english/health/newsid_211000/211032.stm>.

O'Brien, D. 2002. Learn to remember. Presentation to the Memory Matters seminars, Institute for Cultural Research, London University, February 16–17.

OECD. 2001. Knowledge and skills for life: First results from PISA 2000. December 4. Paris: OECD. Abstract available from <http://oecdpublications.gfi-nb.com/cgi-bin/OECDBookShop.storefront/EN/product/962001141P1>.

Oliviera, D. 2001. Letter to the editor. *New Scientist*, October 20, 2001: 109

Opie, I., and P. Opie. 1969. *Games children play*. London: Oxford University Press.

Ornstein, R. 1997. *The right mind: Making sense of the hemispheres.* New York: Harcourt Brace.

Pantev, C., R. Oostenveld, A. Engelien, B. Ross, L. E. Roberts, and M. Hoke. 1998. Increased auditory cortical representation in musicians. *Nature* 392: 811–14.

Pascual-Leone, A., D. Nguyet, L. G. Cohen, J. P. Brasil-Neto, A. Cammarota, and M. Hallett. 1995. Modulation of muscle responses evoked by transcranial magnetic stimulation during the acquisition of new fine motor skills. *Journal of Neurophysiology* 74(3): 1037–45.

Paulesu, E., and J. Mehler. 1998. Right on in sign language. *Nature* 392: 233–34.

Pert, C. 1997. *The molecules of emotion.* New York: Touchstone Books.

Plunkett, K. 2000. The development of the brain and early years learning. Presentation given at the Royal Institute, London, November 16.

Portwood, M. 1999. *Developmental dyspraxia: Identification and intervention.* 2d ed. London: David Fulton Publishing

Quartz, S. R., and T. J. Sejnowski. 1997. The neural basis of cognitive development: A constructivist manifesto. *Journal of Behavioral and Brain Sciences* 20(4):537–57.

Ramachandran, V. S., and S. Blakeslee. 1998. *Phantoms in the brain: Probing the mysteries of the human mind.* New York: William Morrow.

Ratey, J. 2001. *A user's guide to the brain: Perception, attention, and the four theaters of the brain.* New York: Pantheon Books.

Rauscher, F. H., G. L. Shaw, and K. N. Ky. 1993. Music and spatial task performance. *Nature* 365: 661.

———. 1995. Listening to Mozart enhances spatial temporal reasoning: Toward a neurophysiological basis. *Neuroscience Letters* 185: 4–7

Rizzolatti, G., M. Gentilucci, R. M. Camarda et al. 1990. Neurons relating to reaching-grasping arm movements in the rostral part of area 6 (area 6a beta). *Experimental Brain Research* 82: 337–50.

Russ, S. W., A. L. Robins, and B. A. Christiano. 1999. Pretend play: Longitudinal prediction of creativity and affect in fantasy in children. *Creativity Research Journal* 12 (2): 129–40.

Sacks, O. 1985. *The man who mistook his wife for a hat and other clinical tales.* New York: Simon and Schuster.

Salinas, J. A., and Gold, P. E. 2005. Glucose regulation of memory for reward reduction in young and aged rats. *Neurobiology of Aging* 26(1):45–52.

Sapolsky, R. 1998. *Why zebras don't get ulcers: An updated guide to stress, stress-related diseases, and coping.* New York: W. H. Freeman and Co.

———. 2000. Stress, disease, and memory. Presentation at Brain Expo, San Diego, January 17.

Sasanuma, S., M. Itoh, K. Mori, and Y. Kobayashi. 1977. Tachistoscopic recognition of Kana and Kanji words. *Neuropsychologia* 27: 547–53.

Scheuer, L. J., and D. Mitchell. 2003. Does physical activity influence academic performance? *Sportapolis* May. Retrieved from <http://www.sports-media.org/sportapolisnewsletter19.htm>.

Seligman, M. 1975. *Helplessness,* San Francisco: W. H. Freeman & Co.

Seligman, M., R. Rosellini, and M. Kozak. 1975. Learned helplessness in the rat. *Journal of Comparative Physiology and Psychology* 88: 542–47.

Shucard, J. L. and D. W. Shucard. 1990. Auditory evoked potentials and hand preference in 6-month-old infants. *Developmental Psychology* 26(6):923–30.

Simons, D. J. 2000. Current approaches to change blindness. In "Change Detection and Visual Memory," special issue, *Visual Cognition* 7: 1–16.

"Sleepless in Loughborough." <http://www.lboro.ac.uk/departments/hu/groups/sleep/wellcome.htm>.

Späth-Schwalbe, E. T. Schöller, W. Kern, H. L. Fehm, and J. Born.1992. Nocturnal adrenocorticotropin and cortisol secretion depends on sleep duration and decreases in association with spontaneous awakening in the morning. *Journal of Clinical Endocrinology and Metabolism* 75: 1431–35.

Springer, S. P., and G. Deutsch. 1998. *Left brain, right brain: Perspectives from cognitive neuroscience.* New York: W. H. Freeman and Co.

Stein, J. 2000a. The development of the brain and early years learning. Paper presented at the Royal Institution, London, November 16.

———. 2000b. Early learning and the brain. Paper presented at the Royal Institution, London, July 12.

Sternberg, R. J. 1988. *The triarchic mind: A new theory of human intelligence.* New York: Viking.

———. 1996. *Successful intelligence: How practical and creative intelligence determine success in life.* New York: Plume.

Stickgold, R., E. Pace-Schott, and J. A. Hobson. 1994. A new paradigm for dream research: Mentation reports following spontaneous arousal from REM and NREM sleep recorded in a home setting. *Consciousness and Cognition* 3 (1): 16–29.

Stimulating environment protects brain cells. 1999. *Nature Medicine* 5 (April): 448–53.

Study finds key areas of brain smaller in many premature infants. 2000. *Yale Bulletin and Calendar* 29, no. 7 (October 20). Retrieved from <http://www.yale.edu/opa/v29.n7/story4.html>.

Sylwester, R. 1999. In search of the roots of adolescent aggression. *Educational Leadership* 57(1):65–69.

———. 2000. On teaching brains to think: A conversation with Robert Sylwester. *Educational Leadership* 57(7): 72.

Tallal, P. 2000. The science of literacy: From the laboratory to the classroom. *Proceedings of the National Academy of Sciences* 97(6): 2402–4.

Thatcher, R. W., R. A. Walker, and S. Guidice. 1987. Human cerebral hemispheres develop at different rates and ages. *Science* 236: 1110–13.

Thompson, P. M., et al. 2000. Growth patterns in the developing brain detected by using continuum mechanical tensor maps. *Nature* 204: 190–93.

Torgesen, J. K. 1999. Phonologically based reading disabilities: Toward a coherent theory of one kind of learning disability. In *Perspectives on Learning Disabilities,* ed. R. J. Sternberg and L. Spear-Swerling, 231–62. Boulder, CO: Westview Press.

———. 2000. Individual differences in response to early interventions in reading: The lingering problem of treatment resisters. *Learning Disabilities Research and Practice* 15: 55–64.

Torgesen, J. K., A. W. Alexander, R. K. Wagner, C. A. Rashotte, K. Voeller, T. Conway, and E. Rose. 2001. Intensive remedial instruction for children with severe reading disabilities: immediate and long-term outcomes from two instructional approaches. *Journal of Learning Disabilities* 34: 33–58.

Torgesen, J. K., and P. Mathes. 2000. A basic guide to understanding, assessing, and teaching phonological awareness. Austin, TX: PRO-ED.

Water "can reduce brain power." 2001. *BBC News Online,* January 25, 2001. Retrieved from <http://news.bbc.co.uk/hi/english/health/newsid_1133000/1133308.stm>.

Weinberger, N. M. 2000. What the brain tells us about music: Amazing facts and astounding implications revealed. *MRN* 7 (Fall). Retrieved from <http://www.musica.uci.edu/mrn/V7I3F00.html#tells>

Weinberger, N. M, and T. M. McKenna. 1988. Sensitivity of single neurons in auditory cortex to contour: Toward a neurophysiology of music perception. *Music Perception* 5: 355–90.

Wright, D. B., and G. M. Davies. 1999. Eyewitness testimony. In *Handbook of Applied Cognition,* ed. F. T. Durso, R. S. Nickerson, R. W. Schvaneveldt, S. T. Dumais, D. S. Lindsay, and M. T. H. Chi, 789–818. Chichester and New York: John Wiley & Sons.

Yue, G. H., M. Bilodeau, P. A. Hardy, and R. M. Enoka. 1997. Task-dependent effects of limb immobilization on the fatigability of the elbow flexor muscles in humans. *Experimental Physiology* 82: 567–92.

Yue, G. H., J. Z. Liu, V. Siemionow, V. K. Ranganathan, and V. Sahgal. (In press). Brain activation during human finger extension and flexion movements. *Brain Research.*

Yue, G. H., V. K. Ranganathan, V. Siemionow, and V. Sahgal. 1999. Older adults exhibit a reduced ability to maximally activate their elbow flexor muscles. *Journal of Gerontology: Medical Sciences* 54: M249–53

Zohar, D., and I. Marshall. 2000. *SQ: Spiritual intelligence: The ultimate intelligence.* London: Bloomsbury.

Index

The suffix g denotes a definition in the Glossary.

MOVE IT
Physical Movement and Learning

Alistair Smith

There is an increasing body of knowledge which links physical movement and learning. What the best teachers and the wisest parents have believed for years is affirmed in this book of physical activities. The book contains over 100 simple activities, all fully illustrated and with clear instructions. Young children and older learners alike will benefit from practicing them. The book contains sections on—

- Theory of movement and learning
- Lifestyle choices and the importance of play
- Brain breaks for handwriting
- Brain breaks for relaxation
- Brain breaks for numeracy and literacy
- Brain breaks for improving concentration
- Improving coordination
- Building confidence
- Eye patterning
- Links to learning topics
- How to add music to movement

The activities have been successfully used in schools and include many exercises suggested by teachers with whom the author has worked.

Grades K–12
Paperback, 80 pages
ISBN: 1904424740

About the Author

Alistair Smith began teaching after a brief career in post-graduate research and prisons education. He is known internationally as an outstanding presenter, trainer, and motivational speaker and is the chairperson of Alite Ltd., a company he founded to work in the field of motivation, teaching, and learning. Alistair is the author of many books including *Accelerated Learning: A User's Guide*, *Move It: Physical Movement and Learning*, and *Bright Sparks: Posters for Students and for Classrooms to Raise Motivation and Achievement*.